Robert Booth

With warm good wishes

John Hall

John Hall

Gondolas & Grapes

SIBILLINE PRESS

Half-title page drawing by Crispin Mason

First published by Sibilline Press

© 2002 SIBILLINE PRESS

16 Bonchurch Road
London W10 5SD

British Library Cataloguing-in-Publication Data
A catalogue record for this book is available
from the British Library

ISBN 0-9542198-0-5
Printed and bound by BAS Printers Ltd
Over Wallop, Stockbridge, Hants

Contents

Katharine   Nicholas and Charlie   Kate

Katharine

Nicholas

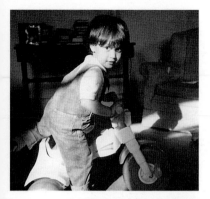

Sam

For my children and their children

Charlie

Kate

Sam

Pliny's
Garden

Introduction

Man is in love and loves what vanishes,
What more is there to say? W.B. Yeats

Standing at the top of a ski-lift on a peak in the French Alps, I gazed into the even more brilliant whites and blues of Italy. Although then, at the age of thirty, I had never been to Italy, I was aware of a well-developed desire to live· and work there: not in the snowy Alps, but down through the sun-haze, in those golden cities whose names I knew so well – Venice, Verona, Cremona, Ferrara, Mantua, Rome. An affair with Italy began and deepened when I started working in Venice, an experiment which turned out to last the best part of a lifetime.

The point of no return, of hopeless commitment, was passed one May day near Rome. I had gone with notebook, pen and reference book to see the Papal gardens in the Alban hills and had stopped for lunch in Frascati. There were white-clothed tables in the dappled shade of plane trees; below stretched a Claude Lorrain view of the *Campagna* to the cupolas of Rome. The resinous scent of cypresses among buildings of sun-baked antiquity, the perfume of the *fragoline* – the little wild strawberries which the waiter pressed on me: I had never eaten them before – and the bite on palate and mind of the cold, pale wine produced an overwhelming contentment. I was hooked.

The Venice work began to flourish and looked like expanding into the field of cultural tourism. And time spent researching this mirage seemed to justify wishful thinking about acquiring a base in Italy. I drove further and further off the beaten track, exploring new territory. As range after range of mountains extended in diminishing intensities of blue, I realised that, as well as discovering new tour areas, I was pursuing something which haunted the memory. A long-standing desire to possess an old house with beamed ceilings, open fires, mountain views – an obsession persisting from a childhood in the North East and North West of England cut by a sudden removal to the suburban South – became Italianised. I keep a cutting from the property page of a Wiltshire newspaper: '*Whether you can afford a palace or a pint-sized pad, the one thing you cannot afford when buying property overseas is to be romantic.*' My motive was actively romantic, and worse: it included a considerable element of some kind of personal psychological quest.

The quest ended in a farmhouse, perched at two thousand feet, isolated at this moment as I write by a mountain mist which muffles the hillside. It is penetrated only by the bell of the Poor Clares from the town above, by the plop of a falling fig and the tap of November moisture dropping from poplar branches onto the leaves below; not everyone's idea of Italy. Our house is in the *Marche* region of central Italy, in the countryside below the walls of San Ginesio, a town of four thousand inhabitants. In the 14th century there were twenty thousand, as witnessed by the walls, bell towers and churches which, mist permitting, form the skyline at the back of our house.

The early years in Venice coincided with my divorce. Our three children, Nicholas, Charlie and Katharine were brought to Italy in school holidays, arriving at Venice airport as unaccompanied minors, departing again with white handkerchiefs held against the inside of the plane window. After the house in the *Marche* had been bought, a hand-built terrace or two later, I married Therese, a black-haired, brown-eyed South American lady and the kitchen filled with delicious herbal aromas. A self-seeded fig tree sprung up miraculously in the courtyard. All plants grew. Bantams, ducks, geese, pigeons, even pheasants, emerged from eggs and flourished and we are overrun with dogs and cats. I became *we*, which meant more than one plus one. Three-year-old Kate came with Therese. And years later the prepotent Sam, born in

J.H., on the right, with some Milanese friends

Venice as if yesterday. These indigenous children went through the
local infant and elementary schools in Venice and San Ginesio until it
was time to worry about their complete lack of written English. So once
again the routine of handing over to air hostesses to go back to school
became part of life. Sam, aged sixteen, now travels on his own twelve
times a year, to and fro.

We occupy that strange status of not native and not tourist. To be
expatriate sounds a little heavy when repatriation needs only the twice-
daily bus to Rome and a two-hour flight. My aunt and uncle, who
loaded a family schooner with couples of animals and sailed away from
Arklow in the thirties, to settle in the savage Solomon Islands, deserved
that name.

'Tell me what it was like,' regularly insisted the eleven-year-old Sam
before falling asleep, wanting to hear about the past, to hear yet again
about air raid sirens, the distinctive sound of German bombers'
engines, convoys on the horizon heading up towards Russia, artillery
shells whistling over our house and exploding at sea during Sunday
morning target practice, our dog being blown up by a landmine while

rabbiting on the sand dunes. These are my memories of when I was his age. What are recorded here are memories of peaceful, unheroic years in the process of acquiring a gold-tinted patina. The halls of memory and imagination are adjacent chambers.

The admirable Prince Lampedusa, author of *The Leopard*, spoke in favour of making the effort to record.

It is imperative to try to gather together as many as possible of the sensations which have passed through this particular organism... All should find it possible to preserve, in some such way, things which, without this slight effort, will be lost forever. So the reader (who won't exist), must expect to be led meandering through a lost earthly paradise. If it bores him, I don't mind.

Writing his rejected masterpiece as he did in the back room of a bar, he must have felt the opposing pull, in the Sicilian midday heat – the impossibility of exaggerating the complete unimportance of everything.

Our dilapidated albums of photos and snaps, the red ones of life in Venice and the green ones of our country life record personal instants. Time is stopped. The quick and the dead are folded together, smiling under cellophane. This is exactly *what we were*, except, as our artist friend Geoffrey put it, finishing a portrait and naming his fee, – 'the result being you are more eternal than you were.' As albums accumulate, the collection of moments in time records the passing of time itself: passing, but always in sunshine. The dark side of the freelance life, the intermittent drizzle of worry and financial insecurity is not photogenic. The same goes for telling, or partly telling: *le secret d'ennuyer est celui de tout dire.*

If part of what follows has a narrative thread, the rest is more ruminative, closer to the pace of browsing in the albums. It is an assembly of selected moments, happenings, places, people; memories turned 'til they catch the light.

1

Point of Departure –
The Orient Express

VENICE-SIMPLON ORIENT EXPRESS. Paris Venice Trieste Athens Istanbul, was indicated over Platform 6, Gare-de-Lyon. What with engine trouble between Victoria and Dover and missed ferry connections, this was the next train out of Paris for Venice. The Orient Express was still a regular, timetabled train, a little tattered and torn and definitely no longer The King of Trains and Train of Kings, with railway enthusiast Boris II of Bulgaria driving it personally across his kingdom. But to be on it, by chance, was an exciting surprise for a young schoolmaster making a break: April, 1964. I was on my way to Venice for the first time – the aim: to turn a dream into a practicable reality – in a week. The conductor had a spare second-class sleeping berth and he gave me a voucher for dinner. A handbell sounded in the corridor. '*Premier service. Le dîner est servi. Premier dîner.*'

Nothing could be more romantic than sitting in the faded blue and gold dining car at the platform in Paris, perusing the menu. A waiter pushed the trolley of aperitifs between the rapidly filling tables. '*Le Kir, Monsieur*', and he placed in front of me the drink which was to mean to me France at the moment before dinner, usually after a day's driving. The next few hours live in memory with the luminous, miniature precision of a Flemish oil painting. The characters were as real as fiction: the ugly lady opposite with her bizarre question and exquisite niece; the tweed-clad English couple with their unstoppable county gossip; the American lady and her daughter; the Italian gallop-horse owner. The electricity failure resulted in candlelight, which glamorises any dinner, especially dinner on a train. The waiters' imperturbably regular pronunciations, as they presented each course, imposed a measured formality on the meal and on the exchanges of conversation.

There was activity on the platform. '*En voiture! En voiture!*' Doors were slammed.

At the small table across the gangway was a remarkably ugly lady. She sat very upright. Round her neck was a collar of very large pearls. Her hands were covered with rings. Sitting at the table opposite the formidable monster – was she Italian, Hungarian, Rumanian, Greek? – was an apparition of delight. Her daughter? Granddaughter?

'*Celestine?*'

'*Oui, Tante Claire?*'

'*Mes… où sont mes…?*'

'*Ici, Tante Claire. Voila!*'

Celestine passed her her gold-rimmed glasses. Celestine was about twenty perhaps, wearing a tight-fitting little black coat and skirt and a white satin blouse. She had a remarkably beautiful, foreign-looking face, dead-white skin, large dark-brown eyes, jet-black hair. Her manicured hands had deep-red nails. She wore one large emerald set in platinum. Her glance had already been turned in my direction for a succession of instants. Tante Claire turned her bulk in my direction.

'*Connaissez-vous Ostende?*'

Which alarming and extraordinary demand was blocked by a tall man, lean of figure, and a tall woman, pear-shaped of figure; he tweed-suited, she tweed-skirted with twin-set and pearls, passing between me and the lady of the question. As soon as the tweeded English had passed and settled into the table invisible to me, behind my back, English voices sounded out loud and clear.

'*Garçon!* Now dear, will you have a dry sherry? *Garçon!* Un dry sherry et un whisky. Vous-avez Glen Grant?'

Another couple followed into the dining car and were put opposite me: a large American lady with rolls of white hair and a dignified aquiline face, and her daughter, a plain eighteen-year-old.

'Excuse me sir. Emmeline, say "Good Evening".' Emmeline said 'Hi.'

'*De l'eau mineral, si'l vous plaît.*' The waiter served the Americans. Tante Claire and Celestine were each sipping a flute of champagne.

I had to stand up to let a large Italian man squeeze past me to the last place at our table, by the window. As he lowered himself into his seat, the lights in the dining car went out. The electricity had failed. There were exclamations, then there was silence into which the unpanicked male English voice behind me continued, addressing his wife, his voice dominating the dining car.

'The Bellaires do not understand the conduct of the world's affairs. In fact they understood them so badly that they had to cross the channel.'

'Not to mention nine lawyers,' now it was the female voice 'four counsels, five judges, together with their respective wives, husbands, sisters and heterogeneous connections...'

General conversation was bubbling back. '*Un piccolo* black-out,' said the Italian next to me. Waiters were carrying trays of candlesticks 'til each table was lit.

'*Che bello*! *Che miracolo*!' exclaimed my sanguine neighbour.

Whistles outside, a last door slammed and the train began to move pulling the candlelit dining car away from those left behind on the platform, waving. Meanwhile Celestine's patent leather shoes were off, her stockinged feet carefully kept from the floor by a napkin.

'*La Ballotine de Sole aux anguilles, sauce caviar.*'

The dish was placed in front of each diner with ritual respect. The candlelight raised dinner to an occasion. There is nothing better than a train journey for sorting out thoughts, ordering plans into notes, into lists of things to be done. My card and pen were already beside me on the table. The American lady opposite was fixing me with a blue eye.

'Forgive what may appear like curiosity in a stranger, but may I ask where are you from?'

I saw dark eyes and a hint of white teeth in the candlelight across the carriage. My glass was filled with white wine.

'*Pouilly Fumé Ladoucette, Monsieur.*'

'And what do you do? I'm Jackie. Pleased to meet you John.'

So I told her about giving up being a schoolmaster – *I'm sure you will be very happy here, and if you are the man I think you are you may rest assured that I shall study your interests* – so had written Canon Shirley, headmaster of the King's School, Canterbury, when he had appointed me fresh from Oxford. Obviously I wasn't the man he had thought I was, as this was more or less the last communication I had from him in seven years.

'Now that's too bad! My husband believed in encouraging young people. When they do good, prais'em. Giv'em confidence. When they do bad, fir'em. That's what he believed.'

Tante Claire was still sitting bolt upright, eating. Celestine's attention was focused on our table. Neither spoke. The waiter refilled our glasses. The Italian was loving his meal. He came from Treviso, just North of Venice. He had been to Newmarket to buy horses. He owned horses – for the *galloppo*.

'Come and see me in Treviso. We will have a wonderful meal at Alfredo's. Best food in Italy.'

'The idea is,' and I fixed my eye on the mother whose eye was fixed on the crayfish on her plate, 'the idea is to set up a kind of pre-university course abroad, in Venice I hope, for people who are taking a 'gap' year after school and before university.'

'Got it! Gee – that's brilliant.'

Emmeline was looking out of the window at the darkness. 'So from January, Jackie,' I was competing with the remains of her crayfish for her attention, 'from January, a team of wonderful lecturers and teachers would open the eyes, ears and minds of all these intelligent eighteen-year-olds to European civilisation.'

'That's what I love: European civilisation. Mr. Vanderhof would have liked your idea John. You go right ahead and *doo* it.'

We exchanged addresses. 'And who knows, Emmeline may well come with you one day.'

As the train headed towards invisible Burgundy, the dinner maintained its momentum.

'*L'Aile de Pigeonneau sur son lit de Choux Verts Frais.*'

'*Le Chateau Branaire Ducru 1958,* Monsieur.'

Jackie looked at the pigeon with apprehension; Emmeline forked at it in horror. It was delicious. So was the wine. My Italian neighbour was thoroughly enjoying both.

'The question of where in the world to set up this abstract plan,' – the Italian's English was excellent and he clearly had an agile mind and was following what I was saying.

'The question had answered itself after not much thought.'

'Italy. *Italia*, no?'

'If you want a beautiful urban environment, if you want History, if you want Art, if you want Music too . . .'

'And beautiful people, and Fellini, and Antonioni, and real coffee, and Gaggia coffee machines and Ferrari cars . . .' He knew my script.

'And don't forget the sun. The Mediterranean sun.'

We both agreed that Italy was the only place. Emmeline perked up at the thought of what lay ahead.

'Germany. Forget it. Germany left a very nasty taste in my mouth. Very unpleasant.'

Martino Tonon – that was the Italian's name, he had given me his card – agreed with my choice of Venice.

'*Firenze.* Florence is like England. Full of English. And Americans.' I knew. Twenty-three English and American institutions existed, even in 1964. And the British Institute. And the colonial English on the peripheral hills – Chianti had not then been sold and bought. It was all too like the Canterbury precincts.

'But *Roma*, why not *Roma? Roma è bella. Bellissima.*'

Would the parents of my future students risk their children on the Via Veneto, where *la dolce vita* was still rampant? Venice was better. Galleries, churches, art, history, music, a university. And not one foreign institution.

'*Giusto! Giustissimo!* You're absolutely right. *Anche Venezia è bella.* Venice is beautiful too.'

Emmeline had come to life. She was interested in Venice. Might she be my first enrolment, my first student?

'A kind o' Junior Year Abroad. I get it.'

'And do you have friends in Venice? Do you have good contacts?' asked Martino, 'good contacts, in Italy…?' The wine glowed through our re-filled glasses.

'Not really. My Italian teacher – I had taken a few lessons – knows a family in Venice. He is something to do with museums. I have the address. And I'm meeting the old aunt of an Oxford friend. She has a palace.'

The cheese trolley was alongside our table. Emmeline said '*Yuk.*' The Americans had had enough and her mother was fiddling for her purse to pay the bill. The lady opposite asked for their bill. I waited to see how Celestine would re-enter her shoes. She re-entered them with a direct smile, at me. The large lady, more expansive still after dinner, again turned to me and again, with a golden smile, put the question '*Connaissez-vous Ostende?*'

And again the tweeded couple intervened, heading out of the dining car without interrupting their own flow of words, '… and fourteen hunters still eat in the stables of the good squire Bellaire…'

'Are you married?' Martino asked, as the lady opposite and Celestine rose from table. Celestine arched a questioning brow.

'*Bonsoir, Monsieur.*' Her voice was low, intimate and her smile distinctly memorable. I confessed to her aunt that I didn't know Ostende.

'*Pouf. Ça ne fait rien.* It doesn't matter at all. Bonsoir Monsieur.' They left the dining car, leaving a vacuum.

'*Quel fromage. Magnifique!*' Martino exclaimed in French. We had reached that stage of a meal when one becomes philosophical. I was thinking how Jeanetta, my future ex-wife, would have enjoyed being there. She loved France and French food and we had enjoyed these things together. Martino listened with the experience of a long and irretrievably married Italian to the strange convictions of youthful romanticism.

'Everyone has problems. All passions cool. Anyway – passion… ma…!' And Martino waved a dismissive hand. He dismissed too the Paris-style existentialist priorities, which still walked in the sixties – to make your own decisions, to determine your own direction, to have courage. Very grown up, we thought then.

'*La Marquise au Chocolat et sa sauce aux grains de café.*'

As for our romantic conviction that a priority of the worthwhile life was a dedication to the Desire and Pursuit of the Whole – Love with a capital L, Martino indicated that it had something in common with the Marquise au chocolat but without its style. To give himself more space, he moved to the other side of the table. As he lowered himself into his seat, the electricity came on again. The dining car lost its magic. Everything was ordinary.

We drank our coffee and paid our bills. We were the last to leave the dining car. With many *auguri* and *ci vediamo a Treviso*'s, we made our way to our respective berths. I had mine to myself, the other bunk being untaken. Before turning in at last I could make my list of priorities and arrive with the sharpest objectives.

One: pensione for students. A *pensione* had to be found for my hypothetical students and one that would provide me with a room for an office. In Venice it would be an inspiring room. I had in mind a *pensione* occupying a dilapidated Gothic palace on a quiet canal. I had already written to every *pensione* which the tourist office listed, naively expecting to get a reaction to the proposal of bringing a group of students for twelve weeks from January, in the lowest season. I was about to visit the five that had replied.

Two: space for lectures. Maybe in the same *pensione*? Maybe on an abandoned floor of the enormous palace where the Scottish aunt lived? An Oxford friend had an elderly aunt who had 'an enormous palace in Venice.' At least she had answered my letter.

Three: find someone who could give lectures in English on Venetian art, someone who could lecture on Italian cinema and someone who could give Italian lessons. The only starting points were the Scottish aunt and the Italian teacher's friend.

In bed I read Osbert Sitwell's humorous *In the Train* chapter in *Winters of Content:* the breakfast with the Americans. And I fell asleep in the company of the passengers in the dining car in *Murder on the Orient Express.* The rhythm of the wheels on the track spread an optimistic torpor. Somewhere in the night I was aware that the train had stopped. Distant voices lowed, like cattle, calling the name of the frontier. '*Vallorbe. Vallorbe.*' There were metallic outside sounds, the tapping of rails, the coupling and uncoupling of carriages. And then again the reassuring motion of the wheels.

In the morning, coffee was brought to my berth. The dining car was gone. The people of last night were gone, as if they had never been there – less real than my late-night fictional characters. The train trundled on across the plain of Lombardy towards Venice. I looked at the card with my notes, one to three. It was real.

2

Venice – The First Visit

As the train moved slowly across the lagoon causeway from Mestre to Venice, I stared out of the window, looking for the first time at the now familiar clutter of cranes and derricks of the docks, and the assortment of bell-towers-*campanili* – and domes rising behind – St. Mark's *campanile* instantly recognisable as the tallest. The sun was shining. Outside the station was water – canal glittering in sun.

The squalid door to the Pensione dei Dogi was in a minuscule *calle* – Venetian for 'narrow street' – at the side of the famous clocktower on the corner of the Piazza San Marco. An unshaven man led me through a grimy reception area, up steep and endless stairs into a shuttered room with a curtained-off washing area. As this was an inspection visit, I turned on the hot tap, and allowed the trickle of water to flow.

Opening the shutters was like switching on the hi-fi at full volume where the ten-part double choir and full orchestra explode in Monteverdi's *Vespers of 1610*. The balustrade outside my window abutted onto the central part of the clocktower where the golden lion of St. Mark stands on a blue, star-spangled field below the bronze moors. Almost in touching distance, the white, upward-cascading sculpture of St. Mark's, Ruskin's 'marble foam and frozen spray', flowered into angels, blue and gold, a frontal to the cluster of parachute-shaped Byzantine domes, each crowned with its three-dimensional Greek cross. Down the Piazzetta, between the two columns, the white Palladian façade of San Giorgio Maggiore and the brick walls of the former monastery stood four hundred yards away across the water, every detail clear in the limpid air. There, behind the firmly closed wrought-iron gate into the first cloister, was the Fondazione Giorgio

Cini. Looking at the famous Palladian façade from my balustrade, in the first hour of the first day of my Venetian enterprise, I had not yet heard of the Fondazione Giorgio Cini. Certainly I could not have imagined that within eight months a shy, un-self-confident school-master would be facing television cameras, microphones and journalists, presenting his creation at a lavish inauguration which the Foundation had laid on in their Palladian refectory, to place our activity clearly on the Venetian map.

The dribble of water still ran cold and the unshaven man showed no interest in having people in his hotel for twelve weeks of the lowest season. So ideas of conducting affairs from this room with a view to end all views had to be abandoned.

Hotel number two was the *Seguso,* on the Zattere waterfront. My second night's sleep was disturbed by deep engine-sounds which set the window and floor vibrating. I dozed through seemingly hours of these mysterious comings and goings of submarine activity until, surprised by morning light, I opened the shutters. Blinding morning sunlight reflected off the Giudecca Canal. The deep channel was throbbing with shipping going down on the high tide into the dog-leg bend by San Giorgio and the Doge's Palace and on to sea through the Lido channel. The building drummed with the propellers of sea traffic. Black and white tugs were at work – *Strenuus, Validus, Maximus, Pardus, Squalus, Titanus* – six in as many minutes, warping through the heart of the city laden cargo boats whose high steel sides dwarfed the line of palaces across the water and blocked out Palladio's Redentore Church as they slid past. As their washes arrived, thin wavelets spread over the paving of the Zattere, where I was taking breakfast coffee, compiling the day's list of things to be done.

I was learning. In hotels in Venice, hot means cold. Boiling – *bollente* – means tepid. *Super-bollente* means hot but is more a concept than a possible fact in the vocabulary of the cheaper *pensioni*. A proud flow of abundant tepid water did not necessarily mean a hot water system which didn't work, nor did it mean miserliness. It sometimes demonstrated a kind of sanity. Here heated children are not allowed to gulp water after exercise and no sweating labourer will down a glass of beer if it's chilled. '*Fa male* – it's bad for you,' like the night air that would come in if a bedroom window were to be left open. As for the American mania for ice and refrigeration – '*Mamma mia!*' The same goes, in reverse, for very hot water.

A *pensione* a day was the plan, trying what seemed the best-placed of those few which had replied to my letter, from the Dogi to the Seguso, from the San Maurizio to the Calcina, from the Dinesen, whose owner had written begging me to buy the hotel and relieve him of the bother of running it, to the Teson next to the public showers, with which we later, perforce, became familiar. The cheapest, the best buy in *Europe on 5 Dollars a Day*, the old Atlantico, with its cardboard room partitions, its dry taps and cavernous dilapidation, was just too far beyond the pale, in spite of its wonderful position on the canal three bridges down from the Bridge of Sighs.

Signor Maurizio, the owner of the little *pensione* San Maurizio in the *campo* of that name, had not only written to me, he had telephoned me in England, saying he had the perfect place. Not his own *pensione*, but another – the Pausania. The Pausania, closed and in a state of disrepair, was full of potential. We inspected it after dark, by the dimmest electric light. A beautiful courtyard with an ancient, crumbling stone outside staircase. No problem about getting it back in working order, Maurizio assured me. Yes, the kitchen too: he could provide meals. Wonderful spaces for lectures. As for my office – a superb room on the *piano nobile* with a window of fully five Gothic arches. This he pointed out to me from the *fondamenta,* the pavement running alongside the canal, outside the hotel. Too good to be true? Elation was balanced by intuitive doubts.

The pensione research went on, the perfect place being always, I hoped, on tomorrow's list for inspection. Of the eight listed none was ideal, two were possible, including the Pausania, but even I, with my inexperienced judgement sensed major problems there.

Another line of research went ahead like an ignited crackerjack. On the first day, I went in search of my Broadstairs Italian teacher's family. The Trentin doorbell was at the last door in a sequence of exceptionally narrow and twisting *calli* in the Toletta area, near the Accademia. After hearing my poor French further distorted by the crackling intercom, Giorgio permitted me, an unannounced and total stranger, to enter the building and rise in a lift to the third floor, where his powerful figure waited for me at the open door of his flat, three-year-old child at knee. I brought greetings from their friend, the lady who had given me my few Italian lessons and this introduction.

I was taken into the flat and into the heart of this famously anti-fascist family, and introduced to the three-year-old Nicoletta, the eleven-year-old twins Silvia and Francesca, whose voluptuous black hair hung straight almost to their waists, and to Giorgio's elfin wife, Picci. Curiosity at the arrival of a stranger, interest in what I tried to explain in my unpractised French – they spoke it well from their time in exile in France – and a remarkably quickly-growing appreciation of what I needed resulted in a major part of what has occupied my life ever since being set up then and there. The whole family were to remain friends that one passed almost daily in the village that Venice is. Francesca, now a mother and a teacher, was an effervescent companion for a Carnival evening many years after that first meeting and as many years ago now.

Giorgio was a civil servant, a senior one, working in the offices of the *Sovrintendenza alle Belle Arti*, so knew everyone in the museum world. He was born and bred in a city where everyone knows everyone anyway, the son of a popular martyr commemorated on a plaque near Rialto, and therefore a much-respected person. He was intelligent, ironic and efficient, knew whom I needed to meet and arranged meetings. In the course of the first of many fine family suppers, he had telephoned, interested, and arranged for me an appointment with Terisio Pignatti, vice-director of the Civic Museums. He had telephoned John Guthrie, a reader in English at Ca'Foscari, the university, who would see me, but would be out of Venice 'til Monday, my last day. He had telephoned Flavia Paulon, organising secretary of the Cinema *Biennale* and arranged an appointment. He revealed to me the all-powerful and vital position of the Cini Foundation and their probable interest in my project: if they said yes, there would be no further difficulties of any kind, although he could not approach them personally, for political reasons: Count Cini had been an important financier in the Mussolini regime. But Pignatti would put me in touch. He knew nothing about the hotel, pensione and accommodation question: maybe John Guthrie could help.

He introduced me to *grappa*, the firewater distilled from grapeskins. After dinner, he strolled me round the nearer parts of his city, his lessons in urban appreciation punctuated by overfilled tumblers of caustic *grappa*. We followed an itinerary of hidden bars and taverns which have returned forever after in dreams as a familiar night-time underworld of dimly-lit male company.

The topography of the lagoon city derives from a series of ancient mud-bank parishes, separated by the meanderings of tidal channels, now bridged and bordered by paved *fondamente* and veined by labyrinthine *calli*, tourist-proof. In the 4th century, under pressure from barbarian invasions, the Emperor Constantine had moved the imperial capital from Rome to Constantinople. A few centuries later, for exactly the same reason, locals from the Veneto mainland cities and villages – people who knew the tides, the channels and the mud-banks – had moved into the safety of the lagoon. They went first to Malamocco on the Lido. After the shock of being besieged by Pepin, Charlemagne's son, in 809 they moved into the central lagoon, to the area known as Rivo Alto – the 'high bank'– Rialto. Giorgio pointed out the vernacular of pink brick and white stone from Istria across the water in Yugoslavia – a stone which is water-resistant and ideal as a damp course. He made me aware of the quality of paving, of the finish of every detail, of every bridge. We stopped by a canal and listened to the irregular hollow knock of a moored *sandolo*, a smaller, sleeker version of the gondola, moved by the tide. In the parish centre, he explained, the highest ground above the tides, the parish church was built on the field left open for grazing – the *campo*: in Venice every square except St. Mark's is still called a *Campo*.

The little Campo S.Filippo e Giacomo was crowded with people dining at the tables outside the three bars, and the space, the size of a tennis court, was filled with the remarkably pleasing sound of human voices talking and laughing. Two black-and-silver-cloaked student-buskers created an instant audience with the most lightly-brushed chord and then enchanted the crowd with their gentle voices and guitars, each chord and syllable clear – the Venetian register.

Many years later, in the countdown row preceding the infamous Pink Floyd concert, there was much discussion of decibels. The Civic Hospital's Audiological Centre showed a scale running from the sound of a person sleeping, through a vacuum cleaner, a pneumatic drill – to a discotheque. It was revealed that in 1638 there had been a complaint recorded in the Senate at the potential damage to the mosaics in St. Mark's by the letting-off of celebratory mortars in the Piazza. Our slow walk back brought us through the empty Campo Sant'Angelo where Giorgio stopped. He snapped finger and thumb together. Three separate echoes returned off the surrounding palace walls. Click. Click. Click. Silence – the Venetian acoustic.

Professor Pignatti received me in his office by the library of the Correr Museum, the window looking out onto the lagoon and San Giorgio. He was a thickset man with a cast in one eye. He spoke English well and had an un-Italian restraint in manner. He listened. He understood. When he spoke it was to the point, in a strong voice, 'from the balls' as they say in Italy. He would be prepared to give a series of ten lectures, on Venetian painting and architecture, from the St. Mark's mosaics to the Fall of the Republic in 1797. He asked what would be the *honorarium*. What I had budgeted for the series of lectures, he told me, would not pay for one of his lectures. I was at a loss. But he would do them, all ten, at my figure.

Without a smile, and without charm but with visible approval and gathering momentum, he telephoned the Cini Foundation. The Director, Vittorio Branca was abroad but the Vice-Director would see me. An appointment was made.

'You must have a centre for your programme. I think the Cini will help. 'Til January, then.'

The next day the appointment at San Giorgio went well. Over Lapsang Souchong and Romary's Tunbridge Wells water biscuits in his sumptuous drawing room of an office looking across the water to the church of the Salute, Professor Nardi responded to my enthusiastic French. He was of the opinion that the Cini Foundation would be able to give us workspace and general support. But he who decides, Professor Branca, was away for a week, until after I would have left. So I was to write a formal letter and he, Nardi, would support it in person. Then this thin scholar, who had slept through the occasion when the *diretto vaporetto* had lost control on the sharp turn coming out of the Rio Nuovo into the Grand Canal and demolished part of the palace below his bedroom, asked exactly what a snapdragon looks like: his life work was on D.H. Lawrence.

Flavia Paulon, the secretary of the Cinema *Biennale*, met me in her office in Ca'Giustinian, the *Biennale* headquarters, a large palace on the Grand Canal next to the Hotel Monaco. A small, vigorous lady of immediate enthusiasms, she said she would arrange for private showings in the *Biennale* cinema, on the roof of the palace, of a selection of Italian films, and agreed to give introductory talks. So Rossellino's *Stromboli*, Visconti's *Senso*, Fellini's *La Dolce Vita* and Antonioni's *The Red Desert* were installed in our programme. Already, back in England, Sir Carol Reed had agreed, if he were free, to run film-making classes with the students. In the lift coming down, Flavia Paulon, after telling me how she had found the Palazzo dei Leonini for Peggy Guggenheim, urged me to explore her region, the Friuli – 'wonderful food, wonderful wine, wonderful people! See you next January!'

The British Consul was away but the Vice-Consul, Patrick Mansfield-Meade was warmly encouraging and his wife offered to help with our students if need be. They repeated the advice sent to me in a kind letter from James (now Jan) Morris, to make sure that everything was legally in order and correct, when setting up in Venice. A Scottish nobleman had recently been made to leave the city for eccentric behaviour. They introduced their nephew Geoffrey, an eighteen-year-old art student from St. Martins, who had just switched to the Accademia in Venice.

Richard Creese-Parsons, who had recently founded the Oxford School of English, soon to flourish in many towns in the Veneto, received with courteous suspicion a new English presence in his territory. I thought that maybe, when the course was over, a little English language teaching…? No.

In contrast to all these unannounced visits, afternoon tea with the Scottish aunt, Mrs. Paterson, had been arranged by an exchange of letters weeks in advance. I followed instructions, past the British Consulate into Dorsoduro, the *sestiere,* or quarter, where foreigners like to live. Through the Campo San Trovaso, past the gondola-making boatyard, smelling of tar and varnish, is the Canal of Ognissanti where *sandoli,* moored together in rafts, lay deftly in the meniscus. On the other side of the canal the twin wings of the French consulate enclosed a garden, whose statuary could be seen through the wrought-iron watergate. Arriving at number 1113, the red stuccoed Palazzo Bonlini, I rang the bell marked Somers-Cocks. The door clicked and creaked open into a dark, dank entrance. A voice echoed down from upstairs.

'Mr. Hall? Come up. Come up – to the second floor.'

I felt my way up an unlit stairwell. The Kensington voice welcomed me at an open door at the top of the stairs. Mrs. Paterson took me through the long *salone,* the central room which runs from front to back of a Venetian palace. The walls were covered with famous masterpieces of Velasquez from the Prado, enormous canvases in black frames.

'Mr. Somers-Cocks – the family own the palace – was consul in Madrid. His wife passed the years in the Prado, making copies,' explained Mrs. Paterson, leading me through into a small sitting room.

'Impossible to heat the apartment. Russian coke is so expensive. Excuse my husband. He always stays in another room.'

In the fireplace logs smouldered, smoke curling out of the chimney into the room. Sunk in a too-capacious armchair with broken springs, balancing a chipped Crown Derby cup and saucer, my eyes running with the acrid smoke, I sipped tea and answered questions.

'You knew my nephew Tim... from Oxford? Or was it at Rugby? You're a schoolmaster. How splendid. Which school are you at? What part of England do you come from? And where did you go to school? Your wife isn't with you?'

Mrs. Paterson was part of the summer English colony, some of whom organised the social side of the national pavilions at the *Biennale*, a world of cocktail parties in the *Giardini* and in palaces.

'So you've been to the Cini Foundation? You must have met dear Stefano. No? Avvocato Rosso-Mazzinghi. No? Of course you'll have been in touch with *Contessa* Cicogna. No?' Mrs. Paterson didn't know Giorgio Trentin. She had never actually *met* Professor Pignatti. She had never heard of Flavia Paulon. Professor Nardi at the Cini? That little man? Met him once, she thought.

'Now do tell me about this fascinating plan of yours.'

A distant bell rang.

'Ah – that must be Christina. I want you to meet Miss Thoresby. Christina *knows* people.'

Mrs. Paterson greeted Christina at the top of the stairs. Their voices were clear.

'So kind of you to come, my dear.'

'So kind of you to *ask* me, my dear. Is he here? What's he like?' Miss Thoresby added, in one of her audible whispers.

'Now come along and meet Mr. Hall.'

I levered myself out of the armchair and got rid of my teacup.

Christina Thoresby

A tall, gaunt lady stood in the door, iron-black hair in a severe bun, dark eyes gleaming like a hare's in March. Was she fifty? Sixty? Seventy? We were introduced. She listened. She was interested in the Pre-University idea. Pignatti? Excellent, the best person you could have. Nardi? Charming, and efficient in spite of a sleepy manner.

'And Peggy' – Peggy Guggenheim, she meant, the rich American promotress of avant-garde art – 'would be interested, and her friends. The artist Santomaso would help. He'd be interested.'

Christina played the organ at the English church so was *ex officio* at the heart of the English community. Each Sunday she ruled from the organ loft, strangulating the vocal chords of the congregation below with the defiant and obstinate slowness of her bar-by-bar progress through the hymns.

'You haven't been to the *Fenice* Theatre? But it's the most beautiful opera house in existence. There's a symphony concert tonight.'

I was able to get two tickets at the top of the theatre, perfect for appreciating the beautiful gilded stucco on the faded cream, green and blue ceiling, and for a close-up of the gorgeous green velvet curtain, embroidered in gold with phoenixes. It took some minutes to recognise the Opera orchestra conductor's rendering of Brahms' First Symphony.

'But he's wonderful with Puccini' Christina said.

In the interval, being in the cheap seats, we couldn't go into the beautiful bars inside the theatre, but repaired to the Bar al Teatro in the *campo* outside, along with the orchestra. Christina greeted a friend, a friend of Peggy's, a journalist from Milan.

'But Peter, the last time I saw you was at the Bestighué Ball – in the Palazzo Labia. You came in on an elephant. I was in domino, with the Begum.'

Draghadze bought *grappas* and gave me his card, which led indirectly to various special visits to Peggy Guggenheim's for my students and me. Later, and for the first of many times over the next years, at dinner afterwards upstairs in the Bar al Teatro restaurant, Christina ordered the waiter to change the wine I had asked for.

'I *never* drink that.' And we were brought something much better and more expensive.

Christina changed little in appearance over the next twenty-nine years, and not at all in manner or style of living. The austere bun, straight from the Close of Lichfield Cathedral, was unmodified by her time in the Women's Land Army, her time as a 'secret' lady with MI5 in wartime London and even her time in Paris after the war, as music critic for the *Continental Daily Mail*. Although a dedicated socialite who in Venice suffered agonies at not always being invited to parties – she was as poor as a cathedral mouse – she preferred intelligent company, especially the company of artists and people in the world of music. She came to Venice from Paris at the suggestion of her friend Peggy Guggenheim when Peggy had bought the palace in Venice and was always at home in Peggy's circle. She had enrolled as a mature student at the Accademia and successfully finished the Diploma course. And she took possession of the organ at St. George's English Church. She lived, with two large cats, Peter and Mike, in a succession of tiny ground-floor apartments where she gave small dinner parties round a low-level coffee table prepared in a grimy cooking area. On these occasions she adulated favourite visiting art historians or music critics and ignored, interrupted or scolded those of us she saw more often.

'Doesn't he know that you *don't touch things* in other people's houses?' nearly made me drop the jade Chinese cat I was ignorant enough to be handling.

But her opinion on anything, from a neighbour to an opera to an altarpiece to the Prime Minister of England was never trite and always reflected the hours which she had alone to brood over things. She was never a prig and accepted the wildest behaviour of her friends and others with tolerant equanimity never shocked, usually amused.

In later years she asked if she might give a lecture to my students, to which I was bound to agree. In the event, this eccentric figure, unlike in appearance and style our normal lecturers from England, gave an excellent performance. She began with Lorenzo Lotto one year and gradually added Pisanello and the big one, Leonardo da Vinci, as she gained confidence. She regularly received an ovation from the students for pluck – she was then in her seventies – and for what she had to say. These were not easy hours for the operator of the slide-projector. Nor for the photographer who had been browbeaten into making extra slides at short notice.

'Get it *clearer*. Much clearer,' she would boom at a student volunteer working the projector.

'I'm sorry. This slide is *very* poor. I *told* Sarah not to do it like that.'

The photographer Sarah would be sitting at the back well prepared for such thanks.

Christina kept the gossip of the English colony as bright as its Georgian silver. Her own contributions were often vindictive towards her best friends and often completely wrong. 'Just like Geoffrey to give a party when he knows I can't come.'

Some people avoided her known tracks at certain times on certain days – the route from where she lived, opposite the Locanda Montin, past the Accademia, into the shops in San Vio and the English church there. A chance meeting round a corner with the tall, stooping figure in a hat, on a walking stick, swathed in scarves and with a capacious bag would lead to coffee in a bar, extended chat and gossip as she shopped and a slow walk back to her flat, carrying her shopping.

The formidable Christina, whose death twenty-nine years after this first meeting seemed a social and physical impossibility, now occupies one of the last plots in the Evangelical graveyard on the Venetian cemetery island of San Michele. Thank goodness. Her rage, had a place not been found near her friends Princess Eristavi and Jenny Creese-Parsons, would have been eternal. As it is, her spirit, which looms round so many corners in Venice, is content and causes less apprehension than sometimes did her living presence.

By Saturday evening everything possible had been done, things having been steadily crossed off the list. On Monday John Guthrie was to see me at the University. The *pensione* situation was still far from settled. About the Cini Foundation I felt optimistic.

Bells near and far woke me to Sunday morning, a white sea fog and the salt smell of the sea. The day was without appointments, apart from having to take a promised call from Geneva. It was a day to drift, to get lost in the city. A desultory current of families in Sunday best flowed into the light space of the Piazza where already the morning sun was unravelling the mist. The deepest bell of St. Mark's spread its vibrations over the city from a *campanile* still lost in whiteness. The red and gold Sunday banners hung motionless down their flagstaffs outside St. Mark's. I wrote postcards to my children from the uncomfortable, cramped luxury of Florian's Caffe.

A Courtauld Institute voice was drawing the attention of her sixth-form schoolgirls to the clusters of pillars round the walls of the porches of St. Mark's – jasper, porphyry, deep green serpentine spotted with flakes of snow, pale azure and white.

'The perception of colour. Ruskin's point. The perception of colour, Jennifer, is a gift just as definitely granted to one person and denied to another as an ear for music. And, Jennifer, the very first requisite for a true judgement of St. Mark's is the perfection of that colour faculty.'

The girls made notes. Jennifer examined her mauve nails.

Sitting among the praying ladies in front of the *Nicopaeia* icon in St. Mark's, its gold bloomed with the light of many tall candles, I heard the outside bell stop. An active silence filled the church, reverberating like surf in a seashell held to the ear. From above the level of the pewter-coloured marble piers and columns, Byzantine saints stared down with hands upheld. I waited for the antiphons of Willaert, the Gabrieli, Monteverdi, the great *maestri di capella*, to break out from the choir galleries, ignorant that the tradition was long dead.

The Piazza was filling with people with the clearing of the sea mist which still lay thick in the Basin. The Palladian church of San Giorgio was invisible. Its fog bell clanged across the water. I pushed open the revolving glass door of the Hotel Danieli and settled into a comfortable leather armchair near the bar in the vast Gothic atrium, a cross between the Raj and St. Pancras. A succinct letter for the Cini Foundation was drafted. The appointed telephone call from Geneva came on the dot and I was able to say that things were looking good. In those few seconds the mist had vanished and San Giorgio seemed to greet me personally across the water. Just up the waterfront tugs were tied up and more names were added to the list – *Carlo, Furius, Cetus, Sirius, Emilio Panfido.*

Monday. In the institutionalised spaces of the enormous Ca'Foscari, the university building, the eagle-headed Scot, John Guthrie, promised me a supply of capable teachers of Italian. He made me triple the length of my drafted letter to the Cini Foundation, elaborating the same simple points and questions into the required rhetoric of the Italian language. He told me to call on Mr. Clementson who ran the Clementson Travel Office: he would deal with my accommodation business and save endless worries.

Time was running out. Mr. Clementson and I instantly got on well together. We were both from County Durham. He took me for a rapid inspection visit to the Pensione alla Salute da Cici. This was the place for us, he told me, without further discussion. The *pensione* was a small Renaissance palace on a small canal. Above the front entrance were a balcony and a five-arched window. My office? Clem explained to Signor Cici that I had a train to catch. We were whisked upstairs and shown rooms at speed. Motionless staff – chambermaids, perhaps Signora Cici herself? – looked round open doors, down the stairwell, like figures from frescoes by Veronese and Mantegna. Clem took me to Harry's Bar for a *Negroni* cocktail and introduced me, in passing, to Giuseppe Cipriani, the founder of this famous bar.

'See you in January', both said.

The tasks of the visit had, more or less, been done: a pensione – da Cici; an English-speaking art historian – Pignatti; a team of Italian teachers – from John Guthrie; a place for lectures – the Fondazione Cini, probably.

In Geneva my Swiss friend typed out the final version of the Cini letter and together we dropped it into a letterbox in Geneva. Then she typed out my letter of resignation to the headmaster of the King's School.

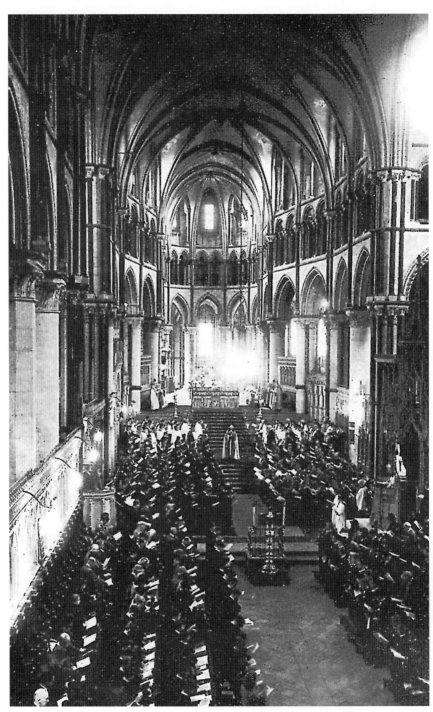

King's School Sunday Matins in Canterbury Cathedral

3

Finishing and Starting

Back in Canterbury a letter arrived from the Cini Foundation saying 'yes'. So in Venice the lights were green.

Canon Newell, the headmaster who had followed the famous or notorious Canon Shirley at The King's School, was visibly unshaken at the news that I was leaving. To break the silence, I pointed out a fault in his and his predecessor's management. How was it that in eight years a budding schoolmaster had not once had a professional conversation with his boss, let alone one on a human level, and not a word of advice, encouragement or even criticism? Not the style of Emmeline's father.

After this, as the silence deepened, the canon's camel-like head tilted further and further back, ruminating. Gazing out of the window across the Green Court, I contemplated a more lasting fault of his predecessor, the bulk of the Shirley Assembly Hall, a large building in red brick in what the architect had proudly called *Hampton Court Tudor* style. This insensitive, unpractical monstrosity is placed in one of the most beautiful English settings imaginable, in the Canterbury Precincts, beside an eighteenth century house, next to the Medieval and Tudor house and garden of the Archdeaconry of Canterbury, near the Old Grange, the Lattergate and the Norman library. The ensemble is dominated by the nave, West Towers and central Bell Harry Tower of the cathedral. These inspiring surroundings are invisible from the inside of this blind building, where seven hundred boys and girls meet each day for morning assembly. The canon spoke.

'Hall – you have done your job. It is enough that you have done your duty.'

On which lofty note my career as a public-school master ended.

The immediate task now was to put together a programme for Venice. A complete study of Venetian or Italian art was never the intention. The idea was to open up new areas of interest, to kindle enthusiasms, to find lecturers with the knack of instilling a feel for quality, of infecting with passion.

The intellectual tone of the early sixties was expressed in the new Sussex University. An inter-departmental concept, Asa Briggs' Contemporary Europe School, was offering areas of study which would go well in Venice. Its theme was the changes from the old European hierarchies of thought and behaviour to the modern. The areas of discussion were philosophy, scientific advance, art, literature, music, society. At that time Art History hardly existed in schools and universities. My judgment, which proved to be wrong, was that Art History would have no appeal to bright school-leavers, though we obviously had to include something – Pignatti's contribution. It was possible to offer in Venice this Sussex-style approach to European culture, ancient and modern, because a friend and former colleague at the King's School was then teaching philosophy at Sussex. John Wilson had no difficulty in recruiting a team of lecturers from Sussex, headed by himself, who could arrange to take time off to come out to Venice.

In my final summer term, the boys of the Caxton Society printed our first brochure, red lettering on the front, black inside on pale blue paper.

The Pre-University Course is a series of lectures on aspects of European Civilization. Attendance at lectures is voluntary. No certificate is given at the end. Equally, it is the experience of living in Venice, out of the tourist season, as part of an active and stimulating group of young people. The Pre-University Course is unique and does not fit into any conventional educational category.

The thin pamphlet was sent out to headmasters, housemasters, head-mistresses, careers masters and mistresses in most independent schools and many state schools. The Canon, rather late in my career, wanted to see me.

'Oughtn't you to have asked my permission before getting a school society to print your material?'

What happened in the next six months, a slow but steady enrolment of students, is by far the most astonishing thing in the thirty-five years of the course's existence. Over many later years I learnt how huge is the chasm between a project, however valid and enticing, and its realisation in the form of people paying deposits and fees. At the time of the launch, the Oxford and Cambridge entrance examination system had just changed. In the then new system, many people stayed on at school after doing their A-levels in the summer for an extra term of special coaching for the Oxbridge exams which were fixed in November. This meant that most candidates, successful or not, now left school in December. So the course was planned to start in January for these people. This was probably the decisive factor. Boys and girls from many different schools enrolled, encouraged by teachers who must have approved of the project. Credibility was provided from the start by the impressive team of lecturers, and in later years by the many head-masters, headmistresses, and university professors and lecturers whose students spoke well of their time in Venice and who were prepared to be listed as referees.

I left the King's School after the summer term and spent a magical Autumn term in the land of Evelyn Waugh's *Decline and Fall*, in a Broadstairs preparatory school. Staff dinner was by candlelight in the headmaster's dining room, with Georgian silver and claret – and port on Saturdays. New to the school at this time was a mysterious, rich man. We both had rooms in the Lodge. He taught French. We had many fine oyster lunches together in the excellent Italian restaurant that overlooks the harbour, and cruised back to school in his Jaguar just in time to tie up the bootlaces of ten-year-olds screaming like starlings in the locker rooms before ourselves taking the field as referees. In January, when I had left and was installed in Venice in advance of the students, he turned up in my absence at Victoria Station, to assist with the send-off of the students – and attempted to seduce my still future ex-wife. Colleagues at this excellent school included the fat man with extra-loud-check tweeds; the thin, peppery ex-army major; the glamorous, well-connected hunting lady from the Pytchley; the hunchback; and the gentlemanly headmaster who introduced his staff to accounts at Coutts. Altogether it was a great deal more civilised, more amusing and more humane than the common room at the King's School.

The post brought bookings for the course in Venice, like manna from heaven. By January, after eight months back in England, the miraculous had happened and the enterprise was about to take off, capitalised by cashing my accumulated pension for £300 and absolutely no private income: a mad risk, everyone said. In preparation for a new domestic life, I had booked for three days, en route to Venice, a service flat instead of a hotel room, in Geneva. I arrived in the dark. Outside the station there were several inches of slush. It was snowing hard when the bell rang inside the flat. She had lost her nerve. It was all off.

So I arrived in Venice two days earlier than expected. A taxi brought me up the stormy Giudecca Canal, spray breaking over the varnished wooden deck, and deposited me and my cases outside the lit door of the Pensione da Cici on a cold, dark winter evening. They were astonished to see me and even more astonished that in a week's time they would have thirty-two clients staying for the twelve deadest out-of-season weeks.

4

Countdown

Through the first nights of the countdown at the Pensione alla Salute da Cici in Venice, as I fell asleep, the bed rose and sank with the movement of the vaporetto, the Venetian public transport 'bus' riding the lagoon swell. Half-awake in the middle of the night, with the window open, the knock of a moored boat and the rustle of tide in the canal reminded me where I was. Bells. At half past six the single bell from the Salute woke me. I could see it flailing the air. At seven the abrasive set of bells from San Trovaso ended the delicious pause between sleeping and waking.

At the end of each day, before going to bed, I walked, wrapped and muffled against the January cold, two or three times round the triangle whose apex is the Customs Point, which sticks out into the Basin of St.Mark's from the church of the Salute, the Grand Canal flowing on the left. Lines of lights gleamed on the water, from the Giudecca island to the right, and to the left across the mouth of the Grand Canal, from San Marco diminishing down the Riva degli Schiavoni towards the Lido. The freezing beauty of the surroundings sharpened the edge of awareness: no Other Half, past or future; an unclear separation from our children; a gaping question mark where a job had been. But, an exhilarating freedom from the limits of life as a schoolmaster and the terrifying exhilaration of the approach, twenty-four hours nearer each day, of thirty-two unknown eighteen-year-old students booked to attend this new enterprise, which had been called the Contemporary Europe Pre-University Course.

Signor Cici

Through the night, the English past flowed and ebbed in the mind as the bell of St.Mark's tolled the hours, recalling Bell Harry and the night watchman who walked the locked Canterbury Precincts calling the hour and weather.

'Twelve o'clock and a fine frosty night!'

The Sunday cathedral service came into my light slumbers, those moments of high comedy when Canon Shirley and Dr. Hewlett Johnson, the notorious communist Red Dean of Canterbury, poured their mutual contempt of each other into bitterly competitive readings of the lessons, loading whatsoever text with personal innuendo.

'Woe, woe unto them that draw iniquity with words of vanity and sin as it were with a cart rope,' declaimed the canon.

'Seest thou a man wise in his own conceit ? There is more hope of a fool than of him,' replied the Dean. The duel was performed in the context of the Medieval architecture and stained glass of the Cathedral Choir, the polyphony of Orlando Gibbons and seven hundred voices singing the great Protestant hymns. Whoever's turn it was to preach laid about the other in scantily veiled words, to the delight of the King's School and the assembled burghers of Canterbury.

In the mornings before breakfast, Cici's voice filled the quiet *pensione*.

'*Pronto! Pronto! Pronto!*' he would shout down the receiver in his broad Veneto accent, as lights flashed on the new telephone switchboard and he inserted leads hopelessly into socket after socket. As the lights stopped flashing one after another he was was left gazing defiantly at the equipment, smoothing back his non-existent hair, helpless without his receptionist Antonietta.

The photo of Cici in the album brings him back to life. He was a small, round man in his fifties, from Dolo up the Brenta Canal, with a glint of gold in his mouth and a prominent gold chain crossing his cardiganed paunch to the mass of keys in his trouser pocket. Every half-hour he pulled out the keys to open the cash drawer and then to open the cash box in the drawer, checking its state. Beside the cash box was a hand gun. He kept a shotgun under his bed. On his own at the reception desk, his mobile features moved from the golden smile of welcome to the frown of concentration when the telephone rang. Although he read and wrote with modest ability and some difficulty, he was alert in the best Venetian business tradition. Every other half-hour he would stand up, put on his black overcoat, his black beret and wind a woollen scarf round his neck and over his chin and mouth. He then walked to the glass front door, stepping outside and looking up and down the *fondamenta* – the canal-side paving, noting the level of the tide in the canal. His bulky wife moved silently about the building in slippers, like a loaded cannon, passing through the reception area into the dining room and kitchen, a professional smile for clients displacing for a moment the conjugal scowl. A pale fifteen-year-old son flitted about in the background.

My bedroom was on the fourth floor, with a window towards the Salute church. My office was the best room in the building, on the first floor, the *piano nobile*, its Renaissance columned and arched windows letting out onto a balcony above the front door over the canal.

In these tense days before the arrival of the students, why Clementson had put us here became clearer. Although the '*vasto giardino*' of the hotel brochure was only a small service backyard, unusable in winter, the position near the Salute, on its own little canal, was picturesque, the price was low and the food in the restaurant was excellent. As I went about my business in Venice, I discovered that *Cici's* was famous for its food and clientèle. I often had lunch there, served by the galleon-like waitress Virginia, who removed the flesh from a fish's bones with consummate neatness. Two elderly *contessas*, a former Swedish ambassador and his wife and a basketball team lived da Cici and took their meals there.

A regular and strange experience was sitting at the next table to the silent Ezra Pound, who lived forty yards up the canal. His companion Olga Rudge talked to him through the meals. His bright blue eyes took in the company, though they never registered any reaction to the passing of thirty or more animated and mainly Aryan students through our dining room into their student dining area each evening, often pausing for greetings and conversation with me and the visiting lecturers who sat with me. On one occasion only was he heard to speak. The chaplain of the English church, Victor Stanley, an American of Orson Welles-like stature and voice, found himself at the next table to Ezra Pound's at lunch. He greeted Mr. Pound and received that slight inclination of the head which could not quite be called a nod. Pound turned to the chaplain and said:

'And what do you think of the Thirty-Nine Articles, Mr. Stanley?'

'You had better ask your friend Mr. Eliot about that,' the chaplain replied, fully aware that these were the only words known to have been spoken publicly by the poet in years.

After three years at neighbouring tables he would return my greetings with what seemed a not unfriendly gaze. I had been taken to his house one evening by John Guthrie, a friend of Olga's. The form was to converse over tea and wine in the master's presence but without expecting his participation. On this occasion he nodded animated approval of Olga's suggestion that she play his reading of his poem *The Bellaires*. Late at night in the previous week, he had broken silence at home, wanting to speak the poem into a tape recorder. His strong voice declaimed this sonorous and ironic pattern of words with perfect intonation and expression.

The San Gregorio, San Vio and Accademia village became familiar. Roberto, another regular at *Cici's*, and I often dined together at the Trattoria ai Cugnai, where the three raven-haired sisters and brother Giorgio serving their clientèle are more or less unchanged to this day, give or take a grey hair or two and occasional replacements of the fish displayed on the same plate in the window.

Of our other local, the Cantinone Storico on the Rio San Vio, today only the faded painted name is unaltered. Sawdust on the floor, the roughest *grappa* at the bar, no menu and no choice: but if you wanted to eat, whatever the family had would be offered. The thirteen-year-old daughter of the family sprawled, Lolita-like, moist armpit hair protruding, at one of the three tables, sucking her pencil, doing her homework. At another, a regular was the sea captain who lived near Sant'Angelo Raffaele. He usually brought one of his monkeys for company: it made alarming forays from its perch on his shoulder.

This was the village of Peggy Guggenheim too, and her family of long-haired Lhasa dogs. Many times each day I passed the gate of her palace, iron wrought in a modernistic style inset with large pieces of coloured glass. At this low season of the year, when the world of glitz was not in Venice, her house was a relaxed meeting place of friends. Bringing Peggy a drink, with lots of ice, in one of the chunky Picasso tumblers, being in the long, modern, white, sunny drawing room over the canal, having supper sitting at an austere Medieval refectory table with high-backed wooden chairs in the small dining room, Picassos on the white walls, was a privilege and pleasure. After Peggy died in 1979, what had been her private house, open at times to the public, often with Peggy sitting at the door taking the entrance money, became an American-style gallery. Controlled by the Solomon Guggenheim Foundation of New York, its name is spelled out in letters large and clear on the canal façade of the palace. The unique personality of the place has gone forever.

'*Venice – Flat to let. Box C 572*' leapt from the small print of *The Times* column which was in the waiting room of the British Consulate, the only time I had looked at an English paper since leaving England. This remote chance opened up another bright dimension and took the mind momentarily off the imminent arrival of the students, now only three days away.

'It's probably Josephine's,' the Vice-Consul said. 'Did you meet her in April? Her husband has died recently. She's had to leave Venice.'

Within three weeks I was Mrs. Paterson's successor, tenant of the large apartment in the *Palazzo Bonlini* where I had had English tea in the firesmoke last April. The owner, Mrs. Somers-Cocks, had flown out from London and gone through the inventory, explained the idiosyncratic functioning of the giant coke central-heating boiler, and introduced Rita. Rita lived in an adjoining house, understood the boiler and would do cleaning. She told me about Silvio who had always been allowed to sleep in the cavern under the stairs in the dark entrance area on the ground floor. Silvio was a frail lunatic who lived by begging, usually in diplomatic French, and by cleaning consular floors. When the moon was full and unclouded, he became charged with energy. I often heard him as he wandered the canals on moonlit nights, and wondered what thoughts were in his head, what his life had been, as he railed in a loud voice and kicked walls. But usually, when I let myself in

Peggy Guggenheim

at night and the tiny entrance hall light-bulb only emphasized the shadows and dimly illuminated me, the intruder, I heard the sound of him turning on his straw, awake or asleep.

The apartment was above the *piano nobile* which was occupied by an elderly *contessa*, who liked to show her signed royal photographs in their silver frames. The palace fronted across a *fondamenta* onto the Rio degli Ognissanti. From the windows I looked across the canal into the garden and palace of the French Consulate, viewing both the preparation of dinners in the kitchen and their social consumption in the elaborate, frescoed dining room. The butler could be seen serving wine at table, stooping attentively to guests' glasses with the decanter, leaving the dining room with unhurried dignity, entering the kitchen, removing his jacket and filling a tumbler from decanted bottles, presumably of premiers grands crûs Bordeaux. Only once did

Palazzo Bonlini

I glimpse anything, from my darkened window, of what the butler traditionally saw. At a lit window, a woman undressed, released her tied-up hair and came to gaze out into the warm night, standing naked at the window. She turned, as someone came into the room and the light went off.

The apartment had the large, simple spaces and convenient plan of the classic Venetian palace and its population of invisible and, in this one at least, benign presences. The main space, the *salone*, ran the full twenty-five yards of the depth of the building, from the windows at the front onto the canal to the taller windows at the back, which opened onto a balcony above the garden. The ceiling was of closely-spaced wooden beams, the floor of slightly undulating *terrazzo*, a paste of ground mortar and marble chips polished to a bright finish which, like water, reflected the light from the windows. The walls were covered with large canvases in heavy frames, those copies of familiar masterpieces from the Prado. In summer, a refreshing movement of air moved in the apartment between the open windows at each end. In winter, icy fronts mixed with pockets of warmth from the central-heating, however firmly the windows were closed.

The day before the students' arrival there was a sense of frenzied activity at the *pensione*, with new chambermaids about, preparing rooms. Whenever I went upstairs, a particularly unshy new chamber-maid dressed in working overall and, it seemed, nothing else, paused in her sweeping or swabbing and followed me with careful eyes.

'*Mi chiamo Lorenzina* – I'm called Lorenzina' – she told me, with a microwave look.

Cici counted his cash and inspected the canal more frequently than usual and had a glass of superior *grappa* brought to me on a round tray. The receptionist Antonietta was in place behind the desk, no beauty but a competent, warm-hearted, bespectacled girl from Conegliano. Cici seemed as nervous as I was, and flashed me many smiles, wondering whether the group would really come.

A young man appeared at the door and struggled in with two heavy suitcases. He looked remarkably like an English schoolboy.

'*Il Corso Preuniversitario?*' he asked at the desk, in newly-learnt but surprisingly fluent Italian.

'*Professore* – is this one of your students?' Antonietta asked me, as alarmed as I was that we had got the day wrong and they were all about to arrive a day early.

All was well. He was the first student and had come a day early as he had been in Munich. He and I had dinner and *grappa* together that evening. By bed time the future Mr. Justice Burton, two of whose daughters have in recent years been on the Course – the third family of the second generation – had offered to meet the students arriving tomorrow at the station and bring them to the pensione. Also to make a speech in Italian on behalf of the students at the dreaded inauguration which so terrified me, at the Cini Foundation. From his experience as head boy at Eton he was far better prepared than I for public ceremonies. From this point on there was no escape. Thirty-one other students would already be en route by train from Victoria.

San Giorgio – The Monastery Island – Where Europe is being Reborn. Venice – Capital of Western Culture. Venice, a living city, continues to make its contribution to World Progress and Civilization. Oxford students at the Fondazione Cini – the first Swallows of Spring.

Headlines and paragraph headings in the *Gazzettino*, the Venetian newspaper, reported our launch in January 1965.

My experience as a junior schoolmaster had not prepared me for being led up the *pietra serena* steps onto the platform of the Palladian refectory, to be seated at a massive high table on a high-backed velvet chair between Count Cini and Professor Branca, the Director of the Foundation, facing a sea of formal faces, flashing press cameras and the illumination of television lighting. The Count and Branca gave speeches of welcome. I duly read my prepared words, explaining the course, and was heavily applauded. The future High Court Judge spoke in much better Italian, as if impromptu, and was received with ecstatic approval. After the ceremony we moved into the series of reception rooms which look across the water, up the Giudecca Canal and across at the Salute. White-coated waiters served a wide range of drinks and delicious snacks. The Foundation's public relations officer, Avvocato Rosso-Mazzinghi was at my side.

'May I present… the Director of the Civic Museums… the Super-intendant of Fine Arts… the Admiral of the Naval College… the Rector of the University… the Assessor for Public Instruction… the Assessor for Culture… the Head of Police… the Italian Cultural Attaché from London… the Head of Radiotelevision… the French Consul…'

And the very British Consul: 'Are there any *important* people among your students?'

Each smiling face, except the British Consul's, offered assistance and special gifts: for our students free entry to all galleries and museums; free tickets to the opera house; tickets for private televised chamber concerts in the Tiepolo room at the television headquarters in Palazzo Labia; the use of the university theatre. The formal meeting became a glittering and thoroughly enjoyable party at which we were the guests of honour. We had all been made to feel that the Island of San Giorgio and the city of Venice was our home.

Professor Branca offered a lift in his private launch. It was dark. We curved across the lights reflected in the Basin of St.Mark's, down the Grand Canal and were landed – I and five students – at Rialto. We finished the evening with a celebratory dinner at the Letizia. Cici's smile that evening was all gold. He had seen us on television and had received the first advance payment. A week later a letter arrived from London by special delivery from the Italian Cultural Attaché.

I greatly enjoyed our meeting and would like to confirm that I am entirely convinced of the importance of your enterprise and shall do my best to encourage it. After a brief conversation I sent our ambassador a long report suggesting he should approach Fanfani, our Foreign Minister.

Later in London financial support in the form of scholarships was proposed by the Italian government but the idea faded with the British Council's dyspeptic lack of enthusiasm to come in on a fifty-fifty basis.

The Venetian lagoon preserved Venice for over a thousand years. There are navigable channels. There are expanses of water only inches deep, covering mud. There are invisible wrecks. There are currents and tides. The mirror surface gives no indication of what is underneath. This was my introduction to Italian politics: stylish, charming, sophisticated – as enchanting and impenetrable as the deflecting mirror of the lagoon. I was aware only of the bright surface.

J.H., Palazzo Bonlini 1965

5

The Pignatti Factor

'Read most attentively the reports of the box office,' Giuseppe Verdi advised a new young director of La Scala. *'These, whether you like it or not, are the only documents which measure success or failure. They admit of no argument and represent not mere opinions but facts. If the public comes, the object is attained. If not...'*

For the next years, by Verdi's criteria, the Pre-University Course achieved its object.

In Milan there had been the Verdi factor. In Venice the Pignatti factor took effect in the first moments of the Course in action and for the next twelve years his introductory ten lectures awoke students to an enjoyment of Art in general and of Venetian painting in particular. Here was a professional and famous art historian, an imposing personality who combined scholarly knowledge with an irresistible and infectious passion for Venice and Venetian art. His lectures, in the private lecture room of the Correr Museum in the Piazza San Marco, began at ten minutes past nine, in deference to the deafening tolling of the bells of St. Mark's at nine o'clock. The *campanile* towered over the lecture room. Allowing time for the last vibrations to be absorbed, he began – and ended exactly an hour later, to rush off through applauding students to his next teaching appointment. He was the first person to agree to give lectures for the Course though the fee was, to him, nothing. He answered letters, kept appointments and his rhetoric was of the heart, not of the convoluted paragraph. He never referred to notes and in the first fortnight had demolished the prejudice that art history was not an activity for clever people – the view current in schools in England at this time. From the first year, the art history content of the Course was increased, by popular demand.

Pignatti was one of the few Italians who lectured on the Course only because very few Italians could lecture in English. In a year when he was in America, his place was taken by the diffident, brilliant and controversial Michelangelo Muraro, who held seminars rather than gave lectures. His most memorable moment was when he arrived in the Correr lecture room with the museum's Antonello da Messina *Dead Christ with Angels* tucked under his arm. This damaged masterpiece, probably the most famous painting in the museum, was then passed from hand to hand for critical appreciation.

The Pignatti Factor, the gift of being able to inspire students, was amplified over the years by a line of lecturers with this ability, starting with the down-to-earth energy of Jennifer Fletcher of the Courtauld Institute. Charles McCorquodale, cream trousers tapering into slim-line, tightly buckled yellow wellies against the *acqua alta*, instilled an appreciation of the difficult virtuosity of High Renaissance art. He expounded the qualities of Leonardo, Raphael and Correggio in a style as elegant, subtle and compelling as the art he described. Charles Hope, from the Warburg Institute, attacked established attributions to Giorgione with the same penetration as his goal-scoring sprints on the football field in our matches against the boys of Gino's Bar. In recent years he has demystified many of the art historians' obscurantist theories, scything the way for the 'uneducated' to enjoy art, rallying the timid with his trenchant opposition to the over-erudite. His fast flow of arguments, backed by uncontestable examples, leave no doubt about the quality of his own learning. At a more measured pace, David Ekserdjian made his impact, his lapidary and nasal phrases highlighting significant qualities in the works of not only the major

Venetian painters. Many will have enjoyed the masterpieces by Cima da Conegliano in the Madonna del'Orto and at San Giovanni in Bragora, pushed beyond mere curiosity, by Ekserdjian's closing words on the lesser painters. 'Give Cima a chance.'

And there was Stella Rudolph. Fashion model, art historian, a mane of long, tawny hair, high cheek bones, hazel eyes, narrow waist, long, fine legs. Her urgent, husky-voiced conversation constantly spilled over the brink into laughter at the ludicrous aspects of almost everything. Stella lived and still lives in Florence. At our first meeting, by the time we arrived in the March darkness in my Mini Cooper at Maiano, a village on the hills above Florence, and went into the snug welcome of the Trattoria alle Cave, the fire of a new friendship was crackling and burning merrily. In the next few afternoons we drove out of Florence to look at Pontormo at Carmignano or to eat *fettunte* and drink the black wine at Machiavelli's farm at Sant'Andrea in Perseceto. The mounting beat of The Rolling Stones and the dreamy sounds of Beach Boys and Beatles on the car cassette player fixed these moments in memory. Stella is half-English, half-American but her mini-skirted walk to the front of the lecture room was pure Italian model on the catwalk at a Pitti Palace fashion show. By the time a hint of expensive scent had spread in the air, she was already several slides into her lecture, the breathless voice machine-gunning the audience with information, interpretations, images, enthusiasm. Stella was always among the last to move off to bed after keeping company in Gino's Bar, where we all, students and lecturers, consumed litres of wine 'til the early hours. A psychology lecturer used to speculate on the statistics of brain cells destroyed during these intellectual evenings. But the next morning, every next morning, when others slept, Stella had done her health exercises and was out looking at Rococo and Neoclassical sculpture and paintings the moment the churches opened at 7 a.m. By the time she had to give a lecture, she had already done a day's Art Historical work on her own account. Living in Florence married to an Italian art historian, young, glamorous, knowledgeable and immediately accessible and sympathetic to students, she answered questions on hairdressers, dry-cleaners, politics, newspapers or anything else with the same informed enthusiasm that she exuded when talking about Piranesi or Piazzetta. Her fireworks illuminated sixteen consecutive years of students.

John Hale's pace was hurried only on his run-in from the Archives to the lecture room which he reached, with just time to down a cafe in the bar, as the hour was striking. Then, when he had recovered his breath and tidied his flowing hair – blond in the early years and now silver-white – when he had crossed and re-crossed his legs, perched on the table in front of the students, an expectant silence would fall. Not for nothing had he been President of the Oxford University Dramatic Society.

'How many of you suffer from the English Disease ? Hands up who has the English Disease.'

More silence, puzzled silence, as he introduced Castiglione's idea of *sprezzatura* – the effortless, versatile polish of the amateur approach. He would tell a lewd, contemporary-sounding story of seduction, in embarrassing bodily detail, before revealing it to be Machiavelli's *Mandragora*: and so, with captive audience, on to Realpolitik. Over many years, always without notes, John Hale lectured as if thinking aloud, inviting students to share his questions, leading them with historical detail into the mentality of the Medici *mafia* in Florence or of the Renaissance popes in Rome. Most years the lecture titles remained the same, but the movements of his thoughts were always different, probing, unpredictable, holding the audience with the quietest of professional oratory. His career, in full spate, was halted seven years ago by a heavy stroke which deprived this most eloquent man of speech. With characteristic courage he was soon up and about again, listening, laughing and speaking words which didn't come out quite right.

J.H., grave-digger poet and Nicholas True

Cold February fog occupying the city after sunset recalled walks on the wild side in the company of Nicholas True. This deceptively young-faced political advisor, speech-writer for many ministers, had for years introduced students to the authentic quality of Byzantine civilisation with his understated style of delivery, a combination of scholarship and dead-pan humour. We shared many interests including the wines of the Veneto, the Venetian language and Venetian life, high and low. What we optimistically called *'the wild side'* was that string of congenial bars, *bacari* in Venetian, which punctuated the back alleys and little squares, from the Mascaron to the Milion at San Giovanni Crisostomo, the Bomba and Vedova off the Strada Nova and down past the Antica Adelaida to the backwaters of the Canal of the Misericordia and the Sensa and on to furthest San Giobbe. These ancient drinking places, with marble-topped bars and wooden furniture, a selection of good wines and traditional *cicchetti*, pulsated with the life of the locality, invisible to the outsider who didn't know the significance of the single dim lantern over a discreet door – the name in faded paint on the wooden lintel board. Locals, Venetian students, the familiar cadence of the Venetian language and the buzz of well-being, a world of hidden *movimento*: anyone might have appeared through the door.

This was the territory of Giorgio, who cruised the bars when his fishing tackle shop at San Felice was closed, self-appointed expert on the dialects of the different quarters of the city; of the ferocious, woollen-capped, duffle-coated, sea-booted retired tug captain whose menacing stare was to be ignored at all costs; and of the Salvador Dali – lookalike grave-digger-poet on the cemetery island of San Michele. And, through the seventies, of the English poet and polymath Peter Russell, on forays from his base on the Lido.

Russell, white haired, white beard blotched yellow with nicotine, a pink face ravaged by alcohol, was a true working poet, embattled publisher of his own self-typed, self-photocopied literary review and bookseller of his own works. The double-doors burst open when he entered, shoulders first, a plastic bag bulging with books for sale in each hand. Once caught by the glittering eye, there was little chance of escaping this ancient mariner. At the level of casual conversation, what he called 'the social chatter-life of the bars', Peter's company was a stimulating pleasure. But when the *Tocai* lifted him into monologue – the ancient racial memory of the Celts, Mabinogion and the Annals of Ulster, religions: Buddhist, Hindu, Zoroastrian, Confucian, Christian, Sofi, Assyro-Babylonian dialects, Sanskrit – 'Of course, no one bothers to learn Sanskrit these days... except me, that is' – few kept with him.

Although there wasn't room in the programme for the '*whole course of lectures*' which Peter offered to give, '*showing how all the scientific and humanist disciplines OUGHT to be a unified single way of thought and practical activity*,' he gave an occasional and memorable lecture. '*Poetry: Bullshit, Games-Playing or Super Knowledge?*' was the title.

'*Please allow me the maximum TIME possible, and let the kids come and go during it as and when they get tired or bored. And if they can take refreshments during it, vino etc., so much the better.*'

An evening slot in the *pensione* lecture room was fixed. He began after an extended dinner with poetry-loving students, a refilled litre carafe of white wine by his elbow. His beautiful voice commanded attention, at first. But as his mind rose away from what was intelligible to his audience, as he explored the dimensions beyond the light barrier and expounded his own theory of unified fields complete with transformation equations, more and more students took him at his word, to come... and go. After the extensive metaphysical introduction and two litres of wine, the second part of the talk was a reading of his poems. Here his voice took on a plangent quality, tears flowed down his cheeks and sobs and strangulated snarls matched his account of seeing Shelley's ghost on the Lido – '*he howled the words like one who was a man.*'

He ended with a characteristic manifesto:

> '*He who counts his pennies*
> *Never made such a rhyme*
> *As I, marrying star and slime*
> *Who have made a God of Excess.*'

Two loyal students brought him away from reeking ashtray, spilt wine and the charged atmosphere of the empty lecture room to join the throng in Gino's Bar, where he returned to earth with an experience of the Italian university system.

'This Ca'Foscari student I had been teaching, very pretty, was in tears. She had been given five out of ten for her thesis on Blake. I rang up the examining professor. "Russell speaking. This is outrageous, the mark you gave Daniela Baldrin – the thesis on Blake. *I* wrote it." The mark was immediately changed to nine, with profuse apologies. "Why didn't she tell us in the first place?"'

After castigating the local university *mafia*, he told much of his life story, including the period of his nine African wives, before walking off

Life drawing at Geoffrey's

into the night to take a late boat from the *Salute* to the Lido, both plastic bags empty. I had acquired his complete works.

'Only girls who haven't had babies have nipples like that,' was the snipy comment of a mother of children looking at a photograph of a life drawing class in action. A dominating full spread of buttocks, a back profile of curving hip falling to thin waist, the top of the torso turned, shoulders lying on a pillow, arms stretched above the head to show two ebullient breasts with conspicuously piquant nipples.

'Wide aperture. Sharp focus on the body. Look at the sharpness of the nipples. Hazy focus on the students drawing the model, on Geoffrey, on the studio, all in less clear focus. Use your apertures. Look at the modelling of the bottom, the strong lighting on the breasts.'

As Geoffrey's life drawing class went on, our professional photographer was teaching other students the art of photography and the art of professional journalism. 'How about a photograph to send to London, to go with the article?' photographer Malcolm suggested to the journalist. The Italian correspondent knew his editor, the editor knew his market and two months later the half-page nude circulated in British staff rooms and common rooms in the respectable pages of the *Times Educational Supplement*. 'Drawn by the Art of Venice' was the innocent title, heading an article on the Pre-University Course.

If Promethean speculation and a rarefied logorrhoea characterised Peter Russell, it was no part of the laconic style of the artist Geoffrey Humphreys. Geoffrey was the young art student I had met at the Vice Consul's, his uncle's, on my first visit. The working day over, Geoffrey's trail was easy to pick up. The traghetto from his palace on the Giudecca brought him to within yards of *El Bottegon*, a bar just off the Zattere at San Trovaso. Here he would bump into the Dutch painter Ysbrandt and cronies of the Dorsoduro quarter. Then his short, round figure, in shape like those wooden Russian dolls which bell out from head down to skirt, could be seen mounting and descending the Accademia Bridge, in winter dress – homburg hat and ankle-length black oilskin coat. A *prosecco* in Paolin before cutting across Campo Sant'Angelo for a serious stop at the Cantine, the bar under the Marcello palace in the Rio terà dei Assassini.

Geoffrey Humphreys

'Well – what have you been up to?' he would greet, with critical accusation, calling the barman to fill me a good *Cabernet*.

'Heard the latest about Cristina… Sandro… Anya…?" he would begin, in almost inaudible, staccato phrases, linked by no syntax and mantled in his Dutchman's English accent acquired from Ysbrandt and the long-absent Dutch mother of one of his children. He would then throw into the mortar a few leaves of wormwood, an eye of newt, a red-hot bud of peperoncino, sprinkling it liberally with arsenic, vitriol, a little imagination and a lot of humour. The finished demolition of character would be presented with a witch's cackle.

'Geoffrey has changed. He's learned it's easier not always to be nasty to people,' someone said. Opinions offered after dinner at the bar of the Chelsea Arts Club need not be taken at face value. In spite of his effervescent malice, there was a warm glow of familiarity in his company, a shared memory of late nights spent together in the bowels of Venice, and his rubbery face exudes a positive pleasure in life.

In the early years of the course, when he too was just arrived in Venice as an art student and was little older than our students, I observed his off-limits cruising in girl-rich Pre-University waters much as the Nantucket lifeguard tracked the approaching triangle of fin in *Jaws*. Twenty-five years on, and he old enough to be the father of the year's intake, my viewpoint was more that of the experienced lion-tamer supervising his drugged but still potent charge as it circles the ring.

'*He liked the English girls aristocratic for preference – his erotic snobbery was the most harmless and comic of vices – and had he not been a penniless nobody 'til he sold his first canvas? In short, the Hon Julia on his left and the Hon Victoria on his right…*' A mutual acquaintance was describing a painter, in his novel set in Venice. The honourables sounded remarkably like my students.

Geoffrey's huge, rented apartment looked across the *Giudecca* Canal at the *Dorsoduro* waterfront. Inside, it glowed with *Lalique* table lamps, lamps covered with fabrics, many candles in branched candelabra, large spaces, large tables, a piano, a cabaret stage with coloured-bulb lighting. Dolly Parton sang from many speakers at a restrained pitch. The walls were covered with his paintings, large canvases, Expressionist fantasies of Berlin-style cabaret scenes: and with drawings which bypassed the titillating implications of brevity being the soul of lingerie. Here was female nude after remembered and recognisable female nude in contorted, explicitly provocative postures. They left an impression of bursting flesh, pouting orifices, of superhuman gymnastic suppleness and endeavour, all bending to the discipline of the artist's pencil.

In recent years, at the beginning of each Pre-University Course, a party was given here for the ever more youthful students, an introduction to the once-younger Bohemian world of Venice.

'Do we call you Geoffrey? It's ravishing, this flat.'

'That's what it's for.'

'Have you noticed,' asked Caroline, snacking in the kitchen, her mouth full of bread plastered with pate, 'there's a bed in every room?'

Edward hadn't noticed.

'And they've all got cords on them.'

At Geoffrey's life drawing classes, good drawers improve their drawing, trying to emulate his fluent line. And pretty girls may still be taught the facts of life. While Charlotte was drawing the model, Geoffrey had dashed off two or three flattering good likenesses of her.

'Would it be possible for me to have one?' she asked, moist blue eyes looking through a practised flutter.

'Sure. It'll cost you £800.'

Not a fate worse than death, Charlotte thought, with mixed feelings.

Besides the Pignatti factor, there were other factors.

With the leave of his House Master, a boy may go out with his parents for a drive when they visit him on a Sunday provided that the drive is in the direction away from London and that it does not entail the missing of any school obligation. The boy must remain in School (Sunday) dress.

1760? 1860? *Nineteen-sixty*. Harrow School Rules.

'What are the Masters like?' my son asked his new class-neighbour on arriving at Chiswick Comprehensive School after rebellious years at a country Public School.

'The Masters? *We're* the Masters.'

In 1967 students arrived in Venice with a completely New Look, with different hair, with *Penny Lane* and *Strawberry Fields*. 1967, 1968, 1969, 1970, creative, relaxed, intelligent, unaggressive. Already, by 1971 the astringent, demolishing humour of Monty Python was puncturing Romanticism and turning towards the shorter mental haircut of the '80s.

Whatever happened to the beautiful, wooden-cased Tandberg tape recorder, donated by Thorn Electronics to our good cause? A cardboard box in the attic has some old spools but there is nothing nowadays to play them on. One is marked 'Peter Russell Interview' – his views on Venice, recorded for the soundtrack of the 16mm film the students shot but never edited together back in London. The 8mm film of the year before disappeared quickly on its round of loans: *Goldpigeon*.

Still-snaps have fixed the villain Michael Burton, in top hat and cloak, by the Moors on top of the Clock Tower, looking across the Piazza with binoculars focused on the shapely Elizabeth Coates, who had persuaded the management of the Florian Caffe to let her appear at a first-floor window in a bikini, in February. Another spool, labelled 'Palazzo Bonlini Music', recalls an afternoon of bright February sun flooding into the freezing apartment where the just-seventeen-year-old Emma Kirkby, already an open classical scholar to Somerville, led a faltering trio of uneven talent.

An old programme records a production in the Ca' Foscari University Theatre of two Pinter plays, a preview of Carmen du Sautoy's memorably sexy performances later on television and in the theatre. Photographs in an album date a production in the Palazzo Priuli of a fantasy version of *A Midsummer Night's Dream*, with gold and silver masks by Geoffrey and Ysbrandt. At this performance, the characters arrived at the palace by gondola, rowed by our gondolier-friend Memmo. To drums and fanfares the cast ran up the stairs into the packed audience room on the *piano nobile*. After the performance Memmo rowed an over-loaded gondola back across the Grand Canal to a spaghetti supper at the house of our bar-friends, Gino and Rosanna. A minuscule student, though one who could control and ride the most spirited horses at his parents' stud in Ireland, was euphorically drunk. Trailing one arm in the water, his head lying in her lap, he professed passionate love to Rosanna, old enough to be his mother.

The sharpest memory of those '70s years when Mike Healey, from the Oxford Playhouse and then the BBC television studios in Manchester, ran wonderful weeks of theatre workshop stays clearly in the mind. Our most beautiful, longest-blondest-haired student descended the marble staircase into the central hall of the dark Palazzo Grassi, dressed in white, lit by her own one candle, reciting Lady Macbeth's sleepwalking lines, execrably. The visual moment held the audience in wrapt silence. This was the old, slightly decaying Palazzo Grassi long before its renovation as an Agnelli-Fiat showpiece.

There is a whole file full of bits of paper, old notices of Healey's other role, as Football Manager in our annual match against the local youth of Gino's Bar.

D Day. FOOTBALL MATCH.

1. D stands for DANGER, DREAD, possibly even DEFEAT. However, today is the day and it is hoped that everyone appreciates the importance of the date-apart, that is, from it being St.Gregory's Day, the beginning of Law Moderation Exams, the beginning of Pass School Groups B2, 5, 7 and 8 and the Matriculation Ceremony. Lest we forget, we ARE British and remain the sole representatives in Venice of a great footballing nation…

2. I perhaps did not make it clear that the football match is Compulsory. The team posted remains completely open to change. Everyone to bring own splints.

3. We still require players with Special Skills. I have mentioned the service a select group of the prettiest girls could render their team (auditions in my room by private arrangement) but we do require girls with First Aid and Nursing experience, trained Masseuses (auditions in my room by private arrangement), those familiar with the techniques of Psychological Warfare and anyone skilled in administering Sleeping Pills (a knowledge of the names of the opposing team could be an advantage).
4. Meet in Gino's Bar at 8pm. Gino is arranging a barge to take us across the water to the Arena.

Signed, Mike Healey' (sic)

The annual eight-a-side match was played by floodlight on the dusty football pitch under the south wall of Palladio's Redentore church on the Giudecca. In spite of Charles Hope's dribbles, Stella Rudolph's American-style cheerleading and Gino's severely supportive refereeing, we never lost by less than ten goals. Except once when we had some large, athletic boys who were cajoled into a do-or-die physical effort by exceptionally persuasive girls. Gino blew the final whistle early just before our fragile lead was lost, after which the cup has remained uncontested on a shelf in his bar.

Gino's Bar was in the Rio Terà dei Catecumeni, right by the back entrance to the Pensione alla Salute da Cici. Isolated in Dorsoduro, near the Salute, for most of the year it did little business – odd coffees and *grappas* for the men who worked in the customs house and for the water taxi drivers based on the Salute waterfront. But while we were in Venice, from mid-January to mid-March, it thrived, from breakfast time 'til at least 2 a.m., packed in the evenings with our students and lecturers.

Gino was a cousin of Cici, from Dolo up the Brenta canal. When we began, at night Gino shared a space under the stairs at Cici's *pensione* with his *fidanzata* Rosanna. Cici set them up in the bar. Congenitally cheerful and hard-working, they provided a second home for all our students and lecturers. At any time of day or night Rosanna would

Students outside Gino and Rosanna's bar 1968

run up plates of spaghetti for the hungry, usually *al aglio e olio* – with garlic and oil – at an unbeatably low price. Jugs of cheap wine were continuously consumed. As the lecturers also stayed at Cici's, they too spent evenings in Gino's, and the effortless, unavoidable familiarity and social intercourse between everyone was exhilarating, especially at a time when in England teachers and taught were separated by nervous incomprehension and sullen rebellion. Plans for expeditions to the Brenta villas, for night picnics on deserted islands, football practices, changes in lecture times, end-of-course travel arrangements – all business was conducted from Gino's.

There were other variations on the Pignatti Factor. Psychological factors. The Venice factor.

'It is not too much to say that in the three weeks in Venice we got across as much as in an eight-week university term', wrote John Wilson in the *Times Educational Supplement,* after the first course.

'A rebirth, a liberation from the limited vision that school had left me with', wrote Sally Cockburn, a former head girl of St. Paul's Girls' School.

The barge left the canal outside Cici's at 6.30 a.m. We crossed the lagoon in thick mist, following the marked channel. As we turned into the Brenta at Fusina and chugged past the ghostly bulk of Palladio's

Renzo's barge on the Brenta

Villa Malcontenta, the sun began to burn through. A day of sunshine, passing villa after villa. A picnic lunch on the barge moored by the Villa Pisani at Stra. In front of me now, on my wall, three photographs of the voyage, taken from the red album. One, facing the stern, of my two children, aged seven and nine, stripped to the waist, each with a hand on the tiller, supervised by Renzo the boatman. Another shows reclining forms arranged on the barge in perfect symmetry. A third looks forward at assorted figures, eating risotto off paper plates, drinking tumblers of wine – students and lecturers. Larry Chase, a Californian philosopher from the University of Kent; Paul Ginsborg, a Cambridge research student now an authority on modern Italian history; Carmen du Sautoy, a future actress; Caroline Villers, a future lecturer at the Courtauld Institute; and the future Museum Curator Nicholas Penny who later wrote:

I owe more to the months spent on the Pre-University Course in Venice than I do to the whole of my time in the sixth form at Shrewsbury or even to my three years at Cambridge. The instruction provided was excellent and also so enjoyable that I cannot think of it as separated from the outings we were encouraged to arrange independently – to the remoter churches of the city, to the Palladian villas of the mainland and to the Villas on the Brenta.

Renzo, his dog and his boat were a regular part of our activities. A tall, lean former professional footballer for Cagliari, he was a typical Venetian freelance boatman, carting whatever was needed – wood, furniture, vegetables. At the beginning and end of the course he would collect the students' suitcases on their arrival at the station and bring them to the *pensione*, and vice versa, running the gauntlet of the porters' and railway boatmen's unionism. Many students remember trips up the Brenta in Renzo's boat, and moonlight excursions on the oily black lagoon, with guitar music and romantic supper picnics on remote islands inhabited only by abandoned dogs.

Renzo married an American tourist, and now, less lean and youthful, parents of a brood of children, he and his wife own a bar on the Fondamenta Nove.

For me personally there were also the wonderful, regular visits of my children Nicholas, Charlie and Katharine, recurring over the years, a pattern of ecstatic meetings of unaccompanied minors at Venice airport, and sad departures. Fitting into this sort of life in Venice was, for them, an exotic contrast to school and home in the Northamptonshire countryside of England. They soon got used to

Brenta picnic

going to bed late when they fell asleep, like Italian children do. They were much befriended by students, lecturers and all our Italian friends. Occasionally we did improving projects, like sketching the facades of all the Gothic churches in Venice. Switching to the Renaissance San Zaccaria guaranteed an appreciation of ultra-complicated symmetry. Eventually they arrived on the course as eighteen-year-old students and now it will not be long before my granddaughter Charlotte, the daughter of oldest son Nicholas, comes on the course herself.

At the end of the course, Cici would offer a special celebration dinner for all the students and any lecturers present, and our friends. We were given Easter lamb or mountain kid as the main course, after the usual *antipasti* and spaghettis and lasagnes. Superior, strong red wine was offered generously and there was a high degree of merriment. English inhibitions disappear on these occasions. A boy approached me towards the end of the dinner, sitting down for a few moments opposite me, a glass of *grappa* in his fist. 'Hey John Hall. I've been wanting to ask you – what do you actually *do* here in Venice? You don't give lectures. You don't tell us off. What do you *do*?' *In vino veritas.* I knew what he meant.

Box office reports had been satisfactory. The number of students rose steadily. Unfortunately, the box office reports are not the only documents which measure success or failure, as the bank manager kept pointing out. It took more than five years to pay the debt which the patient Mr. Clementson had allowed. My amateur costings had been disastrous. The bank manager recommended an accountant who was even more confused than I by working in two currencies with unstable exchange rates, but it took him two years to fade away. His successor, an old Oxford friend, was far too congenial for the job. By the time we had discovered that looking at accounts and evening conviviality didn't go together, we were getting into deeper financial water.

6

Italian Journeys

Mr. Swan, loud-hailer in hand, had gone out on the tug *Validus* to meet his Hellenic Cruise ship returning on the morning tide. We were waiting for him in the Clementson Travel Office in Venice.

8 a.m. Porters at San Basilio. 8 a.m. Busatto barge at San Basilio. Porters transfer cases to barge. Barge transfer to airport. Deposit cases. 9 a.m. Guide, Dr. Ortolani, to San Basilio. Rendezvous with Miss Goodstone, tour manager. 9.30. Morning tour to begin, on foot. 9.50. Accademia. 11.30 Frari. 12.30 Lunch at Giardinetto…

The quiet, North-country voice of Clem went through the arrangements, minute by hour, porter by barge, guide by entrance fee, restaurant by menu – *cappuccino* always included. Lucia, in charge of the Swan file, confirmed each detail. The military precision of moving troops in ships, in lorries, on trains, practised in the African desert and up through Italy in the war, was transferred smoothly into the travel business. The post-war, upmarket London–Mediterranean travel boom was in the hands of friends, a network. Clem had married an Italian, opened his office in Venice and serviced the Mediterranean cultural cruises: the Nile, Greece, Turkey and all Italy for his London friends. Naturally, they all ran with clockwork efficiency.

Clem was from Darlington, where his brother still ran a bicycle shop. The fact that my brother and I had often crossed the Pennines, pushing up the steep hills from Brough to the Bowes Moor summit, then free-wheeling twenty five miles down to Barnard Castle, and knew all about *de Railleur* and *Sturmey Archer* gears was the highest character reference I could possess, in the mind of Clem.

Mr. Swan arrived in the office in grey flannels, bursting navy blue blazer and tie and with a healthy red face – a pickled onion, tomato ketchup sergeant-major type. He lived for his father's brainchild, the Hellenic Cruises. Drawing on classical experts, professors from Oxford and Cambridge who were happy to talk about Ancient Greece in return for a luxury cruise, Swan Hellenic enjoyed the highest reputation. Mr. Swan controlled his relatively well-heeled passengers with the brusqueness of a transport NCO. The retired colonels, canons and Oxford dons and their wives loved it. Over lunch at Swan's favourite restaurant, La Colomba, Clem had introduced me, persuaded Swan to invest some capital in my Pre-University enterprise, and to accept my proposal that Swan should offer an Italian Gardens tour in their Art Treasures programme next year. As a leaving-present from my colleagues at Canterbury, I had been given Georgina Masson's two inspiring books, *Italian Villas and Palaces* and *Italian Gardens,* so I thought I knew something about them.

Long after Swan had retired to his bed in the Bauer Grunwald Hotel, the hard-working Clem needed help in the last phase of a busy day, entertaining the Chairman of Swan Hellenic, who had come in that morning with the returning cruise. In lapses of attention to the Chairman, who was concentrating on the floor-show at the *Antico Martini* night club, I was attending to a sleek hostess who was coiled on a high bar stool.

'Don't you remember me,' she asked. 'Look carefully.'

I was already looking carefully.

'No – my eyes.'

I tried to recall something familiar in that smouldering, sustained gaze.

'Don't you remember dancing with me? At the party with the students at *Cici's*, on their last night?'

She was the once-new chambermaid, Lorenzina. I could hardly believe my eyes.

'I went to Milan.'

Now, after Milan, she was adamant, polished adamant.

'You missed your chance.'

The Chairman and I left together, recommending to each other a good night's sleep, and then going our separate ways. Maybe one last glass with the enigmatic lady, I thought, walking round the block. But as I came round the last corner, I saw the Chairman going back into the night-club. As I walked home through the empty squares, I thought I was looking through an open door into the travel industry, into bright prospects. Lights were out in the French consulate.

As soon as the course was over and the students gone, I headed for Rome. I needed to know much more about Italian villas and gardens for the Swan's tour we had agreed to put together. Georgina Masson received me in her calm, cool, spacious apartment in the stables of the Villa Doria Pamphilij on the Janiculum Hill overlooking Rome.

'Know your Italy' she commanded, like a headmistress. 'Use the old red *Baedekkers* and the *Touring Club* guides. Nothing else. Make lists. Make notes. Visit, visit, visit. There are no short cuts. And read. Pliny. Varro. Petrarch. Alberti.' She gave me lunch in her local *Trattoria Gianicolo* at the San Pancrazio gate. She wished me '*buon lavoro!*' 'And did I know anyone who would like to occupy her flat in the summer, in return for looking after her golden retrievers?'

Classic Italian gardens are clustered round Rome, Florence, Siena, Verona and Lakes Como, Maggiore and Garda, an idyllic research itinerary. They are not, I soon discovered, in the English taste.

The first surprise is the flower fact. Articles on *Perennial lobelias at Longstock Park*, on *The Queen who brought respectability to the art of floriculture* or on *Baskets with staying power* are not a preparation. As D.H. Lawrence found out, ask an Italian what a particular flower is and he will reply: 'It's a flower.' If pressed further he'll say: 'It's a flower that smells.'

Dorothy Wordsworth dismissed the Baroque garden fantasy of Isola Bella on Lake Maggiore as *'the peak of absurdity, a garden not of flowers but of stones, where coloured pebbles take the place of flowers.'*

No one who has seen and smelt the ancient wisterias in the villas outside Florence or cascading over high garden walls in Rome will ever forget them – their exuberance, the intensity of their colour and smell: or the roses at Cetinale; or the lemon blossom at Vicobello; or the jasmine at the Villa d'Este on Como. But it is true that flowers, in the sense of herbacious borders, feature little in Italian gardens. Anyone who tries to keep a garden bright and fresh in Italy in July or August will understand the problem. The climate controls. The Italian palette is shades of green, from the full range of vibrantly scented herbs, through lavender, myrtle and broom to box, olives, bays, ilex, pines and cypresses. They stay green all the year and have an architectural quality well suited to dividing spaces into compartments and to framing views.

A second surprise is the fact that many Italian gardens are in the category of ancient, architectural monuments, works of art, dating from the 16th and 17th centuries. A 16th century architect like Raphael at the Villa Madama in Rome designed house and garden at the same time. Looking at architects' drawings, the divisions of the garden – courtyards, stairs, terraces – look exactly like the divisions of spaces inside the house: in fact the garden was an extension of the house, a series of open-air rooms. A Medici architect confirmed the precedence: *'built things should be the guide and dominate things that are planted.'*

The trouble with planning a practical and commercial enterprise like a Garden Tour, specifically a tour of historic Italian gardens, was the irresistible temptation to immerse oneself in the background, in the mass of contemporary comment, which, as it were, welcomes aliens into the civilized and sympathetic company of garden-makers and garden-enjoyers from these Renaissance centuries.

The view across Lake Maggiore from the garden of Isola Bella

They made it clear that gardens were for social and private use, for living in, not for horticultural expertise, although it is recorded that Petrarch himself tried his green fingers at grafting fruit trees. Attitudes ranged from the somewhat austerely philosophical and scholarly, through the aesthetically sophisticated to the hedonistic, the pursuit of Absolute Pleasure quite up to the intensity of Frankenfurter in *The Rocky Horror Show*: all were culturally light years away from Wisley and the Chelsea Flower Show. Petrarch, in the 14th century, the first humanist gardener, opened up two mainstreams from the classical past. '*I have seen gardens that pleased me deeply. One kind is shady, made for contemplation and consecrated to Apollo. The other is less austere and is dedicated to Bacchus.*'

The more austere current was followed by the early Renaissance Florentines. Cosimo de'Medici the Elder welcomed the philosopher Marsilio Ficino's *Platonic Academy* to the villa at Careggi and then at Fiesole. At the villa of the scholar Bracciolini, called the *Accademia Valdoriana*, founded in 1427, '*no games of any kind were played, as is done in many villas.*' Perhaps in mind was the *Villa Palmieri*, where Boccacio's *Decameron* tales were told, or the exquisitely erotic scene of mixed nude bathing in the fountain of the *giardino segreto* at the d'Este court in Ferrara, recorded in the *De Sphaera* miniature. For the 15th century Florentine, the garden was associated with Cicero's '*otium cum dignitate*' – well-used leisure, and was encapsulated in the Ciceronian pun on the word *cultus*. '*Yesterday*' wrote Cosimo to Ficino, '*I came to my villa at Careggi not to cultivate my fields but my soul.*' Cicero's own Frascati villa was called the *Accademia* and the connection between gardens and Plato's Academy, with Socratic discourse under colonnades and shady trees, was re-established in the Renaissance. Circular fountain basins, box parterres in squares and rectangles reflected the neo-Platonic harmonies of their philosophical theories.

With the ascendancy of the popes in the late 15th century, Rome set the tone and classical antiquity was made officially manifest through the incredible energy, enthusiasm and conviction of the della Rovere

Pope Julius II. *Rovenante* ('demolisher') Bramante, the chief papal architect, was to pull down the ancient, delapidated 4th century Constantinian *Basilica*, the most important and revered church in Christendom, and build a new, centrally-planned Renaissance-Classical styled St. Peter's. He was to join the papal palaces clustering round St. Peter's to the Villa Belvedere at the top of the hill. The Belvedere Court was the result, an enormous built space with three ascending level terraces linked by ramps and stairs modelled on the *Temple of Fortuna* at Palestrina – a major precedent in garden design. Also, he was to build a courtyard in the Villa Belvedere for the display of Julius' superb classical statues, with a special outside spiral staircase so that they could be viewed, without intrusion into the papal enclave, by others. In this space the river gods Nile, Tigris and Tiber became fountains, a voluptuously reclining Cleopatra dripped water from a breast, here stood the *Apollo Belvedere*, the *Venus Felix*, the *Antinous* – model of male beauty; and here writhed the *Laocoon*, reminding Dickens of Scrooge struggling with his stockings. Here was the fragmented *Belvedere Torso*, so admired by Michelangelo. After which, classical statuary, authentic or imitation, was *de rigeur* in the garden.

In 1521 the courtier Castiglione, staying in the Villa Belvedere as ambassador from the refined court of Urbino, where nothing but the best would do, wrote to his mother: '*I am here at the Belvedere which is a comfort to me. Would to God that you had such a beautiful place with its beautiful view and lovely garden and so many splendid antiques, fountains, ponds and running water and, which is better, so near the palace. Through the streets below pass all those who come to Rome on this side and those who go for diversion in the meadows. After supper there come numerous men and women with their follies for my amusement.*'

A Florentine viewed the Romans differently. '*They are continuously in the garden with women, and others similar to them, where they awaken the silent muse with their lyre, giving themselves pleasure and amusement. But, good God, what means they have, to my mind, and how they guzzle after they have poeticised. They have players of various instruments and they dance and leap with these girls in the manner of the Salii or rather the Bacchanti,'* wrote the frugal Agostino Vespucci to Machiavelli in 1521.

In the countryside around Rome there were innumerable magnificent villas and gardens, of which the finest are intact today – the Cardinal Alessandro Farnese's palace and garden at Caprarola, the Cardinal of Ferrara's Villa d'Este at Tivoli and Cardinal Gambara's twin *casini* and garden at Bagnaia.

You who enter here, consider carefully every detail and then tell me if so many marvels are made for deceit or for Art.

The inscription below the Sphinx in the Duke Vicino Orsini's *Sacred Park* at nearby Bomarzo acknowledges the conscious playing between Art and Nature that these creations expressed, as well as something of his contorted mind.

You who wander through the world to see its stupendous marvels, come here where there are horrible faces, elephants, lions, monsters and dragons.

He was referring to the gigantic, grotesque carving of boulders of living rock on the steep hillside below his castle.

In contrast, the garden of Cardinal Gambara was described as:

a gentle and pretty maiden, well adorned with sumptuous and various clothes and also with jewels on her fine head, pearls in her ears and many rings on her well-kept hands.

Born-again Romans, complete with free-standing reproduction statues, busts in niches, obelisks, grotesque heads, sleeping nymphs and river gods, these princely prelates provided gentle stimulation for body and mind. Teasing and pleasing associations and levels of meaning went with the Papal Progresses, the Lucullan banquets and the squeals of the ladies as water, from hidden tricks, squirted up their skirts. In the gardens they walked with an idealised, classical past. In Parnassus, home of Apollo and the Muses, a winged Pegasus struck the ground with his hoof and out poured the freshwater spring of inspiration, Hippocrene. Huge stone acorns, pine cones and water-purifying unicorns took them into the Golden Age, when Nature provided All. The ubiquitous Hercules, symbol of so many patron families, defied the guardian dragon in many Gardens of the Hesperides. Pan, shepherds, goats, satyrs and fauns kept them company in Arcadia, swans, dolphins and cupids welcomed them to the island of Cythera, birthplace of Venus. '*I dare not speak the name of Jesus lest I break the spell*' admitted the very catholic Queen Christina of Sweden, amazed by the pagan spirit of the gardens at Caprarola.

In several gardens their function was inscribed on stone tablets. Some of the most pleasing are at the Villa Barbarigo at Valsanzibio near Padua, the inscriptions now barely legible:

Here a brighter Sun shines its rays; here a more beautiful Venus rises from the sea; here the phases of the moon are more luminous; here Jove plays calmly and his face is serene.

Here weeping has no place and laughter has its home.

To achieve Leisure and Calm is the ultimate purpose of Action.

Sitting in a travel office between Tottenham Court Road and Gower Street, filtering and reducing travel in these realms of gold into copy for a garden tour brochure, focused a mass of new knowledge, about historic Italian gardens and about how the travel business works. Itinerary planning brought compromises. How long the tour should last depended on competition in selling tours: it was decided by competitive costing. What to include, to leave out was decided not by garden historical or even aesthetic importance but by the logistics of coach journeys, accessibility, opening times, airport arrival and departure times.

The brochure, with attractive photos, was printed, circulated and the tour booked up fast, thanks to the reputation of the Swan company and their mailing list of satisfied and suitable customers. I was paid I can't remember what – something per person. The tour went well. Letters of satisfaction came in. An expanded programme was under way for the next year when Harold Wilson's Labour Government imposed currency restrictions on travel abroad. The project had to be abandoned. So ended a short first chapter. At the same time ended the Swan association with the Pre-University Course. Under the influence of the helpful (to me) Mr. Clementson, Swan had invested a little much-needed capital in a Pre-University Course limited company. Aware of his directorial responsibilities and our accounting chaos, he gave up his shares, after insisting that we seriously increased our fees. It was correct advice.

Over the next years parents of students in Venice often asked whether something couldn't be arranged for them. The idea developed, particularly in conversation with Stella Rudolph, of running some tours offering a fundamentally different exposure to Italy from that provided by the conventional tours. Chapter two we named *Italian Journeys*.

The first criterion was that they were to be country tours, in areas not at that time well known. *The Alban and Cimini Hills Tour*, North and South of Rome was based first at Castelgandolfo and from there visited Frascati, Subiaco, Palestrina, Tivoli, Velletri, Fossa Nova, Anagni, and Bracciano. Then, from Viterbo, we visited Montefiascone, Bassano di Sutri, Soriano, Bomarzo, Bagnaia, Caprarola, Tuscania and Tarquinia – most of which, even today, are off the tourist route.

For the tour of Umbria we stayed in the enchanting little hilltop town of Trevi. We arrived from Rome airport outside the gate of Trevi in a de-luxe hired coach with the words *Executive Red Carpet* written down its length. Trevi had never seen a tour group. The coach could not go through the Medieval gate, so we walked with cases to our little hotel Il Cocchetto, a few paces beyond the piazza. During dinner a message was brought to us saying that we were all made honorary members of the Trevi Club for the duration of our stay. The Trevi Club is in effect a bar – the one we had all walked past just inside the gate. The next evening the mayor invited us to a reception in the town hall which he was pleased to give in our honour.

A third tour was the Veneto, based in Bassano del Grappa, and the fourth was *Central and Western Tuscany*, going from Siena into the Maremma near Grosseto and Massa Marittima.

A second criterion was a certain kind of accommodation. International-style hotels were avoided, ancient hostelries favoured, some far more efficient in the days of the Grand Tour than in the 20th century. Bypassed by autostradas, almost all of them have now faded from the Michelin and other guides. The Albergo Antico Angelo, gia d'Inghilterra ed Imperiale – the Queen of England stayed there in 1816 – was *'old fashioned, spacious, with fine, plain rooms.'* The Hotel Mirador, just off the main street, on the edge of the drop down to Lake Albano, had *'simple rooms, with cold water only on tap: there is hot water in the bathrooms.'* The Pensione Palazzo Ravizza was *'a 17th century palace with a shaded terrace-garden and views into the surrounding countryside.'*

Another characteristic of *Italian Journeys* was the pursuit of authentic local food and wine – and wine was included in the price of the tour and was always waiting on the table when we arrived. We ate in many *trattorie* where no English was spoken or written, but we were always looked after with the combination of warmth and natural style which is particular to Italy. At the tiny village of Serrapetrona a local regular brought and offered bottles of his own good wine as a gift when he heard that twenty-five English were coming to lunch. Traditional Italian lunches – *antipasti, primo, secondo, insalata* and *dolce* imposed a suitable long pause in the middle of the day's activities. Time spent over coffee in the piazzas of innumerable little towns was one of the most enjoyable memories of these tours.

Maybe the most important ingredient was the champagne presence of Stella Rudolph. As in Venice, but here on the hoof not in the lecture room, her knowledge of Italian art and enthusiasm for it, and her ability to communicate information and appreciation was an inspiration. Every morning and after lunch we would travel in our coach to look at buildings and works of art, under Stella's guidance. In the evening, after time to recover, we would meet again for dinner. Stella was always at the centre of animated discussion and laughter on subjects often far removed from art 'til the tables had been cleared and re-laid for breakfast, other guests and waiters had gone and we realised with a shock that it was midnight, again.

Many who came on the tours were parents of Venice students or their friends. Some came through the occasional advertisement put in *Country Life* or *The Spectator*, some had seen favourable comments in the travel column of *The Guardian* or *Daily Telegraph*. Numbers varied from fifteen to twenty-five and it was always a pleasure to be with those who came: the judge who had lost an arm near Orvieto in the war; a former head of the College of Physicians who looked on depictions of martyrdoms and cruel deaths, particularly decapitations, in order to observe Medieval and Renaissance ideas of the circulation of blood; the Yorkshire squire and his fey wife who believed that black dogs were re-incarnated Etruscans; the Cambridge professor who ran his college wine cellar; the ninety-three-year-old, agile in mind and body, and her sixty-five-year-old daughter; the naval commander; the colonel; barristers, architects... all Italophiles, all on holiday, all relieved to find such congenial company. Few present will have forgotten the joy of the Derbyshire lady who found a pair of shoes to fit her tiny feet, and the magnificent spontaneous oration of the director of Kay Shoes, holding up the new shoes in our restaurant in Perugia and explaining the fineness of the work and the skills of the maker, unmatchable in England, he said.

Italian Journeys never got going in a way that would cover the expenses of printing and circulation. Our regulars came 'til they had done all our itineraries but we couldn't afford the advertising to widen our recruitment. So the itineraries, the glowing descriptions and the lists of participants were put away in a slim file, an archive of happy memories.

Not entirely inert however. If the idea was good and the problem was only lack of publicity, surely some up-market travel firm might take them up? The Swan mailing list had filled the Villas and Gardens Tour straight away. A letter was written to the London-based Italian firm CIT. They were interested. They wanted four itineraries. Each would be offered twice a year, in early summer and early autumn. Each would be given a full page in their highly-coloured brochure. To justify the cost of the pages in the brochure, each and every tour must recruit twenty-eight people. In the first year CIT expected and required 224 clients: 216 booked. The tours were given a second chance. They reached 220 and were abandoned as not cost effective.

They had a second resurrection following an introduction to the new post – Mr. Swan management of the Swan Hellenic Art Treasures Tours – very sympathetic people to work with. The tours again went well but by this time, the late '80s, Italy had become expensive and what Swan and others were offering in the Middle and Far East seemed better value. So after the travel industry trough round the Gulf War, the *Italian Journeys* faded from the Swan brochure. They now wait for rare resuscitations and re-stylings for American groups, and even perhaps, for the English.

Tours or no tours, the itineraries are there and behind each itinerary was a travel diary of considerable kilometrage, driving, stopping, staying in improbable and remote places, looking at towns, buildings, paintings, frescoes, meeting people. It was in the course of this research that the suppressed dream of living in a house with a mountain view came back to life – a dream which had evaporated in the realistic light of the price of the most primitive country cottage in England. I began to realize that Italy has plenty of mountains quite as grand as Liathach, as sheer as the Cuillin, as wild as the head of

Eskdale. The associations are different. In place of weird sisters on the blasted heath of Rannoch Moor or toe-and-fingerhold dramas roped together on the Central Buttress of Scafell Pike were the ensnaring groves of Ovid's *Ars Amatoria*, the sophisticated villa lifestyle of Pliny, Catullus and Horace and, in place of heather and bracken, olives, vines and sun. The hunt became less casual.

Nine years of intermittent search in the Veneto, in Tuscany, in Umbria, had led up many rocky tracks white with dust or potted with quagmire according to season, into an Arcadian world. Seasonal activities went on as defined in Medieval illuminated manuscripts: the ploughing with sacrificial white oxen – see the photo in the green album of my neighbour Orlando with his team; the broadcast sowing; the grape vintage; the olive harvest; the winter chopping of wood; the killing of the pig; the pruning of the vines trained on trees; the harvests, hay, grain, hay again, maize. The habit grew of driving with neck craned sideways and usually upwards to spot abandoned farmhouses. Engaging in conversations with roadside *contadini* had led into an interior where the stranger was compelled by custom to sit at the family table in the kitchen-living room and accept hospitality – a slice off the homebaked loaf held, for cutting, against the breast of the wife, slices of home-cured ham, a wedge of sharp sheep cheese and a brimming glass of purple wine.

All of which sharpened the appetite for buying what the Wiltshire journalist so unromantically had called a pint-sized pad.

7

Venice – Island of Studies

Having left a life of monthly salaries and the distant prospect of a pension, pitiful though they were, an income for the Autumn was needed, given that there was the hope that tourism would occupy the Summer and the Venice course from January to April. This led to the then still Dickensian world of the London *crammer*, some of them institutions of pleasing eccentricity, individuality and efficiency. After a brief apprenticeship I opened my own mini-crammer, renting by day rooms in the London School of Bridge in the Kings Road. We took students for the Oxford and Cambridge entrance and for the January A-level re-takes.

By Christmas the Oxford and Cambridge candidates knew their fate. In early January the A-Level re-takers filed into the Bloomsbury examination halls, mine, I hoped, like well-prepared racehorses into the starting stalls, blinkered for the sprint. Tutorial files were put away into the cabinet, Venice files put into the suitcase, and the guide books to France came out, the *Michelin*, the *Logis et Auberges de France* and the wonderful guides by Richard Binns. As the regular Labour government January disasters gathered – postal strikes, electricity cuts, dustmen's strikes, and the AA warned motorists off snow-blocked roads, it was the moment of the year to savour, leaving England, heading for Venice.

The early flight on the little *Silver City* car ferry toy aeroplane left at 8 a.m., scattering sheep on the Romney Marsh at take-off from Lydd and putting down across the water at Le Toucquet. Often I was the only passenger. Then South – Arras, St. Quentin, Soissons, Chateau Thierry and the spirit-lifting sign by the road: *Vous êtes en Champagne.* The Rolling Stones and Beethoven mixed with the power of the Cooper S roaring through France as other Cooper S's were beating the Renault Alpines and Lancia Fulvias in the Draguignan mountains above Monte Carlo. The Monte Carlo rally often coincided with these journeys of such clear memories.

Already it was seven in the evening. Torrential rain. The wipers separated clear segments on the streaming windscreen. The headlights lit a smoking road and then a sign, after Chatillon-sur-Seine, to the left off the *route nationale.* According to *Michelin*, the Auberge Saint Hubert was not closed in January. It was a good forty kilometers, curve after curve through wooded hills. Then, Receys-sur-Ours: stone walls, stone houses, a tiny village. The headlights lit the inn sign, which was not illuminated. It looked very closed. But under the arch, in the cobbled yard, was a lit window. The inn was closed for repairs. 'But if I didn't mind a cold room? And something to eat in the kitchen?'

In the large stone-flagged kitchen two enormous dogs of setter extraction lay stretched in front of an open fire. There were four white pigeons in a cage fixed to the wall and four replete builders playing cards at a table, under a canopy of *gitanes* smoke. Madame put a cloth on another table for me and cut slices from a gritty, garlicky *terrine.* Then she brought a tureen of soup. Meat hissed on the fire and then on my plate – grilled lamb. And cheeses. And a jug of red wine. Then profound sleep in a freezing room. In the grey morning, coffee, *croissants* and away in the still pouring rain, back down the curves with glimpses of a trout stream frothing the colour of Guinness.

Passing through France, often entering the Mont Blanc Tunnel in grey rain and wind and emerging into brilliant Italian January sun, and going on down to Venice became a regular and pleasing part of the year. Sometimes the mind was embalmed with the knowledge that everything in Venice had been arranged and there were no visible problems ahead. At solitary dinners en route I studied the list of students I was about to meet – their names, where they lived, their schools, so that usually, within twenty-four hours of meeting them, I knew them all. The enjoyment of the journeys south was always sharpened by the *frisson* of the imminent course. Would it go well? What would the students be like? But in 1972 a considerable problem travelled with me. Where would we hold our lectures? Would I find the *Contessa*? Why had she not replied to my letters?

The courses had begun in the benevolent grandeur of the Fondazione Cini and undoubtedly its highly-publicised hospitality made much of what happened in later years possible: almost every Venetian door was open for us. It was enough to go to the box office of the *Fenice* Opera House the day before, and to present Signor Anselmo with the compliments of the Avvocato, to be given more or less whatever seats one wanted, free. However, in spite of the wonderful rooms offered on the Island of San Giorgio, there were drawbacks for students. The Foundation was closed from 12.30 to 3.30 and there was nowhere on the island to get a coffee, drink or snack. And although the *circolare vaporetto* route from the Zattere must be the most spectacularly beautiful urban public transport experience in the world, doing the journey four times a day was expensive. On sunny afternoons we had compromised by holding seminars in the Zattere waterfront bars, on the wooden platforms built out over the water, with exotic ices or hot chocolate obligatory – so no cheaper than the boat fare. In the evenings, the *salotto* of the Palazzo Bonlini, acrid with wood smoke from the faulty chimney, had been an occasional social centre. Some memorable musical evenings, parties, even cabarets had happened in the dimly-lit *salone*. But the lease of the palace ran out.

Paolo Barozzi was at that time Peggy Guggenheim's personal administrator, a polished young Venetian aristocrat who circulated in the ambivalent world of artists, dealers in contemporary art, patrons, international socialites and those who serviced this society.

'Why don't you rent my little gallery?' he asked me one evening at Peggy's, and immediately took me round to see it – it was just round the corner. It was a ground floor space, the store-room of a small palace owned by his father right opposite the back door of the Pensione da Cici, in sight of Gino's Bar. He had covered the walls with hessian, the ceiling was painted white, a cheap carpet was on the floor but the whole was brought to life by brilliant lighting – bright pools of light from bulbs hidden by the latest in contemporary Italian designer black metal shades. There was no Art on display. It was convenient. We would have the key so could use it at whatever hours we liked. It was an intimate space and it had style, in a contemporary way. And so for three years we held lectures there. Occasionally, *acqua alta* had threatened the gallery, situated in the low-lying Rio tera dei Catecumeni, behind the Salute. Whether the floor remained dry, damp or awash had often depended on our efforts at the threshold with brooms, sweeping back the gently lapping waters. Towards the end of our third very satisfactory year there, Paolo told me he was opening a gallery in Milan, closing the one in Venice.

In the last few weeks that year in Venice I had started thinking and asking around about a space for the following year. One of the two resident contessas at the Pensione da Cici heard of this and, putting on her long mink coat and hat, took me out onto the Zattere – a minute away from the Pensione. 'Your students are so intelligent,' she told me, 'so well-mannered. Come and see what I have here. Maybe it would suit you.' Finding a key in her handbag she opened an inconspicuous door on the waterfront and led me into a superlative entrance hall. A curving iron staircase led up to a huge first floor. She opened shutter after shutter, flooding the place with light. The windows looked across the Giudecca Canal to the Redentore down to the right, to the Zitelle straight opposite and, diagonally to the left, San Giorgio Maggiore – the Palladian trio. The building was empty, unfurnished, totally desirable. And ideal for us.

'The best view in Venice, is it not?' Looking out and down to the waterside paving and a wooden floating terrace, she indicated another humbler building. 'I'm going to make a restaurant there. It'll be much better than *Harry's Bar*.'

'And the price? For our lectures here?'

'Do you like it? Of course it's very expensive. It couldn't be cheap. But we can talk about that. The important thing is that you like it.'

In the last few days of that year's course, at *Cici's*, we shared the exciting prospect over occasional cups of coffee together. Nothing further was established for next year, except goodwill. '"Til next year then,' she said as I was leaving with the students.

During the year I had written to her, but had had no reply. Very few people in Italy replied to letters. As the course date came nearer, I telephoned her at the pensione, but she had left for her villa on the Brenta. So as I drove towards Venice, it was with considerable worry about our lecture space. Approaching Venice, I turned off the autostrada for Dolo and found her villa on the banks of the Brenta. An old retainer answered the bell. The *Contessa* wasn't there. She was with her sister in the mountains, in Cortina. The sister who answered the telephone had immense difficulty in understanding who I was, or what I wanted. But in the end she told me that her sister the *Contessa* from Venice had just gone to America.

'But she had said... she had promised...'

I already had had enough experience of Italy to resign myself to leaving it at that. I never saw the *Contessa* again. A couple of years later the name *Vedova* appeared, roughly painted on the wall by the bell of the obscure door into the magnificent palace. Vedova was a best-selling painter, at an international level, who lived in Venice. And many years later a bar-restaurant did indeed open on the waterfront there: it still exists, but it's not up to the standard the *Contessa* had hoped for.

At this stage it was an emergency. There was no alternative to a serious attempt on Cici himself. Running parallel to the entrance hall of the pensione were two storerooms. When the desperately co-operative Cici realised that without somewhere for lectures we might – *would* – have to change pensione, he gave in. He agreed to demolish the dividing wall, making the two storerooms into one room big enough to seat forty or so students. Knocking down the wall furtively, without planning permission, and taking the debris away by barge to be dumped in the remoter lagoon by night worried Cici, but not so much as possibly losing his low-season customers. His sporting builder was the man who had arranged Hemingway's duck-shooting, the guns dropped off in barrel-butts sunk into lagoon mud and collected hours later after the flight: so he knew well the lonelier reaches of the lagoon by moonlight.

'But what about chairs? Did Cici have lots of chairs?' 'No problem. *Mio zio* – my uncle – has lots of chairs in his deposit. I'll telephone him.'

I had to go round to the *Bar al Teatro* and explain to Cici's rubicund uncle, the owner, what I needed – fifty chairs. The uncle ran the last brothel before the closures in Venice, on the top floor of the building. I never thought of asking why he should need so many chairs. Certainly we might borrow the chairs. Renzo picked them up in his barge and delivered them.

That year we had also used for occasional lectures and social events one of the huge historic Salt *Saloni* just round the corner on the Zattere, '*notwithstanding that it is covered in excrement of pigeons,*' as the official lease from the Town Hall stated. But it had been too bitterly cold that year and had been usable only for vigorous dancing, with mulled wine.

As student numbers rose and Cici's room became too small, we were invited by Professor Pignatti to use his private lecture room in the Correr Museum, under the *campanile* of St. Mark's. Two years later, with our numbers going over sixty, we needed somewhere larger still. At this moment, after so many years, Terisio Pignatti told me of the existence of the *Venice – Island of Studies' Association*, of which he was a founding member. Even though we were in Venice only in the depths of February and March, when foreign academic activity would always have been at its lowest ebb, it would seem remarkable that we could have remained unaware, for so long, of the presence of *V.I.S.* Pignatti arranged for me to meet its secretary, Giorgio Lauro in his animated office then in the Palazzo Priuli, buzzing with Canadian architectural students. Giorgio explained what *V.I.S.* was doing and could offer us in the way of general support and particularly lecture space – precisely what we wanted.

'Sure – you can use the palace. Now. From tomorrow. No problem.'

'The cost?'

'Nothing. Whatever you like – what you can afford. Make a donation if you like.'

Even the bank manager smiled when our numbers went on going up, helped by our rating in the then fashionable *Sloane Rangers' Handbook*, the bible of classy London youth with county aspirations. Buying a hovel in the Italian countryside was becoming a possibility.

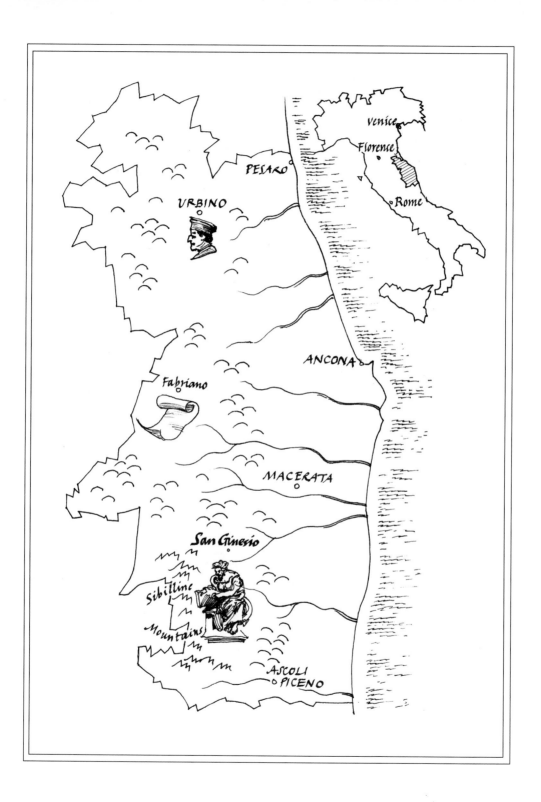

PESARO

URBINO

Venice

Florence

Rome

Fabriano

ANCONA

MACERATA

San Ginesio

Sibilline Mountains

ASCOLI PICENO

8

Arcadia

Anyone looking for a house in the country in Italy soon realises that the tradition of rural architecture in Italy is completely different from that of England. The English countryside is full of houses, large, medium and small, Medieval to Modern, which reflect centuries of comfortable country living. In Italy there is no trace of Chaucer's Franklin, J.P., Knight of the Shire, Epicurus' own son, whose house flowed with wine and snowed hospitality; nor of the land-agent whose house was fair and shaded by green trees; nor even of the country monk who kept fine horses and loved hunting. Neither are there manor houses, rectories and parsonages for younger sons of gentry, houses built by successful sheep farmers and wool merchants or with prize money by naval sea officers or managers of the East India Company. The English tradition of quitting the city and living in the country is exactly the opposite of the Italian, where even landowners prefer to be inside the city walls. Venetian merchants in London in the reign of Queen Elizabeth I complained that it was impossible to get the English to work or do any business between Friday evening and Monday morning. Their love of the countryside took them out of town for a long weekend.

The enterprise and sophistication of Italian Medieval cities is a brilliant chapter in European civilisation. In later, safer centuries merchants invested in land in the countryside round the city, the *contado*, and established a *colonia* – an agricultural unit. They built a house, the *casa colonica*, provided capital and planted there a peasant and his family, a *contadino*, who was obliged to live on the property.

The *contadino* farmed under the rich man's instructions, and half the produce went to the landlord, the *padrone*. The *padrone* lived in the well-paved city and had clean shoes. The *contadino* lived in the country and had to change out of his muddy boots when he arrived at the town gates. This is the *mezzadria* system, which operated from the middle ages. We have watched the last of the *mezzadri* – our neighbours. So the countryside, at least in Central Italy, has no middling houses of quality and antiquity apart from the odd dank mill or uncomfortable tower and is dotted with peasant family houses. In the areas where small-scale farming still flourishes, like the Marches, there is a crop of new, white-painted concrete-framed houses alongside the old stone, brick and rubble ones. As families moved out of the pre-war and wartime *miseria* – poverty – they have built the *casa nuova*, and use the *casa vecchia*, the old house, for the cattle, and for storage. Only the remoter houses are abandoned. These may be buyable, if a clutch of relations, part-owners, who may be in Argentina, Turin and Milan as well as nearby, can be assembled by a lawyer, and brought to agree to sell.

In the earliest years of the house-hunting obsession, in the '60s, I was privileged to be driven round Tuscany by the late Luigi Gori-Montanelli, whose book *Tuscan Rural Architecture* is still the best on the subject. There were beautiful *case coloniche* everywhere, for sale. 'You have to choose which area you like. Near Siena? Lucca? Arezzo? They all have their own characteristics, the houses and the terrain.' This was the period so well described by Raymond Flower in his book *Chianti*:

The cost varied, of course, but in those days, for between £3500 and £6000 you could pick up a good, solid farmhouse with 20 to 30 acres of arable land and woods. And half of Chianti was for sale.

It was at this time that the magazine *l'Espresso* suggested the name Chiantishire.

'*It was pleasant, after all,*' as Raymond Flower wrote, '*to visualise the Chairman of Lazards sitting in the 'bar' at Castellina waiting for the telephone to call up England and settle the details of the merger between Leyland and the British Motor Corporation. It is intriguing to know that just before the 1970 election at which he was returned as Prime Minister, Edward Heath worked out his cabinet with the Chairman of the Conservative party under an olive tree of a farm that Margrave Ugo had made over to the Badia a thousand years before. It is fascinating, when one looks in for a drink, to find the heads of the Central Banks sitting in bathing costumes discussing the European economy.*'

Tuscany was something of a special case. The terrain, which includes extensive rolling hills of scrub oak, although good for small-scale mixed farming, was even better for large-scale development. With the rising fame of the Ruffino straw Chianti flask, there was strong pressure on the *contadino* to sell out to the big wine firms which were planting and amalgamating vineyards on a massive scale. As a result many *case coloniche* were for sale. These were houses of an architectural quality superior to those in most parts of Italy. In the Renaissance, the classical ideals of a refined life during the hot summer in a cool *villa* on the edge of the city, or outside it, came into fashion in Florence. Cosimo de Medici the Elder, described by the socially superior Siennese Pope Pius II as '*more cultured than merchants usually are*' converted several fortified farms into villas in the Renaissance architectural style. Lorenzo the Magnificent built a full-scale villa on the Roman model at Poggio a Caiano. Later, when the Medici had ripened from lean international banking, mean city politics and a viral form of humanism to a Grand Dukedom, European marriages and two Papacies, they turned their attention to the good government and agricultural improvement of their Duchy. They built a series of large villas at the centre of their agricultural and hunting properties, – Pratolino, La Peggio,La Magia, Marignolle, l'Ambrogiana, Monte Veturino, Colle Salvetti – all painted for the lunettes at the villa at Artimino, so many 'portraits' of Medici estates, icons of rural management and power, now to be seen in the *Firenze com'Era* Museum in Florence. The Grand Duke Cosimo's architect, Buontalenti, included designs for the whole range of estate buildings, from villa to stables to *casa colonica*. Many Tuscan city families followed the fashion and the result was the percolation throughout Tuscany of a chaste, austere style of architecture, from grand villa to unhumble farmhouse – well-made buildings of a virtuous simplicity: a well-proportioned main block surmounted by a low 'tower' and on a facade, at ground level, sometimes an arcade with sometimes an arched loggia above.

Rebuild the entrance, repoint the stonework, make good the stairs, replace a gutter and re-design the kitchen. If you spend 150 ducats you could live comfortably, in pleasant surroundings and in style – honourably.

So wrote Machiavelli in the early 1500s, when he had been taken to see a house for sale near Florence. In the late '60s, I didn't have 150 ducats or £3500. When I did, Tuscany was sold and bought – and I don't like colonies.

Autumn and winter reading in London for a future tour and possibly for a perfect future retreat had begun to focus on an almost unknown region of central Italy, the Marches.

'*A March – a tract of debatable land separating two countries.*' To anyone with a sense of history and place, the word has a promising resonance. '*The Marches, a region of Italy, an area of confrontation between Papacy and Empire in the Middle Ages. Every hill became the eyrie of a lord, strongholds were established on crest and spur.*' The Marches – a quadrilateral bordered on the North by the Romagna, on the East by the Adriatic, on the West by the Apennine ridge marching with Tuscany, Umbria and Lazio, and on the South by the Abruzzi.

Curiosity increased as question and enquiry produced an accumulation of enticing ignorance. No one in Chiantishire had heard of the Marches. The rare Italian who has heard of the region may remember the saying *'better a dead person in the house than a Marchigian at the door,'* from the time when the Marches, heartland of the Papal State, provided tax collectors for the formidable Marchigian Pope Sixtus V.

A sentence in a nondescript book on the Apennines stood out from the page. *'From Macerata in the Marches the mountains of the Abruzzi filled the horizon to the brim.'* Almost unknown to Italians, unknown to foreigners: it sounded interesting.

Hugh had been given special leave by his wife to help me house hunt. Although Hugh makes only occasional appearances in these pages, he has been at my elbow through the many years of the book's conception and unurgent gestation. In fact we have been at each others' elbows since Oxford days when Hugh didn't realise for a year that his digs were in a brothel. I have witnessed Hugh's head sink in sleep onto the table in Nick's Diner when he was courting a girlfriend, have handed him the ring at his wedding (and nearly had to double as giver-away of the bride) and have eased the boredom of his long office life with occasional lunches together on fine October days in Charlotte Street, watching the models go in and out. We have together moved his furniture in hired vans, marking the progress from bachelor flat to modest married house to family house and I always hold a key to his front door and to a most genial welcome whenever I am in London. We have walked the bars of Dublin after rugby internationals, watched cricket at Lords and been through the rituals that mark the passing decades. In our more mature years we talk about the books we have read and the ones we are going to write – Hugh being the only one of our circle (of the three) aspiring writers who has actually had a book published – 'til now. Now that he and Georgina have retired to Herefordshire, an annual visit from Italy at the time of the mayfly is becoming a habit, when we spend time disentangling casts from trees overhanging the River Arrow in our quest for its brown trout. So it was natural that he would escort me on a house-hunting expedition to Italy.

The Apennines looking south to the Gran Sasso d'Italia

We soon confirmed that prices near Cortona in the Eastern corner of Tuscany, and even in Umbria, had gone into the For Foreigners category. We had four days left to visit the central area of the Marches, unknown territory.

We came into the Marches by the *Via Flaminia*, the ancient road from Rome through Northern Lazio, the Patrimony of St. Peter, into Umbria and up to the top of the Tiber valley, to Fabriano, city of the great International Gothic painter Gentile da Fabriano and of the manufacture of paper, from bank notes to handmade watercolour papers. Just before Fabriano, we had passed through the *Gola*, the throat where the Roman road breached the narrowest rock cleft of the Apennines, and were in the Marches: '*that other side of Italy, that land of mysterious interest, since I had been told that Cook and his tourists had not found their way thither and that there I should see Italian ways in all their unsullied primitiveness.*' What the Honourable Margaret Collier wrote in 1886 gave a fair indication of what we were about to find in this Paradise Lost.

The *Via Flaminia* continued more or less straight, following the River Metauro, to end in the monumental arch of Augustus at Fano

The Monti Sibillini under snow

on the Adriatic, almost at the Northern extremity of the Marches. On this occasion we did not follow the Roman road to its end. We had time to visit only the central part of the region, the less-known province of Macerata. So at Fabriano we turned right towards Matelica, and were immediately face-to-face with the facts of the region: geography, terrain, history and charm, an almost impenetrable tangle by normal criteria.

From the high spine of the Apennines, running Northwest to Southeast, the rivers flow to the sea obliquely, like the laid-back bones of a fish heading South. The Metauro, the Esino, the Musone, the Potenza, the Chienti, the Tenna, the Aso and the Tronto plunge and flow, bubbling with trout, in a North-Easterly direction. Until they arrive at a very narrow coastal strip and the sea, they run through deep, steep-sided valleys, separated by spurs. Each spur climbs from the coast in a succession of crests, like ocean rollers, to the last and highest one which stands poised, face-to-face with the watershed Apennine barrier, the backbone of Italy. Roads, like the rivers, flow easily in the valleys. More dramatically, and with sensational views of the Adriatic eastwards and the high Apennines westwards, they twist and turn down the ridges of the spurs, like a fluent ski-runner, downhill all the way from the high inland mountains to the sea. But to go, as we wanted to go, across the grain, across the natural flow, forces an appreciation of the region.

It was steep. We drove in deep shadow or into flashing sun. We passed from lush, narrow meadows by the trout-rearing pens through small oak woods mingling with cultivated fields. Caterpillar tractors tilted at perilous angles, silhouetted against the sky, ploughing vertically down, turning over the harvested stubble. Viewed from up on the ridge, a mixture of fields and woods spread on all sides, with always the glint of the Adriatic to the East and the blue haze of Monte San Vicino, the Camerino mountains and the Sibillines to the West. It was an area of small, mixed farms, the precipitous terrain discouraging amalgamation and mass cultivation. On top of almost every hill was a thoroughly-walled town.

In the 10th century Charlemagne's successors the Ottonian emperors from Saxony used the plural name, the Marches, for their feudal *marchesates*, the March of Fermo, then the March of Ancona and of Camerino, almost within sight of each other, but separated by the valleys and mountains into separate political units. The March, as it became known, together with the maritime Pentapolis cities of the old Byzantine Exarchate from Ravenna down into Romagna, had been donated to the Pope by Pepin and Charlemagne after their defeat of the Lombard Kingdom of Italy – the origin of the Papal territorial state. Over the 11th, 12th and 13th centuries, legal ownership was contested, confirmed and disputed many times by emperors and popes, by lawyers and by armies, making clear the distinction between *de jure* and *de facto*. Except on those occasions when they gave complete priority to controlling the region, neither Pope nor Emperor found it easy to hold down such a geographically disunited and inaccessible territory, though the 150 or so walled towns, compared with the mere fifty in the Tuscan patrimony, made it a desirable property. The subsidies demanded from the communes and signori of the March in 1426 came to a total of 40,000 florins as compared with a total of 13,500 which the Rector of the Tuscan patrimony tried to collect from his subjects, according to the historian Peter Partner. Both Pope and Emperor wanted the tax incomes, the armed support and the strategic advantages which possession of the towns gave, as well as the allegiance of the turbulent cavalry gentlemen in their towers and fortified hamlets in the surrounding countryside. From 1294, when the Hohenstauffen emperor Henry VI acquired the Norman Kingdom of Sicily, the March became the essential route for German emperors coming into Italy over the Brenner, going down the Adriatic, skirting well to the East of papal strongpoints near Rome, and so to their golden Kingdom of Sicily. The walled and towered communes themselves, independent by inclination and tradition but realistic enough to trim to political winds, were often able to play papal rector and imperial vicar off against each other as they competed for the valuable town allegiance.

No doubt for the same reason that slowed our driving, in contrast to other parts of Italy, no single family ever dominated the Marche region. The maximum unification was achieved after the pacification of the Papal territories by the Papal general Cardinal Albornoz in the 14th century. 'If,' to quote from Peter Partner's book, 'the *Lands of St. Peter*, *"pacification" is the right word to use of a man who drenched the Italian countryside in blood from the Po to the Garigliano.'*

In the Constitutions which he published from Fano in 1357 he classified the region in cities: *Civitates Maiores, Magnae, Mediocres, parvae* and his lists would make a good groundplan for a guide to the region today. A few baronial families like the Da Varano of Camerino were made vicars of the church, keeping their local imperial titles and possessions in return for payments and military service to the church. They had some sort of sometimes resented control over some of the communes. But many of the communes made separate individual deals with the Roman *curia* and these connections with Rome, as well as Albornoz' legal code, continued until Napoleon and then returned until Cavour annexed the Romagna, Umbria and the Marches in 1866, in the unification process. Even in the anti-clerical Napoleonic interlude, the strong local papal attachment was acknowledged in official proclamations which put the word Religion instead of Fraternity in public notices and proclamations in the Marches: *Liberty! Equality! Religion!*

According to Cavour's successor, the very Tuscan Prime Minister Baron Ricasoli, the Marches *'suffered from a system of government which condemns them to inertia and a material and intellectual prostration in sad contrast to the progress seen everywhere else in civilized Europe.'* Stendhal too commented on the baleful stagnation of the Papal State and the offensive arrogance of even the lowest clergy. Unlike Umbria, which is geographically and politically open, the Marches, in its mentality and traditions still dozes under protective layers of benevolent pontifical dust. Many towns have their daily bus service to Rome – a four-hour journey – but to nowhere else.

We admired the Romanesque abbey of S. Maria a Pie di Chienti and the smaller one of the same period at Rambona. We were surprised by the completeness of the ancient Roman amphitheatre standing in a field by the roadside at Urbisaglia. The quality of the 14th century frescoes in the *capellone* of the basilica at Tolentino, painted to promote the beatification of the local miracle-worker Saint Nicholas made us wonder where the art historians had been – 'til we remembered the roads that had brought us here.

We saw superlative paintings by Lorenzo Lotto at Cingoli, Jesi, Loreto, Recanati and Monte San Giusto, the surprise masterpiece by Tiepolo at Camerino, the exquisite little gallery in a 16th century palace in San Severino. We didn't have time to visit the quintessential Renaissance court palace at Urbino in the North, home to Raphael, Bramante, Piero della Francesca, Castiglione.

Antipasto di Pesce – little plate after little plate of sea delicacies, first cold ones, then hot, followed by *coda di rospo*, monkfish, grilled on wood at the Ristorante della Torre at Numana, looking North to where the cliffs of Monte Conero plunge into the sea, South down the coast, to the Sanctuary Basilica of Loreto, and Recanati and the line of blue mountains behind. Chilled white *Verdicchio* wine. Away from the coast, in the interior, at the Locanda Marchigiana near Sarnano – a selection of home-made *tagliatelli, ravioli, gnocchi* followed by pigeon, lamb, chicken grilled on the embers which fell from the iron bracket fire at one end of the room. And the red *Rosso Piceno* wine of the area.

And farmhouses. Many had the new alongside the old, both in use, a sure sign that tradition not heritage prevails. But we spotted many that seemed abandoned. Humbler than those in Tuscany and with little architectural pretension – the villa civilisation never happened in the Marches – they were in more pleasing and grander surroundings: always the steep fields, the woods, the oak trees and always the presence of seriously high mountains which held snow 'til June.

On our final evening we drove up the steeply winding road to San Ginesio, the highest town in the Marches. Entering through a Medieval gatetower we passed a building with a Gothic arched loggia on ground and first floor and parked the car near the centre of town. It's always a pleasure to walk the final yards up narrow, cobbled streets into a piazza. We had to telephone to book a table for our last dinner in Italy, across the mountains in Umbria.

The piazza was deserted, almost. On the far side a woman stood at the open door of a clothes shop. A short, grey-haired man stood outside the newsagent – *tabaccaio*. To our right, under an arcade, a man and woman stood outside the bar. The piazza was in shade but the tall front of the main church, a giant Gothic polyptich of pink brick decorated with *terra cotta* tracery blazed in the evening sun. But where was everyone, at this evening hour of the *passeggiata?*

We looked up at the church facade, following the upward glance of the clothes-shop lady. In the adjacent bell tower, under the onion dome which sprouted many thriving shrubs, there was movement. A massive bell swung slowly into the sunlight and back into the shadow, silently, regularly. As they caught the sunlight rhythmically, we saw two men, stripped to the waist, controlling the momentum of the bell, pushing and holding its wooden side-frames as if restraining a powerful cart-horse.

The door of the church opened and a diminutive nun in black habit led out two little boys dressed in the slashed yellow and black hose and doublet of the Swiss Papal guard, on either side of another seven-year-old with a wide-brimmed, long-feathered hat.

'*Ecco! Marco! Il principe! Il principe,*' exclaimed the barman's wife, next to us, spotting her son. Then followed a little girl in white with a flowered crown – the Madonna – flanked by two attendants in white and, behind, a flock of angels, all of whom the nun was trying to organise into processional pairs. Four side-drummers and four silver-trumpeters had taken up position at the church door. A resounding bang and a puff of pink smoke above the church marked the detonation of the first maroon, a signal to release the clappers of the bell, which rang out over the town and countryside, the strong men shoving it up to its full arc, pulling it back down to shoot it up on the return curve. As the drums rattled, the trumpets fanfared and the bell made the buildings shake, the nun led the costumed guards, the Madonna and the angels up the *piazza*, leading the procession. Spilling out from the church there followed a hooded and cloaked group carrying a crudely hewn cross – the *sacconi* – followed by another group in blue robes – the *confraternita del sacramento*. A motley of elderly women in mufti – a Franciscan praying lay order – came next. Then came serving boys in lace surpluses, preceding a priest, in front of an elaborate *baldacchino* of faded red and gold brocade over a red velvet cushion on which lay a gilded reliquary in the shape of a golden hand – with San Ginesio's own hand-bones inside. More fanfares, more drumrolls, more puffs and bangs of maroons. Behind the *baldacchino* walked a bent, aged cleric, resplendent in white and yellow robes – the Cardinal of Naples, the barman told us. Then came the marshal of the *carabinieri*, the town standard, the mayor in tricolour sash, the town band in black jackets, white shirts, black ties. At a signal from the big drum, the strains of

Va Pensiero merged into the now continuous vibrations of the tolling bell, which made the piazza hum like a brazen goblet. By the time the population of San Ginesio was emerging from the church into the piazza, the nun and her children had disappeared out of the top of the piazza, up *Capocastello* towards the Town Hall. The people followed the procession. We never learnt what festival it was. A few split off into the bar, their lean, country faces browner than their old tweeds. One saw Hugh and me at the telephone. He stood a yard from us, staring and staring, unsmiling, like an erect iguana, observing two aliens. We had to go.

'I'm sure some of those farmhouses are abandoned. They look absolutely ideal. You'll *have* to come back,' said Hugh, as we drove away, the setting sun slanting across tumbling fields, oak woods and beautifully-placed *case coloniche*. We headed into shadows and turned into the massive Apennines, the Sibilline Mountains, towards Umbria and dinner, and, next day, to Rome and the flight to London.

Before I could come back to explore further, Chance made an entrance in the form of an incredible coincidence. Speaking about lecture rooms in Venice on the telephone from London to Giorgio Lauro, the secretary of the *Venice – Island of Studies Association*, I enthused about the Marches in general and about our last glimpse of it, leaving San Ginesio, in particular.

'I was *born* there,' he said. 'Because my mother was English, during the war we were advised to leave Venice and live in some out-of-the-way country area. We went to San Ginesio. In fact we still go for a family holiday every November.'

November was next month. I gave Giorgio the prescription. At the end of November his express letter came, with photographs of a selection of houses. One in particular he thought might be what I was looking for. And bookings for Venice were looking good.

Contrada Scaletti 84 – (Above) the house as bought 1974

9

Buying the House

An old house, a mountain view, beamed ceilings, an open fire and an isolated position was the prescription. At the end of November, Lauro's letter arrived from Venice, with photos of a possible house in San Ginesio. The next day I arrived at Marco Polo Airport, five hours late but the first plane into fog-bound Venice for three days. Two hours later we were in Lauro's car, driving over the causeway into the sunset, the lagoon a misting mirror of gold and red backed by the softened shapes of derricks, tankers, oil containers and the industrial landscape of Marghera. We turned south-east past Fusina, past the silhouette of the Palladian Villa Malcontenta in its clump of trees and on towards the marshlands of the Po delta. As always in Italy, a drive is a drive through history.

Chioggia and the end of the Venetian lagoon had passed in the last light and Lauro interrupted my slumbers as we crossed the broad waters of the Po out of the Venetian Republic and into the Pontifical State. To the right he pointed out the bulk of the castle of Mesola, the easternmost outpost of the d'Este of Ferrara.

We pulled off the road for coffee in the outbuildings of the 7th century Abbey of Pomposa, one of the unextinguished lamps of learning through the Dark ages: here the Gregorian chant was preserved. On the road again, the long cones of our headlights penetrated the mists, lighting the cats' eyes along the straights and curves of the road embanked on either side above the eel-pens of the Comacchio waterlands. Then we were at a red traffic light. A cargo ship towered above us, moored to a quay to our left. By the traffic light a yellow historic monuments sign listed what there was to see: *Mausoleo di Galla Placidia 5th Century mosaics; Sant'Apollinare in Classe 6th Century mosaics; San Vitale 6th Century mosaics; Battistero Neoniano 5th Century mosaics; Mausoleo di Teodorico 6th Century.* Ravenna – the last capital of the Roman Empire in the west. The bastion for the Byzantine emperor Justinian's reconquest of Italy in the middle of the 6th century. More slumbers in the comfortable leather seat of the old Volvo. The imperturbable Lauro, content to drive with a sleeping companion, had a humorous sense of history and occasion, and woke me to see the headlights illuminate the sign for the River Rubicon, Julius Caesar's point of decision and no return. The fog had cleared and we crossed with modest ambition but great expectations.

We came onto the Adriatic autostrada at Rimini North and entered the Marches. Immediately hills started to crowd down to the road. A yellow moon hung in the sky ahead and lit the crenellations of Gradara Castle on its cliff above my right shoulder. Here Francesca da Rimini fell in love with her husband's brother Paolo, aroused by reading together the story of Lancelot and Guinivere. Surprised in their embraces and slain by the returned husband in 1285, Dante consigned them for their lust to the second circle in Hell – a lesson on which Tchaikovski brooded with poignant relevance. We sped south, past the turning for Urbino, glimpsing at Fano the Roman arch marking the end of the *Via Flaminia*, across the River Metauro where Hasdrubal was defeated and killed in 207 BC., past Senigallia, past Ancona, past the sanctuary basilica of Loreto illuminated on its hill, with the Adriatic gleaming to our left in the winter moonlight.

At Civitanova we left the autostrada and began the steady climb into the interior. On either side of a wide valley, little towns glittered on hill-tops. The valley narrowed, the road steepened. We went through woods and past the grand façade and Gothic door of the Cistercian Abbey of Fiastra. At Urbisaglia the tall ruins of a Roman wall crossed the road, broken just enough to let the modern road through. The moonlight showed a sizeable amphitheatre in a field to the left, sprouting secular oaks. At Passo San Ginesio, Giorgio slowed to a stop, eased the car off the road onto the paving and switched off the engine. 'Ten-thirty and I'm hungry. Now for a Marchigian meal. We're only fifteen minutes away now.'

As we stepped out of the warm cocoon of the car, we breathed icy air tinged with woodsmoke. The *trattoria* was lit by low-power bulbs and was full, at one end, with *contadini* in tweed suits and caps standing crowded round the two tables of card players. At the other end burned a hooded fire, glowing with embers, and there were empty tables. Our entry in the dim light caused a momentary silence and scrutiny from every eye present. Then we were absorbed in the warm, relaxed ambience, the lady of the house being the only female present. Draughts of the local *Rosso Piceno* accompanied home-made *tagliatelli* with generous gratings of truffles. Mixed meats hissed on the grid over the embers and were soon on our plates – pigeon, guinea fowl, sausage, lamb, finished with sideplates of crisp salad. Now almost at the moment of truth, within minutes, possibly, of the end of my search, impatience had gone and I savoured the moment, the *pecorino* sheep cheese and lingered over the first coffee 'corrected' with the local aniseed distillation, *mistra*.

The last fifteen minutes were continuous curves and hairpin bends, all steeply uphill, the car moving between second and third gear. At the first towered gate in the Medieval walls of San Ginesio we bore left, skirting outside the walls and battlements. We slowed and took a turn left, onto a rough, narrow gravel track, white in the moonlight, which passed a sleeping farmstead and then plunged steeply between high, tree-lined banks. Lauro eased the car in first gear between deeply gouged tracks and potholes. We came out of trees into a field in which stood a farmhouse, its long roof of old tiles sloping into the hill. The engine stopped. Lauro looked at me and wrinkled his brow in a question.

The ground was iron-hard and scattered with curds of frozen snow. The moon stood high in the sky, as bright and sharp as a ploughshare, illuminating a massive landscape, from the field where we stood, to the woods falling below us, then, leaving a jump of space, to the hills across the valley and behind them the bulk of the Sibilline Mountains a few miles away. Tiny necklaces of seed-pearl lights hung in distant spaces, defining the many towns that sat on the tops of hills. The air was razor-cold, and carried a hint of cow-byre from the farm we had passed. Above, a firmament of stars blazed. Silence.

The moonlit house stood comfortably in its land, built into the steep slope of the field like a wedge, the three-storeyed valley front reducing to one level of lean-to styes and woodsheds on the hillside. We made careful steps down the frozen field towards the house. A dog barked, shut in the house. Another dog started barking, revealing another farmhouse in the wood below. Dogs from the farm above joined in. A dog a mile across the valley barked and we heard more and more distant dogs adding their voices. As we arrived at the ground-floor stall door, we were startled by the whinny of a horse inside and the panicky clashing of hooves on cobbles.

Lauro turned the car with difficulty and we crawled up the track onto the asphalted road, then still further up and under an arched gateway into the silent town. At the lightless hotel the landlady appeared in dressing gown and scarf and let us in, with the dreadful information that there was another Englishman in town. We were shown to our freezing rooms in the hotel long ago closed after its August month of activity. A final nightcap cognac which Lauro had brought, anticipating the hotel's heating limitations, plus two extra pullovers guaranteed a dreamless night of content. I woke in the dark with freezing ears. What could an Englishman be doing here except trying to buy my house? I retreated under the blankets back to sleep.

Cocks were crowing. A church bell close by tolled. A shaft of orange light coming through the curtain opening put a hard-edged stripe on the bedroom wall from floor to ceiling. It was 7.30. I pulled open the curtains and cleared my blurred eyes. Precipitously below, over the city walls and down in the tumbling countryside, I could actually see my house.

Cappuccini and brioche in the empty Bar Centrale established the identity of the mysterious Englishman, Mr. Peter, a retired Yorkshire solicitor who had bought an old house in the city walls ten years ago. He was certain to be as deeply displeased at the news of another Englishman entering his retreat as I was to learn of his presence. And there was another English connection, I was shown. The bronze statue in the centre of the piazza, in reformation MA cap and gown, was Queen Elizabeth I's professor of law at Oxford University, the local free-thinking Alberico Gentile, native of San Ginesio, and founder of International Law.

I was as ready as possible for the crucial meeting with the vendor, Elio Merelli, who was already outside the house as we arrived, a short, thick man with black moustache and *mafioso* dark glasses. We approached each other across the glassy grass, careful to avoid the *bruttissima figura* of falling flat on the ice, and shook hands. After minimal courtesies, Merelli moved to business.

'First the house – and then we'll look at the land.'

The door and windows had already been opened and the cold, clean air occupied the rooms which were bright in the sunlight, and dry – not a whiff of damp. We went up steps through the door in the sidewall into the living room-kitchen – spacious enough with three windows, the required open fire and hooded chimney blackened with smoke and, also required, ancient beams of unusually twisted and contorted character. In the recess under one window the floor area sloped to the wall and, in one corner was a small hole – the washing up area and outlet. At the far end, a door led to another smaller room with two small windows, one looking directly out onto the mountains. In the distance was the unmistakable Gran Sasso. This was to be my study.

'Electric light' said Merelli, turning a switch which drew my attention to a spindly assortment of wires nailed to charred beams, and one bulb dangling in the middle of the room, its filament glowing red. The steep stairs led up to three rooms under the roof. As we went in, a cloud of pigeons exploded into the outside sunlight.

'If you buy the house, I'll clear out the pigeons if you don't want them.'

The little upstairs rooms, paved in the dusty-pink *terra cotta* tiles of the area, had a certain romantic charm and magnificent views eastwards.

'And the bathroom?'

'None.'

'Water?'

'There must be water here. There always was a vein, running from the top corner of the field, by the big willow, running down near the house, past the willow at the front of the house. You could make a well. And the *Comune* are bringing a water supply to this *contrada*. It's passed the council and should be done soon.' I dismissed thoughts of the Wiltshire Europroperty advisors. The house had a dry, light, happy quality. It was isolated, had mountain views, open fires, old beams.

We went out and down to the lowest level under the living room and my future study, at the front. The first open door was into the *stalla*, a space with cobbled floor channelled for drainage, and a long manger, its wooden edge polished with use by cattle. Fresh horse dung showed it had been used last night. The other door gave into the space below my study – the *cantina*, where a fermenting barrel, three dusty demijohns and the smell of wine showed its function. Both spaces had the calm atmosphere of centuries of unchanged use. In fact, this was the classic *casa colonica*, where the *contadino* lived and worked. Below, his beasts and the wine, then himself and his family in the kitchen-living room and bedroom. Then, under the roof, his grain. Outside, styes for a couple of pigs, a shed for a chain of sheep and covered space for the plough and harrow. Beyond the haystack, a bread oven and another stone-built outhouse.

Outside again, dazzling sun on the heavy white frost put Merelli in his dark glasses at an advantage. As we scaled the icy bank on the other side of the house, a half-blood horse galloped downhill at us with shuddering hooves and whinney, swerving at the last minute to avoid us and plunging to a stop at the bottom of the steep field, snorting and blowing like a dragon.

'Stella. Osvaldo's horse. Osvaldo is the *contadino* who lives in the house below.'

I took this as a good omen, thinking of the human Stella who sometimes behaves in a similar way.

We examined the labyrinth of pigstyes and outhouses which various walls divided into separate spaces under the long sloping roof. In the yard-thick stone wall of the main house were two Romanesque niches, as if on either side of a former altar. Then, in the gloom and muddle of structures, I saw a well-made column of old brick, with a simple but shaped plinth and a simple but shaped capital, built into a temporary partition. Peering through a hole into another, gloomier space, I saw its pair. So this was not *just* a *casa colonica*.

Merelli's sharp eyes and business intuition had been watching my every reaction, ready to raise or lower his unrevealed price according to what I valued. Here he gambled.

'They say it was a cell, that monks lived here, connected with the church.'

Mention of monks and connections with a church would have immediately put off any local Italian, who wouldn't tolerate even cypresses because of their cemetery associations.

'The church?'

'The church over there across the field, Santa Maria delle Scalette. The abandoned church.'

Two fields away a church, early 17th century, stood on a platform of hillside, complete with three original bells silhouetted against the sky. We were in the Contrada Scalette.

I looked again at the buttressing thickening of the house walls on the valley side and various hints of pilasters and structural irregularities, aware that as I added a century or two in my dating of the building, Merelli was keeping pace in millions of lire. Had he been selling to an Italian it would have been the opposite – the older the cheaper.

'It's a good house. It's sound. It's dry. It has the electric current. Do you like it? It's habitable straight away.'

'And the water?'

'Not important. There's water at Osvaldo's below. We'll make a well. It's easy to pump up. Now let's look at the land. Tell me what you want and I'll sell you what you need to go with the house.'

The land which went naturally with the house was a triangle with the point at the top of the hill, the classic shape of a unit of land in steep territory where ploughing has to be done vertically downhill, a furrow at a time. One side ended in a rising cliff, over the top of which looked the bell-towers and walls of San Ginesio. The other sided dropped out of sight down steep scrub. The base was a steeply-falling wood of old oaks. It measured three acres, more or less.

The decisive battle was short and took place in the slippery, sloping field. Merelli had been thinking of eight million lire but was settling for seven and a half – about £5,000. Which presented a problem, I was saying to Lauro, as I had had four and a half in mind, expecting to go up to five. I wanted the place. We were in price range. Merelli had a buyer nearly in his grasp. It took little time to arrive at the compromise of six million three hundred thousand, – £4,200 – if I would share the expense of building a well at Osvaldo's. I agreed to this if Merelli threw in the oak wood, which he accepted.

After the customary pause for second thoughts, we met at six in Merelli's earthquake-proof house in the town, his office walls covered in old pistols, swords, rifles and daggers. His son was an Olympic pistol shot. We agreed that we agreed, shook hands on it and tumblers of Chivas Regal were poured, glasses clinked and the scalding pledge downed. Lauro was invited to type out the preliminary contract, which put down all the details, then and there, banged out on an ancient type-writer. At this stage it emerged that technically the final buying contract would be between me and the Benedictine nuns of San Ginesio. Some years ago, Merelli had bought the property from them at a knock-down price but left the deal suspended between preliminary contract and completion – and now had saved himself a purchase tax and would no doubt be making a sizeable profit.

'And, by the way, when we sign the final act of sale, it's best if we put down a price much lower than the real one. The difference you can give me in cash.'

Understanding, and not understanding, I let Merelli mulch over this momentarily exposed root of the system, which flourishes like bindweed under the surface of every aspect of Italian life.

Two months later, in February, I came down from Venice to complete. We met the lawyer at Merelli's and walked through the rain to the Benedictine monastery, its pointed Romanesque bell tower just visible in the cloud. The heavy door clicked open. We went into a warm, beautifully polished marble-floored hall and were greeted by an old nun and a not-so-old nun, both standing on the far side of a large table which had been placed across the gap in the opening of internal double doors – they are an enclosed order. The nuns introduced themselves with charm and smiles. The older was Assunta Belfiore, born in 1898: she had brought the property to the order as her dowry. The younger was Anita Pacione, in religion Suor Teresa, abbess.

The advocate read the document in its traditional formality and entirety and, when everyone had signed, the abbess rang a tiny bell and another nun appeared with a tray of liqueur glasses, a bottle and a plate of sweet biscuits, produce of the community. The nuns joined us in the decorous celebration and we left: all content with what the deal had brought us.

10

Carnivals – For the Record

The meeting with Giorgio Lauro at the Palazzo Priuli, so casually arranged by Professor Pignatti, seemed to be the dawn of a Golden Age and gave meaning to the enigmatic Italian political theory – the Convergence of Parallels: our coexistent paths had at last met. Giorgio's reign as secretary of *V.I.S.* was interrupted by military service. Having provided a house in the distant Marches more or less at the click of a camera shutter and an express letter, and having promised us space for lectures in Venice as well as the luxurious psychological support of an organization whose purpose was to help us, he disappeared into barracks – entirely against his will, he protested. In his place in the *V.I.S.* office was Renzo Salvadori. And the office had moved to the Palazzo Fortuny.

The '*Venice – Island of Studies*' Association – *V.I.S.* – was the idea of a group of eminent and active Venetians, some, like Pignatti, directors of cultural institutions, others in positions of power in the business world. At this time there was much thought and talk about the role of the city of Venice in the future. They believed that a permanent international academic presence would add a modest but interesting dimension to the life of the city. Venice was an appropriate place to study history, art, music, restoration, town planning, the many aspects of marine ecology – and many other things. From the start, the *V.I.S.* plan was that their idea should be shown to be practicable to a sceptical city council and that then it should be taken over officially by the city and not continue as a private enterprise. That the city politicians' interests were beginning to concentrate not on any airy academic enterprises for foreigners but on the launching of a new-style Carnival, with a capital C as in Commercial, had not yet shown above the surface of lagoon speculations.

An ingenuously active *V.I.S.* committee set about proving that their own idea was possible. The secretary visited universities in Britain, Canada and the United States, offering a Venetian welcome and finding out what was needed. What was needed was a place in which to hold lectures and classes; if possible a room where a communal library could be developed; a liaison service so that foreign institutions could know in advance what other academics would be in Venice, for possible collaboration and pooling of resources and for helping find student accommodation; and, as a luxury, a recreational common-room space for students.

V.I.S. proved that the idea was attractive abroad. To give an idea of the quality as well as quantity of the response it is worth recording in detail the academic programmes which were quickly set up in Venice. From Britain came Warwick, East Anglia, the Courtauld Institute, University College, London, the Royal College of Art, the Architectural Association, the Polytechnic of the South Bank, Manchester University; from Canada, Queen's University, Ontario and the University of British Columbia; and from the United States the Universities of Wake Forest, Cornell, Virginia, Berkeley California and New York. In the year 1971-2 there were 670 foreign university students spending more than two months of organized study in Venice. At one time twenty-seven foreign universities were in action in Venice, which, if it did not make much difference to Venice's problem of diminishing young population, at the very least added to the social chatter-life of the bars.

The Palazzo Fortuny was a crumbling Gothic edifice, hidden down a narrow *calle*. Up the outside stone staircase from the courtyard was a door into the Fortuny Museum, a series of rarely visited rooms. Large canvases of his wife and other voluptuous ladies, influenced by

Veronese and Tiepolo transposed into a Spanish *Belle Epoque* key hung on the walls. They were by the Spanish designer Mariano Fortuny. There were a few elegant lamps with shades of disintegrating silk. His fabulous dresses and fabrics and manufacturing secrets have stayed in the luxury world of commercial high fashion – a world of which there was not the slightest lingering expensive perfume in these ghostly and dusty spaces. Another door from the top of the outside staircase led into the cavernous heart of the long-abandoned palace: huge rooms completely stripped of all decoration alternated with smaller rooms. Hidden, narrow staircases led up to the top floor – more large spaces under the rafters. A door led onto a perilously rotting wooden balcony, poised high above the courtyard.

The palace was left by Fortuny to the *Comune* of Venice, to be used 'for cultural purposes.' The *Comune* were persuaded to let it, on a temporary basis, to V.I.S. in return for their offer to repair the vast roof – done at the private expense of the V.I.S. backers. The top floor of the Palazzo Fortuny became the headquarters of V.I.S.. There was an administrative office under the new secretary Renzo Salvadori. There was a growing library, mainly provided by Warwick University. And there were many spaces – for lectures and classes and even theatrical activities. Here we settled and enjoyed four wonderful years. Part of the attraction was the immensity, antiquity and dilapidation of the building and that we had to manage it ourselves, without cleaners or caretakers: so students in weekly teams gave the lecture room a semblance of tidiness and cleanliness and were rewarded with an invitation to a few glasses of wine, at the end of their duty week. These were the last years of the Burano carnival.

On *Martedi Grasso* – Shrove Tuesday – the last day of Carnival in what turned out to be our last year in the Palazzo Fortuny, we all, as always on the last day of Carnival, came to afternoon lectures in costume. In those days there was only one shop selling masks in Venice, near the remote Ospedaletto, hand-made masks in leather or papier-mache from 18th century blocks. Masks and costumes were

Sarah Quill and Stella Rudolph

J.H.

J.H. as The Doctor

home-made or came from the family dressing-up chest. That year our student fashion was newspapers, sellotaped and silvered, with much facial grease-paint and a fair amount of transvestism. After the second lecture, as the afternoon was darkening, we joined the throng moving away from St. Mark's and the centre towards the north shore, to the Fondamenta Nove and the boats for Burano. In the long interim between the old eighteenth century carnival and the new touristic promotion, a traditional *Martedi Grasso* evening of carnival had grown up on the Island of Burano, far out in the lagoon near Torcello. It was a Venetian affair. Everyone in Venice, and no one else, knew that this was where the action was. The Piazza San Marco was as empty as Mark Antony's market place, with Cleopatra, several Cleopatras, on the other side of town, on the barges bound for Burano.

As the violet hour darkened, Francesca Trentin, the then twenty-two-year-old daughter of Giorgio, my first and most important helper in Venice, crossed the Accademia Bridge to join us. She was dressed as Lawrence of Arabia. The khaki shorts showed off her trim legs. We became part of the bloodstream of the city, moving through the narrow *calli* towards the north shore. We were carried along in the crowd of masked, costumed people; general gaiety mixed with our high spirits.

On the Fondamenta Nove the crowd was dense, noisy, engulfing. Two of the lagoon boats were tied alongside the quay. Laughing, shouting people were crammed together near the gangway. Faces turned to the sound of loud drumming. A tall cross, followed by hooded monks carrying above their heads a black coffin, forced a way through the crowd. The coffin lurched up the gangway. Six crusaders in chain-mail, with silver-painted swords followed. Francesca and I forced ourselves through jammed bodies into the vacuum behind them, up the gangway and on board. The boat was packed, seething with people, shouting voices, singing, musical instruments. A voluminous prostitute with vast breasts bursting a blouse, brightly rouged cheeks and nose, lifted flagrantly a scarlet skirt to where silk stockings ended in a hairy male thigh, and offered Francesca room on the wooden bench.

'Buona sera, Colonello.'

His friend was dressed in top hat, waisted black riding-jacket, white shirt, black tie, white breeches, leather riding-boots and spurs. Flexing her whip, she smiled through caked white make-up at Francesca.

'*Ma guardi Alfredo, guardi. Che bella! Divertente.* Look Alfredo, look. How pretty! How amusing.'

Opposite, a large Arab smiled under his stuck-on moustache. His wife and three children laughed and giggled. The gauze veils didn't conceal the children's ecstasies, or the identity of the family of Claudio, barman at Harry's Bar.

The ringing of nautical bells, shouts and the vibration of engines indicated that the boat was leaving. The aft saloon was packed. At the far end, Beethoven, in black morning tails and waistcoat, high-collared white shirt with disordered Romantic hair falling down over his brow was conducting his neighbours through obscene verse and chorus of a Padova University medical student song. A surgeon, in white robes and hat, gauze mouth-mask, rubber gloves, forceps and stethoscope sung the verses, miming the obstetric details of the song to the general delight and applause. The whole saloon clapped the rhythm and sang the chorus.

We went on deck. Everyone was inside. We were alone. The radar scanner turned on the bridge. We could just see the hissing salt wake below in the lagoon fog. It was cold.

We went into the forward saloon which was as packed as the other. A group of wide-shoulder-padded American footballers with space helmets were playing Scott Joplin on guitar, drums and trumpet. A black-coated black-hatted priest danced, in thirties style, with a petite Franciscan monk, whose tiny waist was defined by the girdle.

'Ciao Geoffrey. Ciao Holly!' Francesca shouted in their ears.

Turks with broad scimitars mixed in the crush with triple Kings-of-Orient. An aeronaut in leather flying jacket and helmet and

Katharine Hall as Lady Death 1983

goggles Charlestoned with a ballet dancer in white tutu. Harlequin, Pierrot, the clown, gypsy queens, Red Indians, clockwork-orange delinquents, prisoners, lepers, national-service soldiers, Afrika Corps tank commanders, and flocks of tiny shepherdesses and Grand Turks moved about the boat, visiting the four crowded saloons, delighted and delighting.

At Murano the boat took on more revellers, before settling for the journey into the lagoon. In each saloon the party gathered force. The entertainers entertained, the entertained joined in with applause. There was movement, changing of places, of neighbours, of compliments. The propeller beat beneath the din of the party.

'Hi Francesca. You look great. Compliments!'

She had noticed a black-coated, leather-belted *carabiniere* patrolling the boat, pistol in holster, plastic eagle-beaked face under peaked cap. Whose was this American voice?

The boat throbbed through the fog, the posts marking the channel slipping behind. The wake of the boat crossed the channel and broke in foam on the lagoon mud, covered by an inch of water.

Below deck again she was offered a swig of *grappa* by a familiar Garibaldi, a professor at the *Accademia* art school. Warmed, she danced a foxtrot with an athletic cloche-hatted, Art Deco sequin-skirted student of architecture. His drag didn't conceal his growing male normality, she told him, smiling into his mascaraed eyes. He closed one eye at her and proposed a rendezvous for next week.

'But next week Fabio – who knows where we may be? We might still be on this boat in this fog, lost forever. Who knows.'

The propellers changed beat, ground to reverse for a moment and cut. There was activity on deck. People cleared misted windows. The boat glided without engine before roaring into full astern, alongside the wooden quay. It disgorged. A united crusade poured along the badly lit unpaved path from the landing-stage, turned right over a bridge, followed a short *calle* between buildings and suddenly was in the middle of the Carnival of Burano. A straight canal, criss-crossed with lights and coloured flags led to the small main square, where all Venice revelled. The tall walls of the church backed the square. Against the wall of the church, on a platform, a rock group was playing, inaudible above the din of laughing, talking and shouting people. Improvised bar stalls with barrels of wine, stalls selling *porchetta*, and, near the band, people dancing. Francesca saw lots of people dressed in tattered newspapers, speaking English, she told me.

'They're ours. Our students.'

A rocket soared and burst into crackling lilac glitter. Another followed, exploding in musical golden clusters. A series of rockets climbed into the misty sky. Golden Rain, Silver Fountains. Detonations. No one, watching the display, would have guessed that this was the last *popular* carnival, the last carnival for the amusement of Venetians, the last Burano Carnival.

Chambers of commerce, hoteliers and shopkeepers' associations were warming to the city councillors' profitable proposals. The image of the Venetian carnival of the 18th Century was not far below the surface, in the collective memory of 'A' Category Europeans, the

Venetian market research experts said. For striking publicity posters, it was enough to stroll in *Ca'Rezzonico*, the freezing palace which is the Museum of the 18th Century. In the smaller second floor rooms are paintings which fix forever the image and spirit of the old Venetian carnival. Pietro Longhi's *A Stroll on the Liston*, or a Guardi painting of the *Ridotto of S.Moise*: the white or black mask, the black hood covering head and shoulders, the black tricorn hat – the Domino.

In the olden days, on St. Stephen's Day, the day after Christmas, a government official announced the beginning of Carnival, that masks might be publicly worn. In the *ridotti* and *casini*, the gambling and coffee and chocolate drinking retreats, only patricians in robes were permitted *not* to wear masks. Masks gave complete class and amorous mobility: anybody could go with anybody. Gondolas were black outside, by sumptuary law, but inside the *felze*, the curtained and cushioned cabin, provided a delicious privacy: the fittings were luxurious silks, satins, velvets, ebonies and ivories. They provided the most intimate privacy.

'*Vien co mi, montemo in gondola, andaremo fuora in mar*' went the *barcarolle* words – come with me, let's get into the gondola and go out into the lagoon.

Casanova's diary note – '*je sortis pour vaguer à mes affaires, c'est a dire, à mes plaisirs*' – *I went out to see to my affairs, that is, to my pleasures*, was echoed by Le Brosse, president of the Burgundian parliament, visiting Venice. '*Nothing can equal the liberty that exists and the tranquillity that one enjoys. Here they don't taste pleasures, they gulp them.*'

'*I passed the gates of the palace into the great square,*' wrote William Beckford on his Grand Tour in the early 1790's, '*which received a faint gleam from its casinos and palaces, just beginning to be lighted up, and to become the resort of pleasure and dissipation. Numbers were walking in parties upon the pavement; some sought the convenient gloom of the porticoes with their favourites; others were earnestly engaged in conversation, and filled the gay illuminated apartments, where they resorted to drink, coffee and sorbets, with laughter and merriment. A thoughtless, giddy transport prevailed; for, at this hour, anything like restraint seems perfectly out of the question.'*

Sequins, ducats, Murano glass, Burano lace, cloth of gold: these are the textures of the Carnival years of the end of the Republic, the insistent memory of the city caught in the flickering brush strokes of Francesco Guardi, – hints of funeral-black among the white highlights.

'I will be an Attila to the Venetian State,' thundered the bullying, twenty-six year old Napoleon, and blew it all away. On June 4, 1797, a thousand years after the coronation of the first recorded Doge, Ludovico Manin took off his doge's hat, handing the white linen under-cap to his valet, saying: 'Take it, I shall not be needing it again.'

In spite of Napoleon, the market researchers were right: the image of Venice as the carnival city lingered in the mind of the world and was brought into focus in the Town Hall. Revive the Carnival! Venice fully booked for two weeks in deadest February! Tradition is Dead! Long Live Heritage!

By the time that municipal thoughts had arrived at this stage, the old-style power of the Democristian party, of the Cini Foundation and of many of the promoters of V.I.S. was gone. The city had moved to the left. To Anglo-Saxons, the left may have overtones of egalitarian, idealistic wishful-thinking. To Italians of this period, it was viewed cynically as an equally corrupt alternative to the entrenched Christian Democrats. V.I.S., whose political image was of the liberally emancipated old order, managed to persuade the mayor and councillors to attend two public meetings, at which they were invited to interest themselves officially in the growing presence of foreign students – particularly by allowing them to continue in the *Palazzo Fortuny*, or another of the empty palaces in their care. The answer was an unexplicit 'No'.

In those days of more naïve enthusiasm, we foreigners were all a little puzzled, even indignant, at the stolid, negative, evasive and platitudinous front of the politicians. We did not understand. They were either locked in a system where nothing was done without the exchange of favours: positions of power or bribes or the expectation of personal financial gain on a scale which only years later, in the corruption cases which filled the courts, began to be known. *V.I.S.* was not in this league, or game. Or they were paralysed in coalitions where a move towards a project of this kind, for foreigners, would have been politically impossible. This was the tense era of the Red Brigades, when each of us was often stopped on the streets by police for identification. It was the time when the drain of young people away from the historic centre of Venice, for lack of decent housing, was in full flow: a decline from a population of 123,000 in 1965, when our course began, to 73,000 in 1993. The city fathers had other priorities, they said, fogging the relatively insignificant side issue of a few foreign academics. This exposure to politics returned my thoughts to the inauguration of the Pre-University Course at the Cini Foundation – the television cameras, newspaper headlines, the fanfares and publicity. In those days, promoting a foreign enterprise would undoubtedly have won political *kudos* and most probably would have released a flow of funds from somewhere to someone.

So the Palazzo Fortuny's doors were shut to foreign student groups and a 'closed for restoration' notice decayed on its door for years after. Occasional photographic exhibitions are held there. Perhaps when the moonlight floods into the top floor, merry ghosts bring it back to life. Tom Hammond, *répétiteur* of the English National Opera explaining the *leitmotiv* structure of *The Ring*; or the composer John Rutter saying that music, like love, is better made than talked about; or the student Molesworth agonizingly struggling through a wildly over-ambitious tenor aria from Wagner's *Rienzi* in one of our concerts; or Charlie Hall and Mary Anne Sieghart breaking down into giggles having forgotten their lines in the Goldoni play hopelessly under-rehearsed by Nick Hawtree; or the resounding laugh of Consul Ray Jacques during the cabaret given by Sandy Wilson, writer of *The Boy Friend*, after his lectures on musical comedy. And perhaps the tall figure of James Sainsbury will arrive late as usual, with his new silver-topped walking stick, wearing his newly-bought silk shirt and tie of the day, wondering where everyone is.

The *Venice-Island of Studies Association* did not die – it faded away. Nine years later, in 1989, a slim booklet was printed, 'V.I.S. 1966-89. *Twenty three Years of Activity of the Venice-Island of Studies Association.*' Pignatti was quoted:

We had conceived perhaps too elitist a project, given the times, and the city rushed towards the ephemeral. Whereas V.I.S. wanted to bring Venice to Europe and the World, the city preferred to bring the province to the Carnival.

Without the help of the *V.I.S.* office and without the work space offered at the Palazzo Fortuny, it became difficult for foreign universities to make plans in Venice. After this, only five foreign academic activities have managed to continue to operate regularly in Venice. The American Wake Forest University has its permanent quarters in the palace of the former American consulate, on the Grand Canal next to the Guggenheim Palace. Germany has its Institute in a palace on the Grand Canal. Warwick rents expensive space in the Querini-Stampalia palace. East Anglia makes do without a lecture base. We were received by the Societa Dante Alighieri for nineteen happy years in the Arsenale until the navy took back its premises. We have been lucky to find another home with the Istituto Artiginelli in the cloisters of the Gesuati on the Zattere. Few Venetians would remember having heard of *V.I.S.*. Only a few foreigners and the *V.I.S.* people themselves would be aware of how the launching of the commercial carnival pushed the idea of an international academic community out of the political agenda. There was in fact room for both.

Years later, after more than twenty recent years with an established and regular place for our lectures, probably the most important of our requirements, the excitement of finding and collaborating with the *Venice – Island of Studies Association* may seem odd. It was a very real

excitement – a period of buoyant expectation, when the directors of foreign programmes in Venice believed that national or international centres – that is, premises in a palace – might be set up. John Hale and Michael Mallett of Warwick University, Andrew Martindale of East Anglia, Abraham Rogatnic of the University of British Columbia and I were the most active and committed supporters of this dream of a kind of academic paradise.

Coinciding with the shutting of the doors of the Palazzo Fortuny in the face of *V.I.S.*, city money went to promote the low-season tourist-attracting 'heritage' Carnival. So arrived the first elephants – and, sadly, the last. But the new Carnival persisted. A photograph from Sarah Quill's picture library shows two elephants walking through the streets of Venice. Another shows Mademoiselle Gruss riding high, balanced on the shoulder of her father, he poised on the back of the circling palfrey cantering round the glittering tent of *La Cirque Gruss* –

The Rhinoceros by Pietro Longhi c.1751

à l'Ancienne. These record the Carnival of 1980, the first of the officially revived new-style carnivals. Many Venetians were familiar with Longhi's picture in Ca'Rezzonico of the rhinoceros which had been exhibited at the Carnival of 1751 – 'an element of sadness and futility in the onlookers.' But they applauded the Gruss family and its elephants, in 1980. 'We'll give it a try' was the pragmatic Venetian reception of this new commercial project launched from the Town Hall by mistrusted and disliked politicians.

To persuade the office-bound Hugh and his wife to visit us in Italy was difficult. February was a possibility. 'But don't come during Carnival. Venice is full of French and German photographers. Everything is crowded – you can't move. The restaurants serve junk. You get nothing of the feel of Venice. Come any other time.'

After the first tentative year, the year of the elephants, of the old-style French circus, of participation of curious Venetians, the publicity machine brought the world to Venice. *Venice and Vienna, Venice and*

Paris, Venice and the Belle Epoque, – a series of themes, a succession of competing organising factions – the *Comune,* the *Shopkeepers Association,* the *Chamber of Commerce,* even the *Biennale.* For years hard rock was piped through the *campi* of the city, until a severe Superintendent of Monuments imposed decibel-controlled 'soft' carnivals. Hotels were filled, and restaurants, and shops. Venetians not in these businesses kept or went away. Burano was dead – an improbable memory – the secret of where modern Venetians used to go at Carnival. Georgina understood and argued for good sense but an element of obstinate perversity is built into Hugh: Carnival-time it had to be.

Venice has always been good visual copy and the media had done its work over the recent years. The traditional Carnival of Venice, Casanova's Carnival, had seeped steadily through Style and Travel colour supplements. Images of black-cloaked, white masked ladies and gentlemen, of incognito assignations at the masked ball in St. Mark's Square, the 'drawing room of Europe' had had the desired effect.

So Hugh and Georgina stepped up out of the airport launch onto the gangplank by the Giardini Reali on the Saturday of Carnival. We had to walk four hundred yards to our flat but four hundred yards in the epicentre of Carnival crowds – along the waterfront of the Piazzetta, along the water facade of the Doge's Palace, over the Ponte di Paglia, the viewing point for the Bridge of Sighs, along the *Riva* past the Danieli Hotel: one more bridge, then escape from the crowds down the narrow, dark Calle del Vin where we lived that year.

Off the gangplank, Hugh and Georgina were already taking snaps. The profusion of fancy dresses, the exaggerated size and magnificence of the costumes produced a cultural shock to anyone arriving out of the February drabness of London and Heathrow. Tall, wide-shouldered cloaks, masks scanning slowly like television dishes, towering headpieces, colours brilliant in the sun: gold, silver, feathers, furs, silks, velvets – a year's preparation, regardless of expense. Movement was reduced to slow motion, communication to sign language, by the weight of the gear.

'But how do the Venetians afford these things? They're spectacular.'

They don't. These weren't Venetians. The Venetians were out of town or at their tills. The attentive ear of hoteliers, restaurant owners and souvenir-mask-shop owners heard with pleasure the profitable sound of landing planes, charter after charter flight, carried the four miles from the airport across the lagoon water, bringing business to the historic centre. The Clementson Travel Office had booked the prestigious Palazzo Pisani-Moretta, had engaged a band, had ordered two hundred white *baute* (the classic plain white Venetian mask of the eighteenth century), and two hundred black cloaks and white lace stocks for a travel agency in Lyons. The Carnival is high tourism.

Having shot the best part of a reel of film before crossing the end of the Piazzetta, we concentrated on getting over the Ponte di Paglia, divided by a barrier at Carnival into a two-way system. Crossing, because of the view of the Bridge of Sighs, is like the approach to the turnstiles when Liverpool visits Stamford Bridge.

'Crowded. But how well-behaved. No drunks. No feeling of violence. Very un-English,' Georgina said.

Off the crowded Riva, in the Calle del Vin, through the glass door of the little hotel there, we saw one of the two voluptuous daughters of the house, Franca, standing on tiptoe to adjust the pearl-bound turban of a Turkish janissary. The hotel was full. They come each year, she had told me, a photography club from Dusseldorf and another from Nancy, she had told us. They're all friends.

'So what do they *do*? What happens at Carnival? What do *we* do?' Hugh was ready to go, impatient for the carnival experience. So off with the Burberry, on with the Domino and out.

'Photograph. Pose. And be photographed.' The delicate music of Vivaldi filled the packed *Piazza*, piped through twenty speakers. Outside the Lavena Cafe, at shoulder-level on a big wooden-wheeled wagon serving as stage, a group was performing a *Commedia dell'Arte* act, declaimed in Venetian, with plenty of slapstick smacks on the face, backward somersaults, tumblings, challenges, shouted secret asides, tears, joy. No one in the crowd understood a word but everyone clapped the rise and fall of dramatic movement.

We levered our way across the Piazza to where the crowd was tightest. Through the thickest ranks of maskers aiming cameras, we could see, in the arcade, the windows of the elegant 18th-century Caffe Florian. Inside, at each window-table sat figures in 18th-century velvets, brocades, powdered wigs, tricorn hats, white make-up, all motionless like porcelain dolls, flickering in the continuous blue bombardment of flash exposures, holding poses. In an oriental pavilion at the Napoleonic end of the Piazza – this year's theme was Venice and the Orient – a string quartet, also in 18th century costume, sitting on gilt and red plush chairs, played the music which was tastefully piped into the square.

At midday on the previous Saturday, to a fanfare of municipal trumpeters ranged on the balcony of the Doge's Palace, a large stuffed dummy in the shape of a Dove had begun its wobbly and jerky descent from the *Campanile,* down the wire which was fixed to the ground between the two columns in the Piazzetta. Thousands of municipal balloons had been released in the Piazzetta. Not quite as thrilling as the live Turk descending by the same route in the 18th century, 'the Flight of the Dove' marked the official opening of Carnival.

The manager greeted us appeasingly at the door of the Hotel Monaco, where we had reserved a table for dinner on *Martedi Grasso,* the final night. But it was not the Monaco I knew and loved, with quiet sitting space to the left, comfortable armchairs in front of a wood fire to the right and a spacious dining room on the Grand Canal at the end. It had been transformed into a mass eatery, with closely placed dining tables in every space. The way through to the dining room was temporarily blocked by a horizontal chivalric horse, caparisoned to the ground in azure velvet badged with estoiles argent. Its rider, dismounted, in crested helmet, visor down, chain mail, dazzlingly quartered shield buckled on one arm, was adjusting the gingling bridle and bit and fluffing the horse's ostrich plume. From underneath the accoutrement in suffocated French, a metal-boxed, male voice was repeating *Merde! Merde! Merde!*

After dinner, we looked through the arcade into the seething mass of tourists in the Piazza S. Marco, packed shoulder to shoulder, swaying to a piped Viennese waltz.

To witness the promised *finale* of Carnival, the procession of gondolas, we made our way away from the Piazza, crossed the Accademia Bridge and went towards the Salute church. We paused in the Campo S. Vio to admire the Palazzo Barbaro across the Grand Canal, illuminated by flaming torches on the balconies. Across the water, we could see the movement of people dancing in candlelit rooms. Here, at least, was a peep at real Venetian aristocrats celebrating the last night of carnival in a suitable and private style? It would have been unnecessarily unkind to our guests to reveal that this palace too had been hired for the occasion by a French travel agency.

The waterfront from the Salute Church to the Customs Point was a magically scenic walk. However false the Carnival may have been, the gleam of the lights reflecting across the water enchanted. Few tourists had found their way over here to watch the procession. A few Venetian families, muffled in hats and scarves, were enjoying their city view and exchanging sceptical forecasts about the punctuality or even the reality of this last act of Carnival. A man and wife and two children came towards us. It was Francesca Trentin and her family.

'And how have you been enjoying Carnival?'

Hugh and Georgina gave their reply of guarded enthusiasm.

'But it's no fun,' Francesca was saying. 'It's not *Venetian* any more. People don't *enjoy* themselves. All these foreigners – they just pay for expensive costumes and take photographs. Did you tell your friends' Francesca turned to me, 'about when we went to Burano? *That* was fun.' In fact it was at a prolonged rustic fish dinner that night in a farmhouse on Torcello, the island adjoining Burano, that she had met her husband. He brought a boat-load of us back across the lagoon in the first light. Although a Venetian, he had risked cutting a corner as the

Student film 1983

tide was in, leaving the marked navigation channel and we had run aground. We ended up to our knees in lagoon mud, pushing the *sandolo* back into the channel.

At midnight the bell of St. Mark's started tolling and Venetian groups headed for home, proved right in their forecast that there wouldn't be a procession of gondolas.

'But it said so in the programme'.

Hugh spotted a shadowy boat rowed urgently by two standing oarsmen, hissing past the Point and turning off left towards St. Mark's. Then came another. And a third. And no more.

The one superb moment of the new Carnivals had been the extravagant closing firework display, set off from rafts off the Island of S. Giorgio, reminding Venetians of their own Redentore festival, and delighting everyone. Ironically – or cynically? – the publicity has worked so well, the Carnival is now such a commercial success that in the last few years it has not been thought necessary to spend money on fireworks or publish any programme of events.

We walked home through the fast emptying city. Bells tolled the first Ash Wednesday masses. As we fell asleep, window panes rattled to the roar of departing charter flights reverberating across the lagoon.

If that is the voice of the querulous old, it is not so different from that of our eighteen-year-old student's in this postscript:

Do not expect Carnival to be like Rio or Notting Hill – it isn't. It is a tourist trap where thousands of foreigners flock to take photos of people dressed as Plague doctors or other bizarre characters. Venice is a particularly surreal city and Carnival fits this. There aren't many places in the world where you can get on the vaporetto with a swarm of grown men dressed as bumblebees, meet Cinderella in the cereal aisle of the supermarket or see the odd five-year-old Venetian dragon strolling along the Zattere. The greatest problem you face during Carnival is the acute sense of your territory being invaded by foreigners. It is strange how quickly Venice becomes your own and Carnival brings this home to you.

11

The Garden of Eden

The house at San Ginesio had been bought in deep winter, when the trees and lanes were bare and the fields slippery with ice. When I arrived to stay in the house for the first time, it was June, 1975 – high summer, and the sun was setting.

The track down was a tunnel between high banks of lush growth – hawthorn, mulberry, elder, wild honeysuckle, dog rose, brambles, between acacia, scent-laden broom, the curry aroma of santolina and the nutty, woodsmoke smell of old oak in sunshine. Rampant grasses grew at the edges and in the middle of the road.

My own territory was hardly recognisable. The two fields stood high with barley up to the shoulders of the rows of field maples on which were trained the vines, in the antique style. The buoyant green foliage of the vines twisted and reared along the wires stretched from tree to tree, like dancers holding hands. The house was surrounded by head-high plants of every kind: thistles, nettles, wild barley and oats, camomile, fennel. A flourishing fig, an improbable weeping willow and two poplars pressed near to the building.

The first of many mental adjustments was made. Before the life of the creative recluse could be lived, before reading and any writing could be done, a path would have to be cut to the front door and owner's rights asserted against a Nature that had almost taken over the house. The scythe before the pen.

Leaving the laden Renault 4 opposite the house, I walked the hundred yards down to the house below, where the road ended and where lived the *contadini* Osvaldo and Rita, and where the key had been left. No one responded to knocking. Then, from outside and below came the piercing voice of Rita followed by her broadly-smiling physical presence.

'O Signore, welcome back. Come, come,' she shouted, beckoning me, a virtual stranger and now neighbour, with the gesture of hand which in England means go away. 'Come down. We're in the *stalla*. A calf has just been born. Come in.'

The stall, the byre which exists under every peasant house, was a Tintoretto nativity scene, lit by a paraffin lantern hanging from a beam. Two white Marchigian oxen stood placidly in line, munching hay from the manger. A third beast, a cow of the same white breed, was couched in straw, regarding us with docile eyes, a tiny, leggy calf lying beside her, too young to stand and draw milk. Two builders' planks on trestles made a table, at which sat Osvaldo and eight-year-old son Claudio while Rita carried in a chair for me. Osvaldo pushed his chair for me. Already a tumbler was brimming over with acetic wine, '*genuino, genuino*' Osvaldo urged, and Rita had sliced bread and was cutting slices of their *prosciutto*: best home-cured ham reserved for special occasions.

The Marchigian dialect, although thrown out as if to carry down several fields, was so thick that I had to intuit most of what was said. It was the custom to spend the first evening of a calf's life together in the stall, the family supping with the animals. The soft light illuminated the white beasts, the wooden ceiling beams and the features of my neighbours: Osvaldo, thin as a rake, hollow cheeks, tawny hair and moustache, shifting, oblique glances from a lowered head, pale-blue eyes light against sunburn, insistent on the customs of hospitality to strangers; Rita, a barrel of muscular torso, bosom, hairy legs, red face, tawny hair and blue eyes. They looked in their late forties but were in their early thirties, shaped by generations of peasant life, their un-Italian colouring a reminder of trotting Goth, resident Lombard and travelling Norman.

Part of my mind was engaged in the limited exchange of sociability. Another part, as the daylight outside had gone, was thinking of spiders, scorpions, moths, millipedes, mice, rats and the range of terrors awaiting me on my first night in the abandoned house. There was no way it could be cleaned up that night. I extended my rights of hospitality a little longer, increasing simultaneously my appreciation of Osvaldo's special reserve *Vin Cotto* – a 'cooked' wine, which he had now brought out – and the probability of a fearless night's sleep – and revealing a weakness.

'Snakes? Yes – *tanti, tanti* – lots of them, but serpents, not vipers. Lots of serpents, very few vipers. Serpents do nothing. But vipers! *Mamma mia!*' Osvaldo had killed one last week. 'But little, little. Like this,' and Rita indicated a length of nine inches. On this subject, every phrase and innuendo of deepest Marchigian was clear.

'The size doesn't matter. If you're bitten… It was in the doorway, here in this *stalla*, in a crack in the wall, just at the height of my ear. The Traitor they're called. If you see them, they don't move. If you take your eye off them, they're gone. But at night – nothing. No one was ever bitten by a snake at night.' On which reassuring note Osvaldo refilled my tumbler.

Thus fortified, I returned up the track to my house, glittering stars above, fireflies around and even below me. The massive key found the keyhole with difficulty and by torchlight I located the bed and unpacked the sleeping bag.

In the early morning, with the golden sun just over the ridge but the air still cool, I borrowed scythe and sharpening stone, rake and pitch fork from Osvaldo and began the first of the sequence of tasks which followed natural priorities down the years.

A path was cut from the front door to the road. Then I worked in a series of expanding arcs from the door to the edge of the area at the front of the house, layering the ground with lush nettles, chunky thistles, celestial blue wild chicory, yellow St. John's wort, tall daisies, buttercups, wild carrots, cow parsley, clover, self-sown barley and corn, and many grasses. And as I cut, the scent of mint, fennel, wild thyme, lemon balm, curry and camomile stood in the air.

Probing a particularly lush area under the willow, the blade touched something hard and uncovered a shallow bottom section of a barrel embedded in the ground, brimming with clear water, tapping the invisible vein which seeped down from the top of the field. This was my washing and shaving bowl for many summer weeks.

Working round to the far side of the house, the scythe revealed the steeply-sloping contours of the surrounding banks, thick with nettles, and released two forgotten stone outhouses and the bread oven from their head-high mantle of convolvulus.

Between the house and outhouses was a small sward of relatively weed-free grass, sloping somewhat less steeply. At the edge of it was planted a tall, twisting pole, formerly the central stake of the farmyard haystack. In a dilapidated outhouse there was a rickety, wooden table, the oxidised remnants of green paint embedded in the grain: a table of impeccable peasant lineage familiar to Cezanne, Van Gogh and every Mediterranean farmhouse. And there were two upright chairs of the same breeding. Blocking up the legs of the table against the slope to something approaching level was the first assertion of my outdoor space. The heat of the sun soon made it unusable.

Indoors was cool, and the small windows let in little light. Everything was further softened by the presence of immemorial dust, the finest powdering from the terracotta tiles which paved all floors and ceilings. At the centre of the living-room-kitchen a fine walnut early 19th century table had already been installed in my absence, sent down from Venice. With the gleaming brass oil lamp, it added a pleasing lustre to the room, in contrast to the shabby old fridge, cooking rings and iron bed-frame which kind friends of Giorgio Lauro had brought down as gifts of welcome.

In the car were what the concentrated mind knew to be the bare essentials of life in the Garden of Eden: knife, fork, spoon, two plates, four glass tumblers in the expectation of company, a mug, a sharp kitchen knife, a coffee percolator, a bowl for washing up and another for washing myself should the natural outside basin run dry. A broom, brush and pan, and a fifteen-litre container for carrying water were bought. As permitted luxuries were added an assortment of insect sprays, night burners, snake serum and syringe. Corkscrew and bottle opener were already at hand. For refreshment and cultivation of the soul there was a desert island library – Andrew Marvell's Poetical Works; Kilvert's Diary; Iris Origo's autobiographical *Images and Shadows*; the Italian Touring Club Guide to the Marches; an English-Italian Dictionary; and a portable Olivetti typewriter.

Busy in the way that only those who have no nine-to-five office routine can be, I let my acquaintance with the place and its inhabitants take a natural, unhurried course. The other occupants of the house introduced themselves – the field mice, the millipedes, the self-effacing scorpions, the fluttering moths and a wide range of spiders. We coexisted, a limited chemical warfare being conducted only against insects that bite by night.

In the evening, after pasta and cheese and red wine, sitting some-what awkwardly on an upright chair or sprawled on the sloping greensward, I watched the day fade over the fields and woods of the valleys and hills and finally off the last peaks of the mountains. In the twilight a regular owl alighted on the haystack pole and shared my company, adjusting the angle of his plate-like face in reaction to the liquid bubbling call of my curlew imitation, perfected on the moors above Cauldron Snout in Upper Teesdale.

In such moments of creative contemplation, the primary requirements of country living fell naturally into place. Outside – level areas, a terrace and shade: trees or a roof. Underfoot – something free of nettles, thistles and thorns: paving. Inside – being able to look and step out to the outside living area, without having to go out of the front door on the wrong side and stumble all the way round the house: in other words, a new glass door. Running water, dust-free interiors, strong electric light were of secondary importance. At this stage, cataracts and spouting storms, hurricanes, black frosts and obliterating snows were unthought of.

When the owl had floated off to the abandoned church across two fields and thoughts rose from practicalities towards the songs of Apollo, the nightingales began in the oaks below and in the steep cliff across the field. They called to each other through the night. As darkness came, the fields around the house filled with the living lamps of a myriad of fireflies flashing above the corn and into the mowed areas looking for the steady glow of their earthbound females. Stars shone brightly through uncontaminated atmospheres. The moon presided, uniting the dun solidity of the wide mountain landscape with the immediate intimacy of the fields, trees and neighbouring farms in a way which would have inspired Samuel Palmer. The beaker full of the warm south was drained. A wandering dog, finding a figure sleeping in the moonlight, barked.

A photograph a year later shows a family group beside the table, squinting into the slanting evening sun, wine-glasses raised in toast to the automatically-set camera. Everyone was in white after being swilled with buckets of heated water. After days of sweat and dust we were celebrating the first use of our personally-constructed level and paved area, at the sloping side of the house. The 'terrace' had two poles planted at its outside edge with wires to the house wall on which was stretched a straw awning for shade. My children, Nicholas aged eighteen; Charlie sixteen; Katharine and cousin Rachel twelve, and myself. The photograph goes straight back to what seems an age of innocence: Edith Piaf, chilled *Verdicchio*, aching muscles.

We spent entire days scraping ingrained paint off the amazingly twisted oak beams of the room, sand-blasting being unknown in these parts in those days; or constructing the drystone outer walling of our terrace adjacent to the house, alongside the farm-equipment space, our future Sybilline room. The stones came from the demolition of internal walls and the infill from rubble, inferior bricks and chunky dust.

We also put in time digging a passage round the top end of the house, to enlarge the two-foot wide, nettle-filled snake pit which

Charlie at work on the terrace

separated its wall from the actual hill. We learned why John Berger had called his book on mountain peasantry 'Pig Earth.' There were more embedded stones, each twice the size of a football, than earth. Pickaxe, pointed spade and shovel were the instruments and an improved physique the result of this brutish labour. It was the ideal preparation for a genuine appreciation of the mechanical excavator, our digger in the not-too-distant decadent future – and for draughts of chilled beer.

Peter, the retired solicitor from Market Weedon in the East Riding of Yorkshire put the new idea, the apple of temptation, into mind. Outside his house in the battlements of the town walls, which look out over the Contrada Scalette, in his garden he had built what he called a fountain. Water issued from the mouth of a stone lion-mask into a stone basin a few seconds after he had emptied a jug of water into the cistern at the top: then stopped. He would then open a tap in the stone basin, refilling the jug with the original water. 'Talking of water', and he emptied a jug at the top and we observed the brief flow from the lion's mouth, 'you could probably run a tube down to your house from Orlando's, the farm above. He has mains water.' Orlando is the *contadino* holding the white oxen, in another photo.

'But Peter. I thought you disapproved of luxuries like water?'

'*Hot* water yes. Ruined the Romans. But cold water's essential. We *always* shaved and showered in cold water in the *Andrew*', as he called the Royal Navy. Pale blue eyes flashing like cannons from Nelson's *Victory* supported the vehemence of his words in a way which was to become familiar.

'You don't know *Unamuno*? *The* Unamuno?' A combination of ardent enthusiasm and withering scorn. Unamuno is a Spanish philosopher. 'A *hat*? I *never* wear a hat' – as if a hat were a rotting carcass. It could so easily have been '*Without* a hat? I *never* go out without a hat.'

Peter had been pointed out to me many times by locals keen to make the introduction. He limped on a walking stick, having had a hip replacement. He wore a white, short-sleeved shirt, faded white flannel shorts and long white socks which set off his leanness and sunburnt colour. His short-cut, greying hair was brushed flat. He could be seen at crossroads in the country, water colour painting at an easel; or sitting in the chairs outside any of the four bars, sitting in the sun, reading a book, making notes with a pencil. His family of stray dogs circled and played like a cluster of flies, barking and growling at passers-by. 'Stupid fools', he said through gritted teeth as a young Italian girl snatched her hand away from a playful dog. 'No idea how to treat animals.'

I had introduced myself, in the end, one morning outside the Bar Centrale. He received me graciously, offering a chair. We instantly discovered common ground in literature, cricket, Italy, Venice. He had first retired to Pellestrina on the Venetian lagoon, but left in disgust when they 'ruined the place' by asphalting the only road. After driving all over Italy on a Lambretta, he had settled in San Ginesio, 'the most beautiful place in Italy.'

In our first months of acquaintance we ranged widely over common interests and I soon knew how to avoid having the conversation stopped; how to keep within the canon of Peter's taste. Unamuno, Cervantes 'in the original *of course*' (who would dare admit to not reading Spanish?), Boswell's Dr. Johnson, Sterne, Macaulay, Carlyle were *in*: Byron, Shelley, Joyce, Lawrence, *out*. And then, the cricketers: Hobbs, Sutcliffe, Verity ('very nice chap. I acted for him') were *in*: Kerry Packer, Lillee, Boycott were *out*. '*I'm not surprised at the oafishness of your metal-batted Australians. I never could stand colonials*' he wrote to me.

The same went, by and large, for women. 'How wonderful to be without the wife of my Scotch friend. She really is the stupidest woman on the terrestrial globe, which isn't meanly supplied with stupid females.'

In the piazza one evening, under the statue of Alberico Gentili, 'almost a co-national' as the surveyor said, the conversation returned to our water question. Our discussion of this hypothetical problem was interrupted regularly by his disobedient dogs which ranged about the piazza making a nuisance of themselves.

'Flavio! Luca! Riccardo! Come here!' – to no effect whatsoever.

A man at the next table involved himself in our talk and said the water proposal would present no difficulties and his builders would do the work. The 'work' was to me a new concept, a surprise. The work he was referring to, apart from bringing water to the house by '*tubo volante*' – a pipe 'flying' at tree-top level, was the entire plumbing of the house, a complete bathroom and kitchen. He was a surveyor and gave an idea straight away of the costs: tubing, bath, basin, bidet, kitchen sink, hot water heater, taps, septic tank, labour. Naïve excitement at the thought of one day maybe having a tap with running water had prevented any thoughts on the inexorable consequences – like the complete plumbing of the house with all the trimmings, including a drainage system. 'Til then, drinking water was carried down from a bar in town in plastic containers: washing water was in the sunken tub under the willow. Here lay that savage building axiom, like a crocodile concealed in a muddy pond – that the smallest building work knocks on to a series of unavoidable other more expensive building works.

These luxurious ideas took up residence in the mind. The prospect of lolling in hot water instead of performing the awkward operation of upending a bucket of heated water over the naked body, standing, often shivering, in long grass, was distinctly pleasing. As for lavatories, we had passed from the pioneer era, when son Nicholas and his school friend Adrian, my future colleague in Venice, had chosen secluded panoramic corners, marked by pit-digging spades. One of the first conspicuous loads on the roof rack of an early Renault 4, on the regular run from England, was a pair of state-of-the-art chemical loos which served satisfactorily in a woodshed. But the cost of these luxuries: hot water and proper plumbing, though the surveyor's estimate was deceptively low, made it an impossibility. Or was it? In London I was told of a noble Dane who would be in Venice in February, who might be willing to make a loan.

The Accelerato vaporetto lumbered across the mouth of the Grand Canal from the Salute, its searchlight probing a freezing February fog. Through the swing doors and in the glow of Harry's Bar, overcoat, scarf, gloves and fur hat were taken off and the barman Ruggiero recommended, for so raw a night, a Rusty Nails. So it was over that fine cordial that I was introduced to the Dane and accepted his offer of a loan which made it possible to begin the works in San Ginesio.

Certainly, with this nibble at forbidden fruit, the family photograph acquired hallowed status, recording golden days when improvements were made by the sweat of our brows. Projects for works to be done, the business of builders and the customs of debts and delays had been unknown and unthought of. From this moment on, all was less pure and simple but gradually more comfortable.

July 7. A round concrete septic tank, a bath with numerous taps and fittings and boxes of ceramic tiles have been delivered to the house. Two five-quintal tanks have been left at the roadside under the oaks on the curve above my field and five hundred and forty metres of black plastic tubing in Orlando's yard. The builders begin on Monday.

That naïve optimism was the first reference to builders in the diary. The surveyor had procured a builder – Giancarlo Porfiri, a clean cut, lean man who worked in immaculately pressed pale-blue trousers and short-sleeved linen shirt. As well as farming and building, he had the cemetery concession, preparing, opening and closing the concrete burial cells.

Orlando had been persuaded to agree to a joint being fitted to his outside tap, from which we could draw water. As Orlando was the tenant of a Roman padrone, on the old *mezzadria* system, we needed the permission of the boss too, who came from Rome on the first Wednesday of the month. We left time for him to finish his business with the barman of Pian di Pieca's wife. The barman could not afford not to look away on these occasions: the Roman owned the bar. When we returned to Orlando's yard, there was the Alfasud with the Rome number plate and the great landowner, Casanova himself, wearing a wide-brimmed white hat, in genial conversation with Orlando – Orlando's wife and daughters kept conspicuously out of sight. This short, plump, rosy-cheeked man in his sixties agreed with instant largesse to our request and filled the extra two glasses which Orlando had brought. He raised a toast to the *Inglese*.

Two weeks after the appointed date, Giancarlo and his overweight, unshaven brother Maurizio arrived at seven in the morning. Maurizio, who practised plumbing, quickly removed Orlando's trough tap and replaced it by one with a junction while Giancarlo began digging in the gravelly, hard-packed surface of the yard, to make a furrow from tap to roadside. With pick and spade a channel was quickly dug, a first length of black tube was sawn off, fittings were screwed in and it was attached to the tap and buried.

An immense length of tube was then unrolled down the road. Giancarlo ascended the first poplar out of the farmyard with prehensile agility and without creasing or soiling trousers or shirt. The tube was lashed with wire to a high branch, then to the next tree and so on down the roadside, to the sharp bend where the road forked, left to me and

Osvaldo, right down to the church, Antero's family, and to the Brandi and Liverotti families. Here the flying tube crossed to the other side, pulled as high and tight as possible to give clearance to the tall loads of hay and straw which came up on lorries from the farms below. From here it ran down the hedgerow to where the tanks had been left under the oak.

Giancarlo quickly had the tanks embedded firmly in level ground while Maurizio fitted a series of inlets and outlets, with a ball-valve to stop more water coming when the tanks were full. Then came the final run of tube, looping down from the tanks via the apple tree, attached to a line of vine-bearing field-maples, into the top of a young walnut tree and finally crossing the road into the poplar and down to the ground in front of the house. Giancarlo walked back up to Orlando's, Maurizio stationed himself with plumber's wrenches by the tanks and I waited at the end of the tube.

Shouts came from above and then Maurizio shouted the arrival of water at the tanks. I ran up to watch the clean, unused tanks filling with clear, cold water. When they brimmed full, the outlet tap was opened, the temporary tap at the end of the tube was opened and water flowed and splashed outside the house. At which miraculous moment the Porfiri brothers sat down under the fig tree and ate their nine o'clock *merenda* – a large roll filled with salami.

But they didn't go. They would start on the rest of the job *now*. As they munched and looked at my house, their thoughts were clear. 'Why don't you bulldoze the whole thing down and start from scratch? It would be cheaper and you'd finish with a better house.'

12

At the Arsenale

The Pre-University Corse

If you do not put your staff in order the chambers maidens will not clean the rooms anymore. It is impossible to walk inside the rooms – signed Laura
If tonight you will make too much noise I will let you sleep in St. Mark's Square. (sic)

This, red felt pen in capital letters pinned on the wall of the reception, is the authentic voice of Signora Laura, the owner of the then Pensione, now Hotel Atlantico. The Pensione da Cici had gone downhill and, after ten years, we had moved across the Grand Canal. The Atlantico, improved since the original inspection visit and a fire, was just behind the Piazza San Marco, fronting onto that small canal which runs along a side of the Doge's Palace. Three bridges up the canal from the Atlantico's bridge, the Ponte del Remedio, is the Bridge of Sighs. The hotel was a vast, cavernous palace, many times gutted and put together again, more or less on the cheap. It had a certain dusty, sleepy, shabby grandeur. After getting to know Cici well, and trying to ignore the increasing faults there, it was with plenty of trepidation that we followed the *V.I.S.* personal introduction to Signora Laura at the Atlantico, and moved there. In spite of various *ultimata*, and as a result of continuous self-interested diplomacy between Laura and ourselves, the Atlantico was still our home, twenty-one years later – and home it was. Cooks: Remedio, Carlino, Publio, seemed to rotate in three-year-cycles, perhaps because the existence of a kitchen in the Pensione

Atlantico was highly illegal: no catering licence. No other guests could have lunch or dinner in the hotel and we had to hand over large envelopes of cash for the privilege. Other changes in staff were rare, and usually in the family, so they knew us and we knew them. Rossi, ancient, thin as a rake, dressed in skin-tight racing-bicycle strip complete with long-peaked cap, ran the bar, compulsively drawing the heads of the young females staying in the hotel – the walls of the bar were a gallery of Rossi portraits. His daughter-in-law Pucci, in her fifties, cleaned floors, made beds, laid and cleared tables with the same elegance as she walked to and from work, tall, slim, permanently blonde and immaculate in her long mink coat. Daniela, grown from a fifteen-year-old to buxom mother, battled with the disorder in students' rooms. At the reception desk, Claudio alternated with Teresa. The night porters, Vladimir and Pietro, were both Rotweilers when in an off mood.

The political closing of the doors of the Palazzo Fortuny, with ourselves on the outside, happened a year after we moved to the Atlantico. Thanks to the Signora Laura, for a year it was possible to hold lectures in the cramped space of an Atlantico dining room. It was here that the magnificently Germanic Else Mayer-Lismann of the London Opera Workshop invoked the atmosphere of the opening of *Rheingold*, with recumbent students flowing all over the floor to her feet.

'Vater! Vater! More vater! More, more, more vater!'

Here Nicholas True made his debut, recording the blinding punitions of the Byzantine Basil the Bulgar-Slayer and Justinian the Second Split-Nose. And here the composer Nicola Le Fanu challenged the ear with Satie, Stockhausen, Copland, Malipiero.

Not all these subjects went well to the churning of washing-up machines and cooks' voices behind a thin partition and the uninhibited clashing of plates, cups and saucers as tables were re-laid in neighbouring dining spaces. To one accustomed to teaching in Canterbury in Medieval classrooms continuously under modernisation, with working drills erupting audibly and visibly through walls during lessons, conditions could have been worse. However, we again needed a new place for our lectures.

Rosella Zorzi, who had been so strongly recommended by John Guthrie and who had led the teaching of Italian to our students in the first years, had been rising fast in the university and was already the President of the newly established Societa Dante Alighieri, which propagates the Italian language and Italian culture. Knowing we were looking for lecture rooms, Rosella offered us the use of the rooms which the Societa Dante Alighieri used in the Naval Dockyard, the historic Venetian Arsenal, established in 1144. At the same time the Monsignor of the church of S.Zaccaria was willing to let us use the *Scoletta*, a first floor room in the building which joins the new Renaissance part of S.Zaccaria to the Romanesque *campanile*: in fact, it was part of the original nave of the early Medieval church. The room was used for weekly lectures by the Circolo Italo-Brittanico, so I knew it well. Both options were excellent. San Zaccaria was three minutes walk from the Atlantico, the Arsenal was ten minutes away. The following year our lectures began in the *Scoletta* of S.Zaccaria. On the first day, Monday, Peter Lauritzen gave his outline of Venetian History from 797 to 1797, in two hours.

A resident in Venice, Peter had arrived from Florence around 1967, a youthful American of Danish extraction, as his fine Nordic profile shows. He was of striking appearance, like an Oberammagau Christ, with a face of crucified sensitivity, chin tipped with a goatee, an elongated body, long hands and the pale colouring of satinwood, glinting with traces of old gold leaf. A year or two after Peter, the slender, elegant, Anglo-Irish Lady Rose Keppel came to Venice. After a mysterious absence, Peter and Rose re-appeared in Venice, having been to London and married there. A photograph in the album taken afterwards in Venice fixes the moment and the image: Rose's golden hair, Peter's golden colouring, the radiant smile of both, taken against the crimson plush, gilt and glass of Florian's Caffe. They bought the *Palazzo da Silva*, the embassy in the 16th century of Sir

Peter and Rose Lauritzen

Henry Wotton – he who defined an ambassador as '*one who lies abroad for his country*'. Their presence added an Anglo-Irish-American flavour to Venetian palace society while for the English community, or that part of it which is centred on the English Church, they provided a point of focus more reassuringly of the *ancien regime* than could any incumbent of the impoverished consulate.

Echoes, in slightly broken English, of the languid fall of Rose's voice can be heard in anglophile *saloni* on the Grand Canal. Peter became an expert on Venice, from art to the problems of the waters of the lagoon and the politics of rival solutions. His enthusiasm made him greatly in demand as a guide for superior English and American tour groups and a lecturer across the Atlantic. The same enthusiasm marks his lectures to our students. 'Amazing!' said and say the students. Rose's inconspicuous good turns among the English community go beyond the requirements of *noblesse oblige*. It was she who dressed Christina for her funeral, fending off one hilarious vulture who was after the silk kimono for himself, and worrying whether she had been right not to put the false teeth in the coffin. And Peter gave a memorable funeral oration in the English Church.

On the next day at the *Scoletta*, Tuesday, our new lecturer Peter Phillips, Director of the Tallis Scholars, began his series of five lectures on Venetian sacred music. In London the highest-quality portable ghetto blaster had been bought, with the assurance that its amplification would fill the dimensions of the *scoletta*. It was obvious in the first sentences of Peter's first talk that he had the attention of the students. There was absolute silence: in fact you could hear the click of a switch as he inserted a cassette. He introduced in words the grand antiphonal choirs of Andrea Gabrieli's *Laudate Dominum* and pressed the button. At which precise second the silence was rent and shredded by overpowering decibels from an electric guitar, blasting up through the floorboards, as if Beelzebub himself were in competition. I was down the stairs, out of the building and into a ground-floor door in seconds. In a small, curtained space below, a mild, bespectacled middle-aged man was giving a lesson to a conservatively-dressed youth.

'But I've been giving lessons here for years. Everyday except Mondays. Didn't the Monsignore tell you?'

The next day, and ever since, all our lectures have been at the *Arsenale*.

The name Arsenale is from Arabic, meaning a building for construction work. The Venetian Arsenale is an immense monument of industrial architecture, its inner basins, docks and shipyards almost as invisible today as they always had been, forbidden by the Republic to be included in old maps and still surrounded by two miles of thirty-foot-high walls and fifteen defensive watchtowers. The vaporetto passes through the middle of the Arsenale without stopping, in at the South gate, out at the North, and *vice versa*, providing a surrealistic view of ghostly, abandoned buildings. At the Renaissance entrance arch, by the white marble lions which once stood at the entrance to the Piraeus, the port of Athens, brought to Venice as war trophies in 1697, a national service sailor lolls on guard, machine gun slung across a shoulder.

It is still a naval dockyard. Tied up in docks on the far side, outside the walls, there are usually one or two tankers having damaged plates repaired by welders. Otherwise, it is empty, watery spaces and acres of dilapidated brick buildings, mainly from the 17th and 18th centuries: the roofed sheds of sixty-six dry docks, of arms rooms, foundries, powder stores, lumber yards, sawmills, oarmakers' workshops and the separate, elongated spaces of the rope makers. As early as the 12th century, the Republic provided an enclosed and protected space where shipwrights, sawyers and caulkers could construct ships. By the 13th century its crowded, bustling industry, with conspicuous bubbling vats of pitch, provided Dante with a simile for Hell – the little wooden entrance bridge to our lecture rooms is still called the Ponte del Purgatorio. At this time its symbolic importance was such that the Horses of St. Mark's, looted from the Hippodrome in Constantinople in 1204, were at first placed at the Arsenale gates. In the 15th, 16th and 17th centuries it expanded fast and a method of modular construction, on a conveyor-belt system, was developed so that a work force of 16,000 was able to produce a hundred fully-fitted warships in sixty days. By the time the shipyards of Tyneside and the steel mills of Sheffield were showing industrial buildings on a similar scale, four centuries later, the Arsenale was in decay. The Societa Dante Alighieri, through personal contacts with an admiral and in return for having restored the monumental entrance gate, occupied a small area above the Naval Library.

Peter Phillips' second attempt was made in the Arsenale, without interference and with instantly-bought new player and speakers. After his quietly spoken introductions, he let the high treble intricacies of Cornyshe's Magnificat from the Eton College Choir Book, or the swelling momentum of Tallis' 40-part motet *Spem in Alium,* or the trumpets, organs and chorales of a Lutheran mass work their effects on an often stunned audience.

After the success of Peter Phillips, more music was added to our programme. Jane Glover, the conductor, regularly reduced large

Rodney Milnes and Christina Thoresby

numbers of eighteen-year olds, and often herself, to tears with the music and story of Mozart. Rodney Milnes, the opera critic, for many years converted addicts of heavy metal to the magical *bel canto* skills of Montserrat Caballe, to the revolutionary drama of Rossini and to the heartrending sadism of Puccini. Hunched over the controls of now the highest-fidelity compact disc equipment, himself hypnotised once again by Wagner's *Tristan* and the musical moral dilemmas it plunged him into, he would often stop it with a health warning: 'Hmmm. Very bad for you. I advise you never to listen to that sort of music again. Very bad for you,' sending his audience away in something of a trance.

At the Arsenale, with Rosella Zorzi in control, we were paying guests since 1981. The lecture rooms were ideal: they were cleaned, there was an office with a telephone and fax and the efficient and charming Marisa and Antonella. As it belonged to the navy, the Societa Dante Alighieri were not in absolute control of what happened inside or outside the building. One year, repairs to the roof above our lecture room, with occasional falls of plaster, and once a moment of visible blue sky, did not help concentration on the lectures: nor did workmen appearing on scaffolding outside a window behind the lecturers' shoulder, cramming their mouths with sausage-filled rolls and talking with uninhibited animation – they couldn't see us. Not always does the heating work. However, we were more than pleased to have a base, and such a historic and picturesque base, for our lectures.

What we included in the lecture menu has varied over the years. There have always been lectures to do with Venetian, Italian and European art. Music has for many years been a major part of our activity. There has always been some introductory or background history, and almost always an ingredient nothing to do with Venice or the arts, such as political theory, economics, computer theory, human biology, psychology, psychiatry – this last proving particularly popular. Like vintages of grapes, the vigour and volatility of the fermentation varies from one year to another. It is true that sun in February helps the mixture to boil and bubble more merrily.

An important and consistent element, the true oenologist's yeast, is the superlative team of lecturers who have come out, almost all of whom have the knack of firing the imagination. Few lecturers can resist an invitation for a week in Venice, to give one lecture a day, though many make sacrifices to arrange to be free to come and give far more of their time to students than the lecture hour. Most of the lecturers, once they have started, continue to come year after year, pleased by the spontaneous enthusiasm of the students: and, as was the case of one young art historian, pleased by the bonus attractions of the hotel where they are lodged each year.

The two daughters came in at eight in the morning, Franca or Antonietta on alternate days, and took up their position behind the reception desk, still drowsy from bed. Thick, honey-coloured hair folded on their shoulders and lay in down on their arms. They were pure Prado Titian, golden fleshed – the art historian's connoisseur eye observed. Each morning, he went out, leaving his room key at the desk, took a walk on the Riva, bought a paper and returned for breakfast.

The younger, Franca, was twenty-eight-years old, in the flush of her prime. Hearing a ring at the bell, she leant diagonally back from the stool, an arm reaching above her head to press the door opener, extended, like *Danae*, open to the shower of desire which often hung over her… visible or invisible, to her? Her light brown eyes always smiled as he greeted her.

Danae – Titian

Venus and Adonis – Titian

'*Buon giorno professore. Come sta?*' she would customarily reply, to his disappointment always using the formal and distancing mode of address (a choice the Italian language allows), as she extended herself again, reaching back and up to detach his room key from the pigeon-hole hook. 'Here it is.' Taking it, he was for a second in her musky atmosphere. It made his day.

'*The nude which your reverence saw at Pesaro in the apartment of the Duke of Urbino looks like a nun beside this one.*' And he thought of the d'Este ambassador's report on Titian's slowness in delivering the *Bacchus and Ariadne*: '*I have been to see Titian who has no fever at all: he looks well, if somewhat exhausted; and I suspect that the girls, whom he often paints in different poses, arouse his desires which he satisfies more than his limited strength permits.*'

Antonietta was ten years older and presented herself with more unambiguous allure – a more open blouse, a mini skirt which made casual conversation difficult. '*Because the figure of Danae, which I have already sent to Your Majesty, is seen entirely from the front, I have chosen in this painting to vary the appearance and show the opposite side.*' Antonietta was perched on the reception stool. He looked at her, like at Titian's Venus, from behind, from the breakfast area, allowing Titian's contemporary to make a point. '*Venus is shown from the back. One can see even the slight compression of her flesh caused by the weight of her body as she sits.*'

The pensione was always spotlessly clean, warm in winter, air-conditioned in summer, ruled by the feminine professionalism of the two and their elegant, slim mother who would, when necessary, press a suit for favoured customers. He sent them Christmas cards and they exchanged the correct, friendly conversation of hotelier and regular customer. 'Una persona squisita' – an exquisite person – the mother said of him, receiving the flowers he sometimes gave when he left.

'If I were to present a copy of the forbidden *Postures*, explicit erotic engravings by Giulio Romano, explicit sonnets by Titian's friend Aretino, to which would I give it?' he asked me as I walked with him to the vaporetto, when he was leaving, after another year of wonderful lectures perhaps stimulated by frustrated fantasies. Ezra Pound settled for a cerebral solution.

It pleases me to be among beautiful women.

The purring of the invisible antennae
Is both stimulating and delightful.

And so some major blocks in the enterprise seemed to be in place. A brilliant team of lecturers had been formed. We had a stable space at the Arsenale. We were happy and at home in the Atlantico. Students continued to enrol, occasionally providing a flash-flood of funds towards doing-up the house in San Ginesio. And at last I was in the hands of an excellent accountant, a thin Australian of sixties-hippy vintage whose chief hobby was viticulture and oenology. He had no nerves about increasing pre-university fees in line with our running costs and with private schools. We were able to pay back the noble Dane and to have the house at least plumbed and wired for the arrival of our first guests: Hugh and Georgina, our carnival-battered friends.

13

Snakes and Leaks

The serpent basked in the sun, its flaccid, four-foot length extended on the warm tiles of the outhouse roof. This snake and I shared, with an occasional fox, the habit of enjoying the earliest morning sun, when the air was fresh and clear before the heat of the day and before the builders came. Hugh and Georgina, who had pronounced that Venetian churches would look better without *campanili*, would certainly not appreciate anything so superfluous as a snake. They were due in six weeks time. I measured the snake, like the prison hangman, unseen. I remembered that the chop must be near the head or the one reptile would renew itself into two, 'each as mad as a cut snake' as they say round here.

The snake barely had time to contract its musculature when I struck. The head part lanced with lightning speed under the tiles, leaving a smear of blood and the long tail writhing on the roof. I swept the tail onto the ground with the shovel and, with a convenient bamboo, catapulted it into space towards the cornfield below. By a whimsical fluke, the flying tail wrapped itself round the one electric wire in the vicinity and stuck there in mid air. Giancarlo and Maurizio were less amused by the comic element of the dangling tail

'But the head. You can be sure that snake is still alive. And very poisonous. And very angry.'

'But it wasn't a viper.'

'Doesn't matter. The serpents, when they're damaged, become poisonous. With their anger.'

Against the deadline of the arrival of guests, work proceeded to a pleasing pattern. Giancarlo and Maurizio, like all Italian builders, worked with enthusiasm. Foot-wide channels for pipes were hammered and chiselled down the face of the house and in the thick inside walls, reducing the building to a perforated, war-shelled wreck, with heaps and piles of stones, bricks and rubble everywhere and the air dense with white dust and mortar. Face and chisel confrontation with the irregular obstinacies of an ancient building was accompanied by variations on the *'porca Madonna'* repertoire of oaths and blasphemies.

Demolishing walls is a satisfying activity, good for body, soul and mind. As the Porfiri brothers hammered and chiselled and plumbed, I dismantled the complicated walls and enclosures under the long roof which slopes up to the main block of the house – the former wood store, pig styes and farm implements shelter. This searched out and tuned every muscle in my body. The possibility of causing the roof to collapse sharpened judgement and alertness. And it provided something of the Michelangelo-esque mystery of slowly releasing the form imprisoned in stone – the form of the future Sybilline room. A thumping hammer knocked down recent, high brickwork, making holes to look through into other chambers. A sledge-hammer demolished divisions of rubble and mortar, leaving me wading up to the waist in crumbling masonry as the itchy dust settled. Then, levering the first separation with the sharp end of a pick-axe, blocks of shaped stone were lifted out and put into piles for future use. As generations of improvised walls were reduced to the ground, the structure of the total space showed those two well-made pillars of old brick and, in the thick house wall, the two arched niches on either side of where an altar might have been, which had probably increased Merelli's asking price. The farm implements shed opened onto the grass and nettle area above our primitive terrace. A momentary vision of polished terracotta flooring, white walls, a big fireplace, the view of the mountains through the glazed doors onto the colonnaded terrace was interrupted by shouts from outside. Curiosity had led Giancarlo onto the outhouse roof. Lifting tile after tile, he had disturbed the severed serpent.

'*Porco Dio!* It's *monstrous!* It's long – like this,' indicating a good half metre.

'*Porca Madonna!*'

It had disappeared into a fissure and down into the outhouse.

In Venice on fine mornings people sing: the bread delivery boy; the plasterer on his scaffolding; the boatman taking vegetables to market. So to get them going, the gramophone had been wired to a table outside. Giancarlo and Maurizio, engaged on the quieter business of tiling, had been subjected to music, from *Tristan* to *Tosca*, from the *Messiah* to Monteverdi, from *Grease* to Scott Joplin to the Rolling Stones to the Beatles. The litany of '*porca miserias*' was quieter, in tune with the tiling.

'But don't you like it? Don't you like music?'

'Bella! La Musica e bella. Bellissima.'

'But don't you sing? On a wonderful morning like this? In Venice, they sing.'

'They're Venetians. We others – *noi altri* – we don't sing.'

With pointed spade and angled shovel drains were dug for our future kitchen and bathroom. A large circular hole had been started for the septic tank. The Porfiri brothers had left after the day's work and I was excavating the final three feet. Digging myself into the bowels of the earth, out of sight of everything except the evening sky and the walls of blue-streaked clay, the soft thud of the spade was interrupted at intervals when it hit stone, one of the rounded merds that lie buried in the earth. A pause for leverage, muscles pumping iron.

I felt the vibration of approaching machinery and climbed the ladder into the evening sun spilling down the barley-field. Osvaldo, cigarette in mouth, was riding into the top of the field, mounted on a primitive two-stroke reaper-and-binder which sounded like a petrol-powered heavy machine-gun. Rita, her brother Lino, neighbour Antero and son Claudio trotted alongside.

The reaper made its first swathes round the perimeter of the field, reaping a track of barley and disgorging string-bound sheaves. As Osvaldo rode the reaper, tilting uphill and downhill at precarious angles, weaving between the lines of field maples linked by vines, the men followed, collecting two armfuls at a time of sheaves and propping them into stooks. Rita, bent low, her bottom jutting towards the sky, worked fast round the extreme edge of the field and near the tree trunks, cutting with her sharp sickle the inaccessible barley. With every round of the clanking and creaking machinery, more generations of the family materialised from the countryside like leprechauns, to take part in the harvest. Osvaldo drove off, leaving the stooks standing on fields smooth as lawns. Rita called me over to join the throng assembled on the ground under the walnut tree. The bottle of *vin cotto* was passed from male to male and swigged. Santina distributed crackling pieces of pizza.

My camera shutter clicked, fixing the present smiles of a fast-passing way of life, recording an apparently harmonious clan on home soil: they represented two thirds of the remaining population of our *contrada*, the last of the *contadini*. As well as living with the uncertain and hard conditions of agriculture, viticulture, and the bringing up of children, they had had to be self-sufficient roadmakers, ditchers, builders, terracers, ladder-makers, chairmakers, makers of forks and rakes: and the women span, wove, dyed, made baskets, stitched fur, made clogs and knew about herbal medicines.

There was Rita's brother Orlando from the farm above, his wife Gina and teenage daughters Mara and Mariella. Orlando, thanks to his padrone's meanness in providing up-to-date machinery, was the last in the *contrada* to work with the white and silent oxen. Both girls are now married and in towns. Mariella showed the change in style of life on a visit home, poised awkwardly in tight-fitting silk dress and gold high heels, dragging in a chain of reluctant sheep from the damp field. Rita's

Our neighbour contadini 1975

other brother, Lino, and wife Ida, are still *contadini*, but the children are now in town: hairdresser, university student and street cleaner respectively. Antero was in his thirties, Osvaldo's boon companion and soon to be 'uncle' of Rita's new child, the oldest of the Montanari clan from the house below the church, and the only unmarried one. Small, agile, a Chinese slant to his eyes, he was the merry bachelor, owner of a shotgun, shooter of predatory foxes by torchbeam and a late-night card player. Now, still a bachelor, he works as a builder's labourer, white-haired, and in his spare time is our right-hand helper. His trim sister Santina, is married to Secondo, the blacksmith and plumber from the house by the church, now a free-range chicken establishment. Of their three girls, two are gone to the factories and the eldest has opened an ironmongery in San Ginesio. All are now married.

On the edge of the group, the nimble, bright-eyed old Montanari parents, who would have found fewer surprises in the time when their church – our deconsecrated church across the field – was opened in 1635 than in the world of their children. The old man had been brought home from Macerata hospital to die. We had heard the bell toll. Then

Our neighbour Orlando 1975

Nazzareno the simpleton, whose voice still carries down into the countryside from the town walls every Tuesday and Friday crying *'Pesce fresco!* Fresh Fish!' for the itinerant fishmonger, came running to our door, by mistake, asking for the dead. We showed him the right house, across the field, below the church. We duly paid our respects in the crowded house, the old man lain out in his unfamiliar best suit amid florist's flowers. Four candles burned at the corners of the bed. The wall mirror was shrouded by a sheet. Nazzareno was kneeling, his duty to repeat the *paternoster* through the night. We imitated others who took an olive sprig from the bedside table, dipped it in the bowl of holy water and with it made the sign of the cross over the body. Orlando, Lino, Osvaldo and Stefano carried the coffin out of the *Collegiata*, Antero following, tears streaming, with his mother and then all the familiar faces of the harvest field.

In the centre of the photo, the masterful Rita, Chaucerian in ruggedness of character and physique: petty thief, malicious gossip, dishonest, generous, tender-hearted, humorous, ambitious, no longer on speaking terms with her neighbour brothers after cheating them over buying a piece of land. Rita used to slaughter our fowls, stringing them up by the legs over a clothes line in her yard, before slitting their throats near the bubbling cauldron.

'Better them than us' she smiled sadly, putting the knife in their throats without much precision, 'poor beasts,' and she threw the dying creatures into the boiling water to soften the feathers for fast plucking. Rita and Osvaldo were long ago evicted from the house next to ours.

Merelli, their *padrone*, who had set them up with goats for a joint cheese-making venture, had found himself buying his own cheese in the shop. Rita was *furba* – cunning – a double-edged word used with venom or amusement according to point of view. Merelli, '*baffi di ferro* – moustache-of-iron' was even more *furbo*.

Not in the family group, behind the single lens reflex, I, the outsider, from *America*, as they called anywhere outside Italy, meaning Argentina, where so many Italians had gone. How I happened to be here was entirely outside their experience or imagination. They did not try to think about it.

Osvaldo returned with the tractor pulling a flat cart. As the light went, it lumbered up and down the slope, followed by the merry chatter of the harvesters loading up the sheaves, and the children playing in the newly-shorn field. As the pile grew, sheaves were forked up to Antero who adjusted the load under his feet. When the sheaves were gathered, with Antero and many children on the wobbly top, we drove off up the road in starlight, all of us attached to various parts of tractor or cart, into Lino's yard. After unloading and stacking, we sat in the cobbled space enclosed by the group of houses, on upright chairs or old car seats, among the geraniums planted in oil drums.

Blue days turned to white haze and an ominous stillness hung over the countryside. At unexpected times, the bells of all the churches pealed together, to shake out the thunder and hail storms building up in the sky. The hail was a dire threat to the grapes now big and coloured on the vines. Hens and geese lay spread-eagled in the dust under trees. The tall-chimneyed threshing machine moved from farmyard to yard on contract, each yard in turn a hive of industry, ending in suppers outside at long trestle tables. In the dark, families relaxed, reassured that for this year they had escaped damaging storms. Now only the maize, the sunflowers and the vines stood at risk. Snatches of conversations from invisible families, sitting out in the cool of the night, floated down across the fields to me, sitting on my own proto-terrace.

The Porfiri brothers put in pipes, drains, wires and closed gaping holes. A bath, a basin, a bidet, a lavatory were installed, Giancarlo revealing to me that this was the first plumbing Maurizio had ever done. A corner of my new space had been paved and a kitchen sink, gas cooker and water heater connected up. On harvest days I cleaned, graduating from barrows of heavy stones and rubble to dust pan and brush to wet swab. Days of silent and clean work followed as one of the upstairs rooms was transformed into a bathroom, with gleaming tiles. Water flowed out of taps, the lavatory flushed. The water heater was plugged in and the needle climbed to hot. After luxuriating in deep hot water and using every accessory that Jermyn Street can provide, I was ready to be taken out for the traditional dinner which builders give clients.

They arrived, not in the usual *cinquecento* but in a black Mercedes: their second car. To their amazement, and thanks to the Dane, they were paid in full early in the evening, before pastas and grills and draughts of *Rosso Conero* had undone the knots of linguistic difficulties and we had sailed into a fine celebration. Several coffees 'corrected' with *mistra* and glasses of *Amaro Sibilla* later, Giancarlo roused his drowsy brother and drove us back.

At last the day arrived. Heat and haze had intensified. The bottle of champagne I had bought for this occasion was put in the fridge to chill. After yet another bath with all the trimmings, I put on white trousers and shirt fresh from the cleaners and set off to the nearest station, fifteen miles away, in the battered but well dusted Renault 4.

At 6.30 the station bell rang. The station master, in shirt sleeves and braces, put on a tie, put on his well-pressed uniform jacket and his hat of office with patent-leather peak and applied himself to turning a wheel fixed to the station wall. This, I learned, lowered the level crossing barrier a mile up the line. He then brushed the platform with a soft-bristled broom and awaited the evening train from Fabriano. In the distance the single-carriage train appeared on the single track-line which joins the interior of the Marches to the rest of Italy. By way of Fabriano, via Foligno, via Rome Termini via the Leonardo da

Vinci airport at Fiumicino from Heathrow, direct from Stockwell, my two friends stepped down onto the tiny platform exactly on time, at 6.37 pm.

Pleased with their snug room and the welcoming dram of *Lagavulin* and the hot water, they followed me down the steep stairs, into the newly paved kitchen area, across the cobbled farm-implement space – the future Sibilline Room – across a couple of yards of steeply sloping grass, onto the terrace. With the three cane chairs I had bought, it seemed small.

The mountains were lost in a bruise-coloured haze but the view over the nearer countryside was spectacular. The Pastoral Symphony, '*the awakening of cheerful feelings on arrival in the country*', together with cold Bollinger quickly set the occasion into convivial fermentation. Already Hugh was sparking with ideas about how to bring under control the bank of grass between the terrace and the outhouses. Frequent lightning lit the clouded mountains and distant thunder rolled nearer. Low black clouds surprised us, riding over the house from behind like scouring witches, with turbulent air and an occasional splash of rain. We moved off the terrace into the cobbled farm-implements shed, to the well-prepared dinner of welcome: white cloth, candlesticks, shining glass for this special occasion.

We finished the smoked salmon and I was pouring the Chablis to the strains of '*festive assembly of country people*' when the room went brilliant blue and a crack like a giant bullwhip split the air. The head of thunder, which had detonated over the house, reverberated away and returned in echoing waves off the mountains, leaving us in candlelight and without Beethoven. The electric current had gone. I had given Hugh the first possible origin of the name of our mountains, from a belief that the Virgilian Cumaean Sybil had transferred to a cave under the summit of our mountain.

'And the other version?' Hugh pursued his question about the name of our mountains, helping himself to the cold chicken. Outside, the rain started. In seconds the clouds opened and water fell in torrents.

'But did you do this all yourself? The tarragon sauce is superb.' Georgina looked ravishing, gleaming black hair brushed smooth, brown shoulders bare in the candelight and a glint of discreet country diamond at her ear.

'The other Sibyl is in the *genre* of chivalric quests. Venusburg. Errant knights from Germany. Tannhauser. First the terrors of the cave, the screaming winds, the devil's bridge, dragons, the clashing metal doors. Then, gold, glittering lights, luxury. And the naked queen herself and her girls offering unimaginable delights.'

Drops of water splashed near my foot and became a continuous column.

'The wine's excellent.'

'Have some more. It came direct from Chablis. A lovely village – all stone houses. And quite a nice hotel.'

Another explosion. We all saw the bolt of lightning go to ground just over the brink of our field. Thunder rolled away like surf breaking over the countryside. Another rope of water was falling steadily near Hugh's left shoulder.

'Where was it we stayed Hugh? Not Chablis. Some wine place. On the top of a hill. Rather a nice little town.'

The torrent redoubled its force outside. Two more columns of water were falling in the Sibilline room. Then a metallic dripping started in the kitchen sink and became a steady drumming. I went to put in the plug to save it for the washing up.

'Sancerre.'

'That's it, Sancerre. Shall I help myself to some more chicken? Hugh, do you want some more?'

A different note indicated a new leak onto the tiled floor of the kitchen area. A wind had got up and rapidly had become a whirlwind. Continuous flashes of lightning showed rain lashing horizontally outside and a capricious eddy blew out the candles.

'If you don't mind, I think it would be more comfortable in the library.' I lit a hurricane lantern.

'Do you want to move? I'm fine here.' Georgina put a cardigan round her shoulders, with best British *sang-froid*. Through the large opening, the future glass doors, we could see the rain hissing and veins of lightning going to earth with thumps, cracks and the full tympany of the storm. The Sibilline room was leaking like a sieve.

In the 'library', the former living-room-kitchen, the candles again burned calmly. Rain outside turned to hail. The loose window panes banged near breaking point at each thunderclap. The house rode the storm like a ship at sea, its wooden joists and beams resilient, its thick walls ballasted in the earth. We proceeded with the white peaches. Hugh's curiosity returned to the Venusburg question.

'And why the German connection, here of all places?'

By the time I had explained the Germanic etymology of the word Marches, our region, told him that the Emperor Frederick II Hohenstauffen, *Stupor Mundi* was born in the market place at Jesi not far from here, Hugh's ranging mind had gone to his distant classical education. Fine wines often stimulated his poetic memory and Bacchic moments in Horace would float to the surface.

> '*Nunc est bibendum, nunc, pede libero*
> *pulsanda tellus, nunc Saliaribus*
> *ornare pulvinar deorum*
> *tempus erat dapibus, sodales.*' (1)

I was wondering how much it would cost to mend the large Sibilline roof. Georgina looked increasingly alluring, like the Sibilline queen of our mountains.

'I forgot to tell you. From midnight on Friday to midnight on Saturday, the queen and her ladies turn into snakes. But the enchanted knights are compelled to continue the orgies with them.'

Georgina, following a mistaken thread, asked if there was any naughty life in these parts. Hugh had on his late-night smile of contentment, as he pulled cigar fumes through the nose of cognac.

> ‘Quo me, Bacche, rapis tui
> plenum? quae nemora aut quos agor in specus
> velox, mente nova?’ (2)

With guests asleep in bed and the storm over, I stood at the front door. A quarter moon looked through a ragged sky and the night was loud with waters. Our gravel road was still in flood, inches deep, curving down past the front of the house. An unofficial town sewer, which usually trickled past the house below and disappeared over the edge into the wood, was a roaring cataract. I dreamt of a storm of musical grandeur which resolved into a profound, majestic calm. In the morning I found my bedroom light on and the cassette finished: the electric current had returned. As for the roof, it had to be done. And then there was the garden enclosure idea. The outline of a large construction crocodile was beginning to show, an inevitable sequence of expenses ahead.

After pottering round the outside of the house after breakfast, Hugh came in holding awkwardly between two twigs a desiccated severed serpent’s head.

‘You seem to have snakes.’

(1. Horace Odes Book 1, 37. *Now is the time to drain the flowing bowl, now with unfettered foot to beat the ground with dancing, now with Salian feast to deck the couches of the gods, my comrades.*

2. Horace Odes Book 3, 25. *Whither, O Bacchus, does’t thou hurry me, o’er-flowing with thy power? Into what groves or grottoes am I swiftly driven in fresh inspiration?*)

14

The Last Fountain

All traffic was stuck in a freezing Bora blizzard on the Adriatic autostrada, snow compacting to ice on the long incline up to Fano from Senigallia. Word among the lorry drivers was that we would be there for at least three hours. I was on my way back to the students in Venice after a brief visit to San Ginesio. However, as the *Circoli Italo-Brittanico* in Venice had asked me to give a talk in a couple of months' time on *The Englishman's House in the Sun* – a subject popular in England as escapist winter reading, time on a blocked motorway could be put to use. What better occasion to reduce to bare essentials, to clear and simplify cluttered memories of the long process of building and re-building in San Ginesio? Icy and increasingly alarming isolation concentrated the mind. After the Porfiri brothers pioneer work, the story fell easily into three phases, the eras of three master-builders, Gabriele, Franco and Mario. It's a short story of how one expense committed us helplessly to another. But it had a happy ending – in a beautiful garden, a modest and habitable house with the most magnificent view imaginable and a place of retreat from England in a future crisis.

When chains of rain from the leaking roof come between you and your friends at dinner and there are no dry places left into which to shift the table, the idea of treating the place simply as a summer camp becomes questionable. With running water from taps, fitted bathroom and even a working kitchen of sorts all in place, is a rain-proof roof a necessity or a luxury?

The builder said… but not the Porfiri brothers. They had promised to do future work but they never were available. They had land and there was always too much farm work to do. By what they had already done they had obviously paid out the favour they owed the surveyor who had put them our way.

Not Tiburzi either, whom Peter, our English friend, had engaged on my behalf in our absence. When he didn't turn up, which he had promised to do, in the week after Easter, and he had been tracked down, he said he had far too much work to do. He too had land to farm. But Gabriele: he said he would do the job. Gabriele was twenty, of legendary physical strength, had learned the trade under Tiburzi and was now working on his own account… as from that moment, we afterwards discovered.

Gabriele had the torso of a Marchigian bull. He discussed in detail how to get the main beam of the pergola up into position with the massively heavy beam itself poised on his shoulder as he lit a cigarette. His soft, slow smile was marred by a few missing or rotten teeth. Asthmatic and diabetic, like many in Italy he drew a disabled pension, meanwhile working against doctor's orders. For most of the three-and-a-half years he worked for us, he was also constructing his own *casa nuova* alongside his father's *casa vecchia* – the old house – against the dreaded day when his engagement had to turn into marriage. Putting off completion was one of his specialities, as a builder and as a *fidanzato*. However, in spite of his bovine form and slab-like hands, his eye could work the spirit-levels and the fine, level wires of the *muratore*. He had worked under Tiburzi who had worked under Fefe Sensacqua, the acknowledged old master mason of San Ginesio. Gabriele took on his fifteen-year-old cousin Giorgio, and Ugo, a gnarled seventy-year-old *contadino*, also a relation, as labourers.

The general outlines of what had to be done had been established in creative discussion with Hugh and Georgina. They were too polite to state the obvious: that the roof over kitchen and Sibilline space had to be mended. Inspired by the two fine old brick columns inside the

Sibilline, Hugh suggested building a matching pair outside on the terrace, and making a beamed pergola from the outside columns to the house to give shade, with roses and vines.

As for the 'garden', the small stone buildings across the grass sward from the house and terrace could be partially dismantled, leaving a curtain of their outside walls. This could then be joined to the house at each end by new walls, forming an enclosure or courtyard – all that was needed at the moment in the way of a labour-free garden. Hugh had done a watercolour sketch of the project which now hangs framed on the study wall.

Gabriele had said: 'If you want to make a habitable space under the sloping roof, with a kitchen area at the front and, at the back, a room, the Sibilline Room, open onto the terrace and the view, it's pointless replacing rotten beams and adjusting tiles. You need to do the job properly. You need a *solaio*.'

A *solaio* is a system of roofing a space by placing concrete beams at close intervals, each beam-end resting on the wall tops. The gaps between the beams are filled with *terra cotta* blocks which fit neatly into the pre-cast grooves in the beams. The flat covering is then finished with a skim of cement. He was right. And he hadn't suggested knocking the whole place down.

'Costs?'

'Little. Pay when you like.'

Having won the first point by simple logic and good sense, Gabriele had made a second suggestion. Instead of making a sloping *solaio* to preserve the original sloping lean-to roof, why not make it level? And build onto it another floor, with two bedrooms and a bathroom between? Which of course would have given us a superlative bedroom looking straight out at the mountains. It had seemed stupid not to do it.

'Costs?'

'Little. Pay when you like.'

Gabriele's suggestions coincided with the increasing presence of the South American Therese, whose passion for our house – 'I love every blade of grass here' – blew away any falterings or pusillanimities on my part or Gabriele's. The snow falling, on one of our winter visits, and I suggesting a comfortable hotel for the night, Therese had insisted on staying in the freezing house, more a building site than a house. We had to climb a smooth cement ramp as the stairs were being re-made. We finally settled to sleep in fur hats with the ear-flaps down. There was no glass in the window frame. Soon after, at the beginning of the eighties and the Gabriele era, Therese and I had walked from the Town Hall to the Chelsea Arts Club with new gold rings on our fourth fingers. Therese had spotted, on the pavement, a tiny and auspicious gold pendant in the shape of a heart. Although the tutorial business kept us in London from August to January, we were more and more in Italy. So the house became a household and the symbols of domesticity were installed sooner rather than later: a washing machine, dish-washer, deep-freeze, vacuum cleaner, even a television – and double-glazing in the windows.

In the course of the next two years, looking for ways to improve our income, we were possessed by an insane and long ago abandoned idea of running the rapidly expanding but very small house as a minuscule but expensive country hotel, an idea which drew a characteristic comment from Peter Young, who wrote: '*Keeping a hotel is, as W.G. said of putting the other side in to bat, one of the things that should often be thought about but never actually done.*' Before giving up the project, with Venice numbers on the increase, we had also replaced the two floors of the original living part of the house with *solaii*. In the old system, to make a floor division, porous *terra cotta pianelli* were laid on wooden spars laid across oak beams, giving the house the flexible, resonant, hand-made feel of a hearts-of-oak man o' war. The *pianelli*, when walked on, exuded dust as from a powder puff which in time filtered down through cracks into the rooms below. In our work, the old beams had been taken down, replaced by invisible concrete ones, and then re-fixed below the new ceiling with a purely ornamental function, though not without endless discussions and meditations on authenticity and architectural honesty. Modern easy-to-clean floor tiles replaced the old *pianelli* which began a new life as the paving of outside terraces and courtyard.

Gabriele's role had been to change the house from a cube with an attached wedge shaped outhouse – the Sibilline room and its sloping roof – into a double cube.

Work in progress

The Cortile finished

Improvements which the Wiltshire properties-abroad writer would have valued.

As Gabriele, Giorgio and Ugo had been working on *solaii* in the house I had been dismantling, stone by well-squared stone, the little outhouse buildings across the sward and thinking about making the walled garden enclosure. Gradually a problem revealed itself: the sward was not flat. Walls from outhouse perimeter to the house would undulate like Hadrian's Wall in wildest Northumberland. The house was on a steeply-sloping hillside.

'Not a problem' said Gabriele, and introduced me to the idea of the *motopala* – bulldozer, and *scavatore* – excavator, and the version which combined both, one implement at the front, one at the back. This monster cost per hour what a labourer cost per day, but in a morning could reverse the slope of your boulder-embedded field, and turn a mountain into a molehill, or *vice versa*.

One damp morning in April the Viola brothers had arrived with their two machines and began their mesmerising work. No mere blunt instrument, these docile giants could edge out and lift a specific small stone, could tease out by the roots a tree for re-planting, the jaws working with the precision of a surgeon. Of all the construction skills – making a tall, straight column with old bricks, paving a floor with *terra cotta pianelli*, plastering a bulging wall, making a fireplace and chimney that draw and look well – the work of the bulldozer was the most creatively pleasing: it had a unique degree of excitement, speed, scale and instant achievement, especially when measured against seasons of pickaxe, spade and shovel. Concentrated supervision was essential. How far down to go, how steep to make a bank, how wide to clear a pathway, these were decisions of the moment, depending on judgement of eye as the work was happening and a focused idea of the final plan in the mind's eye.

When the roaring giants had gone and the silence returned with the smell of fresh earth, there was an immense sense of satisfaction balanced by amazement at what had been perpetrated. The grassy sward had gone, replaced by a level earth floor of what had become, in an hour, a *cortile* – a courtyard – unpaved.

On the house side, the comic remnants of our original terrace wall were suspended, like clothes on a washing line, head-high above the new floor, with two metres of fresh earth below where the stonework finished. A ladder was needed to ascend out of the cortile up to the terrace and house. On the left side of the level space was an eight-foot precipice of sheer earth, gashed from the hillside. I was looking at the physical facts which dictate the style of the classic Italian hillside garden. To achieve any flat area – a terrace or courtyard – a wedge has to be cut out of the hillside. To shore-up the sliced earth, walls must be built. Different levels need flights of linking steps. Bare earth, mud in wet weather, needs paving. The Medici garden-architect had made the point to Duke Cosimo: 'Things built come before things planted and are more important.' The truth and expense of this fact stared us in the face. So began our simple garden, essentially a stone-built container inserted into the hillside with a few earth borders left unpaved for

Excavating the Round Fountain

planting, built-in fountain basins and unlimited wall-tops and paved surfaces for *terra cotta* vases.

From our demolition of parts of the outhouses we had the stones for walls and steps, and, from inside the house, the *pianelli* to pave the courtyard. In the angle between the new steps and the terrace we had constructed a rectangular fountain basin, and a second in an angle of the peripheral outbuilding wall. Submerged electric pumps circulated water from the basins via pipes in the stonework to emerge through the mouth of stone masks, a face like a Fury below the terrace and across the courtyard a face like King Edward VII by sunlight, Neptune by moonlight. A buttress of the outhouse we had built up like a small turret above the level of the walls and it later became a dovecote.

With the mad small-hotel idea still visiting our minds at moments of financial worry, sitting on our newly-paved terrace in the shade of our new pergola above our new cortile where two fountains trickled just audibly, we had realised that something more had to be done. Above all this, above the beautiful new stone wall, a steep sweep of rank grass and nettles still continued upwards, far too close to the terrace for high-paying hotel guests. We needed another wedge taking out of the hillside.

A year later the bulldozers came again. In an hour another upper terrace, the size of a tennis court, was levelled. On the hillside we didn't make a vertical cut: we had no stones left to build another big wall. So it was sloped upwards and in front of the slope we planted forty-two straight cypresses, ankle to ankle, to grow to a formal hedge screening the bank. In the centre of the terrace, a circle of white chalk was sprinkled: diameter four metres. In twenty minutes a neat cylinder a metre deep had been excavated to make the round fountain basin, the third fountain. Gabriele cemented it and lined it with *pianelli* – in his own increasingly slow time. Four plane trees were planted to square the circle of water, following the younger Pliny's description of his favourite part of one of his gardens. The terrace was floored with washed gravel and the framework of a pergola erected, to carry roses and wisteria, covering the whole bare, exposed, empty-looking terrace. Gabriele, hunted and winkled out from jobs all over the countryside, built steps at the end of the terrace, up to what we called the meadow or orchard – the continuation of the steep field above the cypress escarpment.

In the following year, returning from Venice in March, we had been followed by a pair of stone statues, bare-breasted ladies, Summer with her roses, Autumn with her grapes, to place at the top of the steps out of the new terrace. Bought in the Palladian-villa countryside near Treviso outside Venice, where the demand for statues for the many villas has never died out, they were hand-sculpted by artisans to 16th century classical patterns, price according to weight. Adrian, my new assistant in Venice, had been staying with us and between us we had moved the statues on wooden rollers to the bottom of the steps. In spite of his strength, a sulky Gabriele said he needed two tough helpers – Adrian and I didn't count – to get them to the top of the steps, and he didn't know when he would be back with two tough helpers. Adrian

The Round Fountain – Winter

was piqued. He tilted a statue enough to insert a shallow brick under one side of its base. Then he tilted it the other way to insert another brick on the other side, then again, to a second layer, and so on. Step by step the statues rose and finally they were wobbled up onto the prepared platforms. A triumph of mind over matter.

During this year, 1983, things had gone from bad to worse with Gabriele as he had been getting more and more building jobs all of which he had tried to keep going at the same time. We could never track him down, to get him to come and finish various small jobs he

The Round Fountain

had left unfinished. Our season was always limited by having to go to England early in August, which added to the frustration. So Gabriele's spell with us had come to an end, amicably enough for him to offer us the traditional builder's dinner. He had arrived to collect us in a Maserati belonging to Walter the plumber, who had come too. At the end of a fine fish dinner at Civitanova, Gabriele had ordered for himself a finger of iced lemon vodka, downed it, folded his arms on the table and went straight to sleep. 'At midnight he has to sleep, wherever he is,' Walter explained.

Walter had been brought along to drive us back. 'Terrible driver, Gabriele. Shouldn't be allowed on the roads. The countryside is littered with his write-offs. It's his diabetes and the pills he has to take.'

We had, without trying, been following the advice of Alberti, whose *De Re Aedificatoria* of 1452 was the handbook for Florentines aspiring to the villa culture in the antique Roman style. Although we did not have the prescribed *'view of some city or town,'* thank goodness, we saw the glittering lights of innumerable small towns on distant hilltops, by night. We had *'in the foreground, the delicacy of a garden.'* Our new dove-cote was now *'near water and moderately high, so that the pigeons, weary from flying and from performing their winged gymnastics and clapping, will gladly glide in to land with outstretched wings.'* Our colony of pigeons, as white as driven snow, had flourished and multiplied so well that we had no need to bury *'the head of a wolf, sprinkled with cumin seed, inside a jar that is cracked so that the smell can escape, to attract pigeons away from their previous homes.'* And, as Hugh and Georgina would testify, our country house *'was in a location where family life will not be plagued by visits from passing acquaintances.'*

The continuing series of improvements which had started with the need to mend a leaky roof had not come to an end with the demise of our builder Gabriele. A feature of the house which we had particularly liked was the local style of having a long, sloping roof covering various sheds, leaning up to the main block of the building. We had removed this and, by adding the extra floor, had been left with a rectangular house. Months in London had provided pause and objective distancing but had not stopped brooding creativity. Bookings for Venice were going well. Why not restore the sloping-roof finish to the house? We could do with a garage, though our dilapidated Renault 4 and museum Fiat 500 had never spent a night under cover. With new builders, this time a recommended firm, we had discussed the idea. No problem. We needed to bulldoze a chunk out of the hill to make room for the new garage and leave a space to walk round the house.

'Cost?'

'Little. Anyway, pay when you like.'

A familiar tune, but the new builder, Franco, built supermarkets, shopping centres and brand-new cemeteries. His little was not Gabriele's little. But we were decided. In the course of the next summer the new garage had been built, complete with a fine sloping roof and arched doorway, restoring the vernacular farmhouse look.

My married son from America, seeing the cars standing awkwardly on the polished paving, had said we needed a large drawing room more than a garage. So, after installing five weathered, extremely long wooden ceiling-beams – for looks only – and a generously-built fireplace, all we needed were the carpets and furniture. The cars had to live outside again.

However, in torrential rain one day we had watched from a window in our new bedroom the latest escarpment carved by the bulldozer into the hillside melt into mud and start slipping down towards the new garage's end wall. A retaining wall was needed: and why not extend it beyond the width of the house and garage, to secure the hillside end of the terrace, meeting up with the end of the cypress hedge? We could face the terrace part with stone, making a last, fourth, small fountain. A small, concrete retaining wall could safely be left to the builder to do before we came back.

This was the most expensive mistake. When we had returned in January the retaining wall had indeed been made. But it was not the four-foot high wall I had visualised. It was a sheer ten-foot of gleaming white reinforced concrete.

'Well – you weren't here. I did it as if it had been my own house. No more worries about slipping land.' The cost had been as much as making the garage and far more than the original cost of the house and three acres of land. 'Doesn't matter. Pay when you like. Pay when you can. I'm not worried.'

Something had to be done to mask the glaring wall of concrete which closed our terrace at the hill end. The construction of a

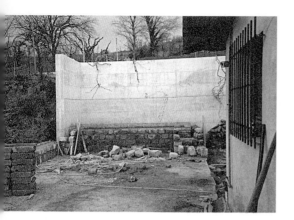

The Last Fountain complete

monumental fountain, the *last* fountain, hiding the concrete in noble stone was the solution- phase three. Here the area for ideas and precedents had to be Palladio, Bramante, Alberti and back to Vitruvius. Because of the uncompromising scale of Franco's wall, it had to be far larger than one's British reticence would have dared to make it.

The builder Mario had been booked for this crucial job well in advance by a surveyor. Mario was an expert with stone. I was surprised when he turned up on the appointed day: builders usually don't. He was a lean, sunburnt, fair-haired, blue-eyed man in his late thirties. He had looked at the tall concrete meanly, like one of the *Magnificent Seven* weighing up his contract. He had looked at my artist's impression of the monumental fountain to be built and raised a questioning eyebrow. He drew the building outlines onto the ground of prepared cement and surveyed the pile of stones I had procured. Then he began. First he mixed cement, not with a machine like most builders, but with shovel and hose. Then he began to place the stones and proceeded, course by course, to erect this relatively large edifice. As it rose in height, he pushed stones and cement up steeply sloping planks in a wheelbarrow. He worked silently, entirely on his own, from 7 a.m. to 7 p.m., with the usual breaks, for three weeks until the fountain was finished. In the album is a photograph of him standing in front of his work with his wife and two blonde daughters, the envelope containing his immediate, total and unexpectedly prompt cash just visible in the pocket of his immaculate linen shirt.

To my surprise, the Anglo-Venetian audience had been interested in these not unusual experiences of an Englishman in country Italy. Questions followed, and answers as far as possible. There was a certain incongruity in talking about such country matters in the parish room of the ancient convent of *San Zaccaria*, the same rich convent which had donated their orchard, the future Piazza San Marco, to the Doge at the end of the 12th century. At the supper afterwards, Christina Thoresby revealed that she had been in the Land Army in Cornwall during the war, and loved the country. A couple of days later, she handed me a card.

'I think this might have served as the text for your talk.'

It was Madame de Stael's definition of happiness: *'a constant striving after some desirable object with a constant sense of progress towards its attainment.'*

The 'garden' followed by necessity. As our farmhouse and garden is wedged into steeply-sloping land at two thousand feet, and commands an immense view southwards, there had never been any question of making a garden in the soft, gentle English style. It would have withered away, botanically and aesthetically. The practicalities of the sloping site and of land sliding under rainfall had forced on us classic architectural solutions: retaining walls, terraces, steps. The framework of the garden was architectural and the garden and house were interlocked: every room on the garden side of the house looked and led out onto the terrace, the courtyard, the round fountain and the view.

Not that we haven't planted. Years later, clumps of cypresses and bay trees frame recommended views. The forty-two little cypresses are now a dense wall closing the top terrace against the hill. The roses *Kiftsgate, Mermaid, Albertine* and *Celine Forestier* cover the pergola over the round fountain and the plane trees give deep shade. Wisteria, honeysuckle, jasmine, roses, box and cypress give scent. Masses of geraniums, petunias and plumbago, in *terra cotta* pots, watered every evening, give brilliant colour for the season. With the plashing water of the four fountains and stone statuary *al antica*, we have a classic Italian garden, as dictated by terrain and climate.

On golden evenings, we sit under our four plane trees by the round fountain, a combination so warmly recommended by Pliny. Although we have a fair tangle of unofficial roses and some Irish informality in the upkeep of borders and paths, we feel in sympathy with the Italian and Roman tradition. We look towards our Monti Sibillini, where the Cumaean Sybil took refuge from Christianity, and are modestly proud to have made a garden in the old style. Knowing the *real thing* keeps us aware of the cottage scale of our own creation.

However, sometimes, when the moon is full, and if a bottle of 1964 Barolo has been decanted, our vision becomes hazy and an invisible garden emerges. Our statues, from the artisan workshop near Vicenza, can merge in the mind's eye with those Castiglione admired in Bramante's Belvedere courtyard. A flight of steps built in local brick can carry up round the side of the Dragon Fountain at the Villa d'Este in Tivoli. The trickle of water from our fountains evokes the insinuating cascades at the Villa Lante at Bagnaia.

'*Costruire e un dolce impoverire,*' wrote the Florentine Luca Pitti at the beginning of the 15th century – 'building is an enjoyable way of getting poorer' – a fair comment on our many years' labour of love.

If we want praise, it comes occasionally, backhandedly, from the rare local visitor who is amazed to find any kind of garden in the despised countryside: '*Che bello! Un vero giardino al'inglese!*' How beautiful! A real English-style garden!

Shakespeare, Adrian Wilson and J.H. in the Kings Road office

15

Decline or Fall?

Our Venice student numbers had increased slowly but surely, and our modest little tutorial college in London stayed alive, just. We were heading for ninety students in Venice when Adrian Wilson – a school and university friend of my son whom I had known and liked since he was thirteen – joined me as an assistant. Adrian looked at the flat in Beaufort Mansions, and at the tiny spare bedroom piled with filing cabinets.

'You can't run a business from here.'

So we rented a beautifully decrepit, sunny, noisy office in the King's Road, alongside the London School of Bridge, whose spare rooms we used for our tutorial classes. Opposite our windows the punk with the red, yellow and blue Mohican crest sat on his bench, with his black dog at his feet, 'til they removed the bench. Until then the bookings and circulations and administrative jobs had been done by Fleur Augarde, paid by the hour, from her house in Oxford. With a London office we needed a secretary and had a succession of efficient and charming part-time ladies.

It was very good to have a co-pilot in the cabin. The skies were ours and the sun shone. But we were aware that over the horizon, right in our path, a year away, was a massive storm in the form of a fundamental change in the Oxford and Cambridge entrance system. The seventh-term-entry was to be abolished. These seventh-termers, those who could afford to stay on at school an extra term after taking A-levels, were our tutorial college bread-and-butter and the greater part of our Venice recruitment. Both our activities would be slammed and there was nothing our accountant could do about it. Do you grit your teeth, shut your eyes, pray, grab a cognac? Do you change course?

We did everything, veering, banking, drinking creative bottles of wine in Charco's, spiralling with imaginative, inventive activity. The archive of old prospectuses tells the story.

Adrian and I had forecast that the school leavers, now all leaving in July, if they were going to take a 'gap' year, would not want to wait 'til January to begin our established Venice spring course. So we invented an autumn course. First time round it was in Avignon and Paris. Then Avignon-Paris and Bruges. Then we went for the exoticism of Spain: Toledo, Seville, Granada. Nothing, we believed, having checked these places out, could be more exciting, nowhere more wonderful to be, in the autumn. The place names themselves vibrated attraction. So much so that we agreed with our graphic designer to have the names up on the office window in big art lettering: Venice-Florence-Rome-Avignon-Paris-Bruges-Amsterdam-Toledo-Seville-Granada, and we threw in Cordova for good measure. The Mohican-tufted punk waved enthusiastically as the words went up. But the Sloane Rangers – our office was in the heart of their habitat, in the block between Peter Jones and the youth-trendy hairdresser Sissors – didn't start flocking up our narrow stairs.

At this time we were approached by an American lady: would we like to run a summer course, for Americans, whom she would recruit, together with Brits coming through us? This resulted in some wretched summer collaborations, producing little income and considerable compromises.

However, some of the Americans liked what we did and encouraged the idea of some promotional visits to their schools. So several trips across the Atlantic were made, to schools in New York, Washington, Philadelphia, Boston, Atlanta, Kansas City, Charlottesville, Los Angeles. I went as far west, in Canada, as Victoria, Vancouver Island, and, via Toronto, to the eastern extremity of Canada, to Halifax, Nova Scotia. Speaking there at the Headmasters' Conference of the Canadian Independent Schools was the nadir of educational experiences. Here, canoeing, sailing, and rowing ruled. For them, Italy meant greasy-haired, money-grabbing wops. The vibrations in Halifax were worse than at the Schools Summer Programs Fair at Baltimore, where my 'stand', table, chair and pile of brochures, was next to that of a Wyoming Summer Camp outfit luring punters with a penned live sheep.

From somewhere the idea had been planted that the quality of an enterprise should be visible in its printed presentation. A graphic designer from New Zealand, a most likeable and talented artist, had launched us on a series of brochures and posters of superlative quality. We believed that they truly echoed and represented what we thought was the style, flair and quality of the programmes we were offering. We saw the point of the theory that 'the medium *is* the message.'

And what beautiful brochures! No longer the hand-typed, black instant-print on pale-blue paper, run up after the pubs closed by Fergie of Truexpress, Oxford, which served for so many years. We had a very stylish shiny dark-blue folder, white lettering, and inserts; then, an unusual square-format booklet with a colour photo on the front and back, and architectural line drawings in with the text in dark green, in dark blue, in royal blue, in grey: a new colour each season. Then, after visiting Los Angeles, a big poster with strong vertical drawings of an Ionic column, a violin, an artist's paintbrush, in blue, red and yellow, symbolising architecture, music, painting – California-style we were told. Finally, a last-resort, bad-taste yellow poster, covered with photos of the students in action, produced *by* students, *for* students, with their comments:

'A great way to spend a year off.' Not our style, we were told by an East-Coast American supporter. It wasn't. The printers' bills were massive.

Then we hit the storm: the predicted change in the Oxbridge entrance system came into force. From 91 students we went to 70: then to 48 and to 35. When is decline fall? The autumn courses had got off the ground, but barely. Summer programmes happened if the Americans came but as often as not a terrorist act or a political crisis or a dollar crisis spread panic and they cancelled: and there were never enough British students who wanted to do a summer course. If we hadn't tried all these expensive solutions, we would have wondered later whether we had not missed an opportunity.

At this point, with bank overdrafts running at twelve per cent, our accountant had come into action, bringing into focus indisputable financial figures and spelling out the decisions which needed to be taken. They were unpleasant ones. The most loyal Adrian, the office and its secretaries, expensive pamphlets, even new projects had to go. So did our flat in Beaufort Street. We were lucky having a house to move to in Italy. I was more than lucky to have a wife of ferocious loyalty: when the going gets tough the tough get going, was her style. At the beginning, as the tide of success flowed, I had occasionally been undeservedly accused of having business flair whereas in fact the course had begun through chance personal circumstances at what happened to be an ideal moment. Just as the establishing of a certain Oxbridge entrance system had provided students, the dismantling of the system took them away.

Businessmen said advertise. We did. It produced no results. I visited schools, talking about Venice and the course. Everyone loved looking at slides of Venice. A few signed up. About eighty per cent hear about the course through friends and the social network of parents' dinner parties. None of us thought it a good idea to lower fees by lowering what we were offering. Contrary to the cliché, we believe that price competition is bad for the buyer – the quality of the product has to be reduced. We sat tight, I and family in Italy and accountant Daryl in Peckham or Melbourne, trusting that the English tradition of sending their young to Italy would continue.

The suddenness of our drop in numbers, together with our expensive failed attempts at lift-off in France, Spain and America left us facing the certainty of falling short of being able to pay the accommodation of the coming course in Venice. We needed a bridging loan. The Clementson office, with new young directors and themselves reeling from heavy fines for years of tax evasion, couldn't help by giving us time to pay. With the bank we were at the end of the road. To our and Clementson's amazement, what seemed to be the absolute last and most improbable resort, the formidable Tuscan, Laura, owner of the Atlantico, said yes, she would let us pay over the coming years. There was a slight chance, I was able to tell her, that I might be able to pay off a large part of the debt soon. I was in contact with an American garden club about an Italian tour. It just might come good. So the next course went ahead, thanks to Laura.

But as Frankenfurter said to Brad in *The Rocky Horror Show,* 'it's not *all* bad.' Therese's pregnancy was more the result of idyllic country life than a do-it-yourself way of boosting future bookings. Towards the end of the course she knew that her time was come. The case was packed, waiting, and the telephone call had been made. It was 2.30 a.m. In the frosty silence we heard the engine of the water ambulance prising its way through the moored vessels in the Rio della Tana half-a-mile away and the hollow bump of boat on boat as it got nearer. Then, out of the window, we could see it tying up twenty yards away at the end of our Corte Nova.

We went downstairs and met them as they were searching with torches for the door number. Therese did without the Sedan chair. We walked down the courtyard and helped her into the snug cabin of the Blue Cross launch. The engine was started and we bumped along the shadowy back wall of the Corderie of the Arsenale, past the new Palestra, under the bridge of San Biagio and into the sudden brilliant moonlight. As we went into the open water, the launch accelerated and described a celebratory arc, wake smoking behind, the hull tilting to show San Giorgio Maggiore, the Salute, the Doge's Palace incandescent in the full moon. Decelerating, the bow dropped and we chugged into the Rio dei Greci, under the familiar bridge and leaning campanile, past the Questura and Squadra Mobile, into a labyrinth of shaded waters 'til the open space of the Campo di San Giovanni e Paolo came up on our right, with the bulk of the basilica and Colleoni riding high

(Above) J.H. and Sam 1985. (Right) Therese and Sam.

on his plinth against the bright sky. We passed the front of the Scuola Grande di San Marco, now the Civic Hospital, our destination.

Past the chapel and morgue on the side canal, through the Dominican cloister, into the warmth of the maternity ward and straight into labour under the attentive care of the midwife from the Friuli. A telephone call to the sister's room on the floor above, where I had been sent for a coffee, brought me running down the Renaissance stairs to find the head already out. Seconds later our son was exercising his lungs.

That was already fifteen years ago – another four years before he, the seventh child, goes through the course: a booking for 2004.

An American garden club on tour

16

Villas and Gardens – Touring American Style

Tours for the English and tours for Americans are planned differently. It's a question of spending. English travellers ask for modest, inexpensive hotels and don't complain about… in fact, they don't complain. By contrast, the Americans don't like to find that there is a better, that is to say more expensive, hotel in the area. As the tour-planner's income is based on a percentage of the overall costs: hotels, meals, private motor-launches, entry to private palaces and the paid presence of Princesses and Contessas, there was considerable satisfaction in casting off from the landing stage of the Hotel Serbelloni in a neat, white motor-launch with the ladies and a few gentlemen of an American garden club on board and, for the moment, *pleased*. Forgotten was yesterday's tantrum at the coach's difficulties in manoeuvring the final curves in the narrow road to the hotel in Bellagio, coming from the airport at Malpensa. The *Aretusa* had tied up below the hotel terrace as the party was finishing breakfast. Captain Mario was resplendent in white nautical kit. The launch was immaculate and the ladies, in wide-brimmed hats and smart shoes, dressed for Fifth Avenue, exclaimed contentedly as we purred out into the lake. It was the end of May, a morning of translucent clarity, the bows cutting into the mirror of green mountainside, dark blue mountain tops against blue sky, sharper in their reflection than in the reality, rising sheer from the lakeside across the half-mile of water.

This was the first day of the garden tour, crossing Lake Como from our base in Bellagio to visit the Villa Carlotta at Cadenabbia, decades after the pioneering tour for Mr. Swan.

So far so good – from a chance meeting with an American lady at the Chelsea Arts Club to staying with her friend the outgoing Garden Club secretary in a Brahmin house on Beacon Hill in Boston to dinner with the incoming Garden Club secretary at the 20th floor Energy Club in Dallas,to Malpensa airport and now to Bellagio. Laura and paying the Atlantico debt was in mind and in sight, but still a long way off, at the end of the tour. Tours can explode and disintegrate along the itinerary if things go wrong. Always clearly in memory was the occasion when I stood on the red carpet under Peruginos's *Adoration of the Magi* in the National Gallery of Umbria, announcing that 'we have a new hotel' to an American museum group who had given me twenty-four hours to upgrade from their hotel in Perugia, or the tour was off. (When we arrived in the best and most expensive hotel in Umbria that evening, there was no water, hot or cold: the town pipe had broken.)

'Don't mess about with hotels' the old-Texas secretary of the garden club had told me at our business lunch at the Hollow Brook Country Club, a couple of miles outside Dallas. On the way out of town in her Cadillac she had shown me over the deluxe hotel in the Crescent, a building complex owned by my neighbour at table the night before.

'We always stay in the best.'

'And they don't expect ever to carry a case', her husband added, as I bit into a memorably juicy Texan steak in Palm's restaurant that evening.

'Sure you wouldn't prefer a Bourbon on the rocks with that?' Another glass of *Cabernet Sauvignon* was brought.

Captain Mario brought the *Aretusa* smoothly alongside the landing stage below the Villa Carlotta.

With a few exceptions, the lake villas are in the neo-classical style, with Romantic landscaped parks, exotic collector-trees and stunning lakeside settings. The Villa Carlotta, built in 1745 for a military marshal, was given as a wedding present from her mother to Carlotta, Duchess of Saxe-Meiningen, in 1843. In the house is high quality *Empire* furniture, refined sculpture by Canova and Thorvaldsen and windows with magnificent views across the lake to the Villa Melzi. The terraces in front of the house, linked by steep stone stairs which drop in ramps to the round fountain and wrought-iron gate onto the lake, are in the classic Italian formal garden tradition. Uncommon roses climb stone walls and pleached terrace alleys trap the scent of lemon blossoms: clusters of lemons hang overhead. At one end the terraces merge into a wild garden, with paths meandering among clumps of azaleas and rhododendrons. They lead into a gorge of giant vegetation, tree ferns, towering trees, birds calling in a green forest, a luxuriant micro-climate. Botanical names on discreet labels pleased the horticulturists. Leaving by the terraces and architectural stairs, we saw Captain Mario and the *Aretusa* through the wrought-iron gate, waiting for us below. On board again, Roberta my assistant and I distributed glasses frosty with chilled Antinori dry spumante and chilled blood-orange juice.

As we proceeded on the bosom of the lake on board our private launch, clients sipping *mimosas* in the shade of the awning, thoughts floated to *The Wages of Fear*, a classic French film where a large reward was offered to whoever delivered a lorry-load of nitroglycerine, which would explode at the slightest bump. This was the Rolls-Royce version, familiar to anyone who has worked in the highly explosive field of American tourism in Italy. Bumps include Italian interpretations of the description *air-conditioning*, ice-cubes in water jugs: lack of, other people's rooms with better views, meals taken at a leisurely pace, narrow, unsurfaced access roads to famous gardens and villas and weather – bad weather. The conspicuous white block of the Grand Hotel Victoria at Menaggio growing smaller as we moved down the lake reminded me of a major weather bump which hit not me but another tour leader. Staying at the Grand Hotel Victoria a year ago with Therese, reconnoitring the area for the present tour, we had driven up a series of steep curves into the mountains which rise behind Menaggio.

Walking the last three-hundred yards through the narrow, cobbled street of a tiny village, we came round a corner to the granite house of the Baron. Its wild location gave it the atmosphere of *Wuthering Heights* crossed with *Dracula*, Italianized by a Renaissance order in portico and window pediments. The pulled bell rang distantly, dogs barked and an old female retainer appeared under the arch of an outhouse. We hacked out of her flinty dialect the information that the Baron would be returning from Milan that evening as he was receiving English visitors at the garden the next day. We were allowed through the arch to have a quick look at well-trimmed lawns running along the fenced edge of the precipitous gorge, where gardeners maintained specimen plants and shrubs by means of rope ladders, grappling irons and a kind of bo'sun's chair for the former President of the Lombardy Horticultural Society, the Baron's father. A thunder-clap drove us for shelter from hail under the arch. As we dined that evening at the Grand Hotel Victoria, checking it out for our future Americans, a procession of gaunt ladies in long dresses and gentlemen in dark suits and ties filed past our table, smiling like the Apparitions at Macbeth, and disappeared into a private dining room. 'The Society of Dendrologists', the head waiter told us, with awe, 'visiting our local gardens. From England.' All next day a storm had volleyed and thundered, its centre of gravity emptying itself over the Baron's territory, at the moment of the dendrologists' visit, we discovered. Dendrologists didn't complain, I imagine. Here and now the sky was cloudless as the launch turned a promontory and moved in towards the little harbour of the Villa Balbianello. A gardener was waiting with a boathook.

The Villa Balbianello, on the headland of a steep, wooded promontory jutting out into the lake, makes a perfect visit. The group of buildings – a minuscule harbour and church, two modest attached houses rising one above the other culminating in a superb and spacious loggia or portico – can be visited by boat and by appointment only. The *raison d'etre* of the 'villa' is the portico, built in 1787 for the Cardinal Angelo Maria Durini for fine dining and entertaining: placed on a platform-terrace at the highest point, it commands surpassingly beautiful views across, up and down the lake. Perfectly-kept paths wind among pollarded planes, oaks and occasional cypresses, from the harbour up to the terraces round the loggia.

Leaving Balbianello, the *Aretusa* glided past the watergate of the Villa Balbiano itself, one of the few 16th century villas in the area-restrained, attracting no mention in guide books, lived-in and private, which brought to mind an occasion in London when I had been taken to lunch to meet an English garden writer known for prickliness, in the hope that he would arrange entrees for me to certain private gardens. To get conversation going, I had asked him what he considered the most important qualities of an ideal garden. The conversation was closed, as by a wrought-iron gate, by his unhesitating reply, repeated three times. Privacy. Privacy. Privacy. Many of the important historic gardens in Italy are in the guide books or permissions to visit can be arranged. A few millionaire industrialists are sensitive about snoopers but most Italian owners follow a long, liberal tradition. Julius Caesar bequeathed his garden on the right-bank of the Tiber to the Roman people. In Rome, bankers, cardinals, princes and popes followed suit.

I, Custodian of the Villa Borghese on the Pincio, proclaim the following: whoever you are, if you are free, do not fear here the fetters of the law. Go where you wish, pluck what you wish, leave when you wish. These things are provided more for strangers than for the owner. As in the Golden Age when freedom from the cares of time made everything golden, the owner refuses to impose iron laws on the well-behaved guest.

The future pope Urban VIII was following the generous attitude of Pope Julius II who had the architect Bramante in 1504 build a special entrance so that visitors could come to look at his great collection of statues without intruding on the papal gardens. About the same time Cardinal della Valle had carved his *Lex Hortorum* at the entrance wall, dedicating his garden '*to the enjoyment of friends and to the pleasure of citizens and strangers .*'

Perhaps female aristocrats were always more tetchy.

'*In the evening we went to the Villa Ludovisi belonging to Prince Piombino: his mother, a ficklesome old lady, has the key and seldom permits anyone to see it.*'

Lord Herbert's account of 1779 was an uncanny anticipation of an event in the present tour. A year before the American tour, the Marchesa Chigi showed us round the decaying but fine garden of the Villa Vicobello. The view from the terraces, of the towers and turrets of Siena framed between ancient trees, now has, in the foreground, the railway station, extensive sidings and a busy peripheral road. The tall Marchesa led the slow procession among the overgrown parterres, magnificent *terra cotta* vases with lemons, up and down mossy stone steps, past a cracked and empty stone water cistern. The Marchesa, back as straight as the tall walking stick she planted at each step, followed by a black labrador and two white Maremma dogs, was assisted by a gardener at her elbow. She stopped frequently for the gardener to light the next cigarette in the chain. Her neighbour Lady Lettice Lane, my friend and helper who had arranged the introduction, followed, tiny in stature, also using a walking stick. I hovered with a camera. Occasionally a noble smile broke out over the severe face of the Chigi.

'But June is *now*. What? What?'

Half-deaf, she could not understand that we were talking about next June, next year, not next week, though her English was perfect.

'Ring me. Certainly, you may bring them. But not into the house. The garden only.'

Lettice and I had kept up a discreet countdown of reminder letters and telephone calls so that when the tour had started up in the Lakes, everything was prepared for when we came down to Siena. When we arrived at the Siena hotel there was a note for me to ring Lettice urgently. The Vicobello visit was *off*. The Marchesa had a party that day: the family was staying.

'Maybe you could come some day next month?'

'But… '

As our launch moved in towards the Hotel Villa d'Este, past water-ski-jump ramps, past moored yachts to a bustling marina of white-painted landing-stages, a fervid anticipation possessed our party. The Villa d'Este was Mecca, Eldorado, the Ultimate. On landing, our ladies and husbands fanned out over the beautifully cut lawns, Nikons snapping in all directions. A natural impetus carried them into the spacious reception rooms of this grand hotel, down wide stairs to luxurious rest rooms from which they emerged recharged.

'But John – this is *wonderful.*'

'John. This is *fantastic.* Now *this* is quite something.'

By which I understood that it had been a mistake to choose as our base the Hotel Serbelloni, whose slightly faded grandeur, superior views and more old-world clientele seemed dowdy compared to this. Having made the first mistake, a second mistake in the tour operator's rule book was to let them see what they might have liked better, what was even more expensive and therefore more desirable.

Our group moved towards the dining room, very much at home among the cosmopolitan hotel crowd: Japanese, Arabs, a bevy of Parisian-chic young Oriental ladies – the entourage of the Prime Minister of Malaya – and other Americans. The dining room was a conservatory looking out over lawns with beds of brilliant scarlet flowers in the Manchester municipal park style of the Villa Taranto on Lake Maggiore. A cold lunch was served with that understated style and courtesy that distinguishes the best *de-luxe* hotels in Italy.

Behind the present grandiose façade, constructed when the place was turned into a hotel in 1868, and behind another three centuries of decay, alteration and enlargement, there was an original villa built from 1568 for the Cardinal of Como, Tolomeo Gallio, owner also of the Villa Balbiano which we had just sailed past, another villa on the lake at Gravedona and two palaces in the city of Como. A secretary of state to Pope Gregory XIII, he was in Rome at the time when the greatest villas and gardens were being built, the Farnese's at Caprarola, Gambara's at Bagnaia and the *real* d'Este's at Tivoli. All that remains of his garden here is the green ramped staircase which climbs the hillside from the side of the villa. Water cascades at each side down carved stone channels from a *Nymphaeum* where a giant Hercules hurls Lichas into the water basin. From the *Nymphaeum*, the eye drops down the staircase, flanked by massive cypresses, to the lawns and scarlet flowers where once had been a formal *parterre* – and on to the lake and the hills on the far shore. The cardinal would surely have pointed out how the little Garrovo stream, which gave its name to the villa, a spirit of Nature untamed, gushed from the trees and rocks of the precipitous hillside before being shaped by Art to run in the curling stone channels from the *Nymphaeum*. He might have enjoyed telling his Comasco neighbours the fanciful symbolism of the water gardens at distant Tivoli, just designed by his colleague the Cardinal of Ferrara.

After the demise of the Gallios, through the procedure inheritances, and after twenty years on loan to the Jesuits, the Villa Garrovo came at the end of the 18th century to the Milanese Marquis Bartolomeo Caldarara, the main *Maecenas* of La Scala theatre. He married the young, beautiful and aristocratic Neapolitan Vittoria Peluso, an occasional dancer at La Scala. Vittoria adored the villa and cared for its garden and park. Before the death of her husband in 1806 she had fallen in love with the glamorous Domenico Pino, an inveterate gambler and womanizer who had been cut off by his family until, at the age of 37, he had enlisted in Napoleon's army, covered himself in glory and rose to general and then Minister of War in the *Regno d'Italia*. The Tristram Shandy-like outcrops of miniature castles, battlements and bastions built on the winding paths which criss-crossed the wild Garrovo hillside were *La Pelusina*'s gift to her new warrior husband, each fort representing a conquest of his Spanish campaign. At the villa, he re-enacted his victories, borrowing students from the Collegio Militare in Milan, some to be defenders, others, arriving by boat, attackers. It ended in tears, with Vittoria having to sell the villa to pay the general's gambling debts. In 1815, on her continental travels, Caroline of Brunswick, the estranged and ardently social wife of the Prince Regent of England who was staying on Lake Como, often visited the Villa Garrovo and she too fell in love with it. Vittoria reluctantly agreed to sell only to please the princess, she professed. During Caroline's wild residence, an attendant abbot encouraged her wishful thinking that she might be descended from the ancient lineage of Ferrara, calling her 'the fairest blossom of the stock of Este.' So she renamed the Villa Garrovo the Villa d'Este.

After the light lunch there was strolling on the deep-piled powder-blue carpets of the reception rooms, collecting of brochures of the hotel and buying of postcards – which gave me time to learn from the head gardener how he made the jasmine climb so effectively out of *terra cotta* vases up invisible frames. It was generally agreed that the *historic* garden, the water staircase up to the *Nymphaeum*, could be viewed adequately from the lawn by the lakeside. As for the statues, they had the postcards.

A light breeze ruffled the lake, a perfect movement of air. Chatter slowed into lethargic contentment as the boat drew away. The *Aretusa* crossed the head of the lake, the city of Como off on the starboard, the bows pointing towards Torno and the gloomy Villa Pliniana – Pliny wrote about its extraordinary natural fountain, which gushed three times a day. The present villa was built in the 16th century by a noble-man on the run from rough justice. It appealed to the Romantic imagination and was visited or stayed in by Rossini, Byron, Shelley, Stendhal, Liszt. Uninhabited for half a century, it was dilapidated and long ago was closed to visitors. On our reconnaissance, Therese and I had encountered snakes and barking dogs. We had pulled a bell at a high, closed gate. We had shouted. No one had answered.

As the company snoozed, I rehearsed the few points I had planned to make as we passed the villa associated with Pliny. Much of our knowledge about ancient Roman villas and gardens comes from the letters of the Como-born Younger Pliny, written in the 1st century A.D.

All Renaissance gardens emulated Roman gardens, so this seemed an appropriate place and moment to make a rapid introduction to the historic Italian garden. 'Who was Pliny? What's he got to do with gardens?' and so on.

A post-prandial snore from one of the Natchez party was increasing steadily. I hadn't said a word yet. Captain Mario slowed the launch and, as we stood off the Villa Pliniana, cut the engine. We were in dead calm water, the villa mirrored in the lake. The total silence woke the company. It was the perfect context for my introduction. At the first mention of the name Pliny I detected an increased attention. At the second, the faces of the ladies from Georgia were becoming purple with concentration. Maybe we should have done this before lunch. There were tears in their eyes. They burst into uncontrollable sobs, paroxysms – of laughter.

'Oh John… '

They were speechless, more sobs. The rest of the group was now relaxed, wide-awake.

'Oh John. Pliny. Pliny. It's *too much*. In our afternoon cartoon series, on Atlanta TV… there's a dog. A very cute dog. Called Pliny.'

Collapse of entire party!

Our next stop was Lake Maggiore to visit Isola Bella. Once a spine of bare rock half-a-mile long, an elongated triangle in shape, in 1630 Count Carlo Borromeo began converting it into fantasy – a palace and garden floating in the lake. The design principle was the ship, the Roman war galley, with the battering ram low in the water at the sharp end, then the palace as a kind of for'ard bridge, then the hull rising in terraces, ten of them, to the poop at the far, stern end. Named after his wife Isabella, the count and then his son Vitaliano supervised the building of immense grottoes, vaults, buttressing walls and the transportation of every cubic metre of earth, so that the gardens were planted by 1670 and most of the palace finished. Less than a hundred years before, the Borromeo family saint, Carlo, had admonished his fellow cardinal Gambara for his expenditure on his villa at Bagnaia near Rome. Here, at Isola Bella, regardless of expense, are coral-covered grottoes, flights of steps, stone balustrades, statuary, obelisks, terraces ending sheer above the blue lake. The plan ascends in a theatrical crescendo, past the fountains in a hemispherical wall to the final terrace, the 'poop' platform. Here, the Borromean unicorn and gods, goddesses and *putti* on top of columns, sail against the sky, like the ship's stone crew. The figurehead, the Borromean crown, bore the family motto: *HUMILITAS*.

The bare bones of the original garden plan were quickly softened by growth. Already in 1685 Bishop Burnet of Salisbury raved.

The freshness of the air, it being both in a Lake and near the Mountains, the fragrant smell, the beautiful Prospect and the delighting Variety that is here makes such a habitation for Summer that perhaps the whole world has nothing like it.

Even the critical Burgundian President de Brosses, in the next century, admired it.

Some parts of it are really exquisite, like the bosquets of pomegranates and oranges... and above all the great berceaux of lemon and citron trees covered with fruit; another place that is worthy of fairies, who have transported here a portion of the ancient gardens of Hesperides.

In spite of Ruskin's verdict on the Islands: '*the Eden of Italy*', a 19th century English painter spoke for many Northerners, seeing Isola Bella as '*worthy of the extravagance of a rich man with the taste of a confectioner.*'

The buffet lunch with the Roman Princess at her country castle near Siena and the candlelight dinner in the town palace of another Prince and Princess were enjoyed by all. A glamorous younger member pleased the Prince by her informed interest in his Purdey guns. In the flurry of thanks and goodbyes after a merry evening, the Princess opened my envelope. 'Didn't I say – we'd prefer it in cash?' I came back the next day with a fatter envelope

There was incomprehension that a garden so famous as that of the Villa Gamberaia outside Florence was approached by such a tiny road. We had to use minibuses that day. At the Villa Geggiano in Chianti there was beautiful 18th century wallpaper in a fragile, precarious state. 'Why don't they tear that down and have it replaced with an exact reproduction? It's such a mess.' At Asolo, near Venice, how come a five-star deluxe hotel like the Villa Cipriani can't be reached, right up to the front door, by coach? All they have to do is knock down a town gate and widen the road.

As defusers of bombs, Roberta and I waited at reception after the allocation of rooms on arriving at a new hotel, the classic flash point. A couple of minutes after we arrived at the Villa Cipriani at Asolo, a legal-looking husband returned to the reception area.

'John – we've got a problem. There's a *bug* in our room.'

The manager personally dealt with the ant with an aerosol insecticide and experienced diplomacy.

Our last visit was to a secret garden owned by a senator on the island of Torcello in the Venetian lagoon. I had planned a glorious sunset over the water, and dinner in Hemingway's famous Locanda Cipriani. It rained steadily, which did not deter the ladies, dressed for dinner, from following the senator's wife round the extensive garden, high heels sinking into soggy, salty grass.

After the excellent dinner with the senator's wife as our guest, speeches of appreciation and toasts all round, we were taken out under umbrellas and helped into the launch to return to Venice. I noticed the tide was low and ebbing. There was *grappa* on the breath of the skipper and his mate. They had been drinking through the period of our garden visit and dinner. We packed into the cabin, the windows opaque with condensation. Squalls of rain drove against the windows as the boat left the canal and hit the buffeting waves of the open lagoon. *Bonhomie* reigned in the cabin. I was surprised when I felt the bows rise and the launch accelerate, illegally leaving the marked navigation channel. We slowed, equally suddenly. I could see into the compartment, where the skipper's mate was standing up in his oil-skins, peering ahead where the spotlight penetrated the driving rain. The launch was accelerating and slowing, casting to starboard and to port in a thoroughly unconfident way. Inside, nobody seemed to be noticing. Merry chatter continued. A lady from Essex, that yachting harbour of millionaires' white clapboard houses on the Connecticut coast, shouted to me over the talk of Harry, Hemingway and tomorrow's TWA flight.

'John – do you *know* this driver? If you ask me, he's casting for a channel. Good luck to him!'

Exactly what I was thinking, remembering when our doctor had arrived at 2 a.m. instead of at 11 p.m., having run aground returning in his boat from an island visit. He had waded half-a-mile through lagoon mud, in his new Church's shoes, to find a fisherman to help pull his boat free. Nobody else was aware that now, below the thin boards of the launch, we were within inches of disaster.

The next morning they waved goodbye as another launch took them off to the airport. The nitroglycerine had not exploded. At the Hotel Atlantico, Signora Laura was glad to be paid a considerable part of the debt she had kindly allowed, to tide us over a critical pre-university year.

17

Absolute Beginners in the Vineyard

On moving permanently to Italy in 1989, after the dogs came the vineyard.

Our vineyard is planted in the sloping field across the gravel road which passes in front of the house. It is backed by a sandstone cliff, eighty feet high, bristling with trees, shrubs and plants, and all the animals, birds and insects, large and small, that go with them. Above the cliff, against the sky are the Medieval walls and bell-towers of San Ginesio. We are on the Southern slopes. Exposed, in the eye of the sun, the vineyard looks out at the long line of the Sibillini Apennines, the Abruzzi mountains eighty miles away on the horizon, in the general direction of Rome, Sicily and Africa. The bulwark of the town hill protects us from the worst blasts of hail, snow and ice driven from the North East across the Adriatic on the *Bora* wind. Our cliff also functions as a solar storage heater-radiator. In a position theoretically too high for good wine-growing, the vineyard has a benign micro-climate.

We planted the vineyard by courtesy of our former neighbour *contadino* Osvaldo in 1989, when we came to live here full-time. When we had bought the farmhouse, two fields and a wood fifteen years before, we had let Osvaldo go on working the fields, preferring to see them cultivated rather than abandoned and running wild, knowing full well that this gave him peasants' rights to the land. There was no shortage of people pleased to tell us this. However, to the incredulity of all our country neighbours and the hardly-concealed wrath of his cunning wife Rita, when we said we wanted to use a field to make a vineyard, he didn't ask for the expected pay-off in return for leaving the land: and with his tractor he did the preliminary work.

The few remaining ancient vines, trained on 'tutor' field-maples and strung in the old Roman fashion, gnarled branches meeting each other on wires stretched between the 'tutors', were pulled out: a sad but necessary action. The field was ploughed. It was deep-drained by a tractor pulling a sharp-pointed torpedo-like 'mole', a *reputatore*, which burrowed to a depth of a metre and a half, its sharp knife edge cutting a grid of subterranean slit-channels. The deep-ploughed furrows were left to break and crumble through the summer, were harrowed fine in autumn and the lines for the four future rows of vines were marked out with red and white plastic tapes. Ideally the rows should run north to south, for maximum sun on both sides of the vines but in a countryside so steep that each year farmers are killed by their tractors turning over on them, the slope of the land dictates a compromise.

A neighbouring *contadino*, the woodman Nello, took me up to the mountains above Montemonaco to select chestnut poles. At this time the European Community were paying farmers to uproot the vineyards which twenty-five years before they had paid them to plant, so there were plenty of now-disused concrete poles to be had for nothing, but we eco-aesthetes preferred wood. It was a great moment when, after two days of continuous quarrelling, Nello *dell'avvocato* and Pietro *il Conte* – 'son of the lawyer' and 'the count', their ironic nicknames – showed proudly their finished work: the four rows of poles, through which the vine-support wires are threaded marching up the slope, the geometry perfect from top to bottom, side to side and diagonally.

'All done by the eye.' The mellow Nello allowed *Il Conte*, so nicknamed because of his arrogant and hypercritical manner, to have the last word. '*Ottimo lavoro* – an excellent job.' The Count gave himself the benefit of any possible doubt. They were praised and paid.

Preparing the vineyard

Although Nello and Pietro had managed to find areas of dispute, the planting of chestnut poles in straight lines at regular intervals, the rows wide enough apart for a tractor to work, is not an operation requiring choices or controversial decisions or discussion about alternative ways of doing it. From this point on however, in the progress over the next years from the cultivation of the vineyard to the production and preserving of wine, almost everything was to do with choice, with method and almost everything we did isolated us from the advice and understanding of our neighbours.

Just as our neighbour builders had thought us mad to renovate an old house – 'better bulldoze it and build a new one, cheaper too' – so our peasant neighbours were emphatically against our planting a vineyard at all – too much work. For our neighbours, wine, often mixed with lemonade, is the cheapest liquid to go with a meal. Every *contadino* is proud of his own wine – *genuino* – untouched by stabilising substances, maturing from mildly acetic to total vinegar as the barrel is consumed from the tap between vintages. The concept of wine as high hedonist culture, or even as a pleasing addition to a meal, does not exist. The making of *vino cotto* – 'cooked wine' – in this area, the boiling down of the wine and sealing the residue in a barrel for at least a year, is a traditional alternative to vinegary wine.

Our first step out of line, after planting a vineyard at all and not using throw-away concrete posts, was not to go down to the Tolentino market on Tuesday and buy whatever variety of vine-stock was there – bunches of *Riempibotte* – 're-fill the barrel' – classic local peasant vinestock, or, in a good week perhaps *Trebbiano* or *La Gallopa*. We gave some thought to what vines to plant.

'*A wine's varietal make-up is crucial, a far more important influence on the flavour and character than geological wrinkle, accident of climate or craft in the cellar.*' Jancis Robinson, the wine journalist, was our first source of instruction. '*The grape stock alone determines perhaps 90% of the flavour of the wine.*' Wanting to believe in Jancis Robinson, we decided to plant four rows, each row of twenty-five vines, each row a different type of grape. We hoped that we would finish with an interesting blend. It was to be red wine. Of the vines chosen, two were French, one Tuscan and one semi-local: not an orthodox selection by local habits.

Cabernet Sauvignon had to be one. So many winter special-occasion dinners in London, with pheasant or mallard or teal, had been graced with the names of the Medoc parishes and chateaux. Merlot was to be included, with less conviction, but in appreciation of the classic claret combination. A second bottle of Marchese Antinori's *Tignanello*, ordered by my eldest son in a little back street *trattoria* in Parma when cheers from the nearby stadium announced another goal against Fiorentino, won the day for the Sangiovese grape. *Tignanello* is Antinori's Sangiovese-based riposte to his neighbour's world-beating *Sassicaia*, one of the first wines to be made in Italy with the foreign Cabernet Sauvignon grape. Italy scored again as we read in Burton Anderson's book *Vino* of Edoardo Valentini's production of a magnificent red *Montepulciano d'Abruzzo* in Loreto Aprutino, just over our Southern horizon. So the Montepulciano grape was included – nothing to do with the town of that name in Tuscany. We later found support in Columella, a Roman agricultural writer of the first century A.D.

It is the part of a wise farmer to plant that vine which he specially approves. It is also the part of a man of foresight to set out different kinds. So let us be content with a sort of quartet of champion vines.

A telephone call was made to the Cooperative at Rauscedo near Pordenone, north-east of Venice, *the* vinestock growers and grafters. They confirmed that all these types of vines should do all right in our location. A small parcel arrived at the post office in San Ginesio, cash on collection – our hundred chosen vines with their fingers coated in wax for frost protection. Pietro the Count was to plant, with me learning alongside. But instant action was restrained. 'We'll do it next week when the moon is right. Just before the full. *Barba Nera.*'

If Jancis Robinson was our first reader, the second was the only book I had heard of in English on viticulture, a deeply serious book produced by the University of California Press, Berkeley, Los Angeles. *General Viticulture* by Winkler, Cooke, Kliewer and Lider is based on scientific measurement, statistics, a handbook for the wine industry of the Lower Sacramento Valley, the San Joaquin Valley, the Imperial and Palo Verde Valleys and even the Salt River and Yuma Valleys in Arizona. But it did have surprisingly low-tech primitive black and white close-up photos of vines, against a white background sheet for clarity, in their various stages of growth. It showed, with pictures, how you plant, what you do each year as the new vines grow, how you train them and how you prune them.

Our third help, often basic instruction, came from Daryl-the-Fax, my Peckham-Melbourne-based accountant, a surrogate vinegrower-oenologist. '*A bud is a small lump which forms in the Autumn, then swells up in Spring and from which a growing shoot bursts. The flowers will drop off in June, leaving tiny berries. Don't have frost or heavy rain while they are flowering.*'

Clare, Therese and Daryl-the-Fax

As beginners, we tried to follow the book. Everyone around, all our neighbours, had generations of vine cultivation in the blood. As an early 19th century historian wrote: '*our contadini, instructed by their elders, know the practical execution of what Virgil with sublime mastery taught in his Georgics.*' Everything they did was in a time-honoured tradition and didn't need thinking about. They had never met anyone who didn't share a common knowledge of vines, let alone a viticultural deviant or free-thinker. In every *contadino* kitchen, on the walls of every *consorzio agrario*, every seedsman's shop, every mill, every ironmonger, alongside the picture of the Madonna and the Milan football team is the agricultural calendar, *Barba Nera* – Black Beard, to whom the Count had referred.

Barba Nera, an Umbrian Wise Man of the 18th century, wrote down the traditions and folklore of the agricultural year as did the classical Roman agronomes Cato, Varro and Columella. *Barba Nera*'s calendar, printed every year, is a ready reference on country life. It gives the ascent and descent of the Moon into the zodiacal constellations, a reminder that the Earth signs, Taurus, Virgin and Capricorn are right for the root, the Air signs, the Twins, the Scales and Aquarius for the flower, the Water, the Fish, the Crab and the Scorpion for foliage and the Fire, the Ram, the Lion and the Archer for fruition. Into this calendar is set the equally important tracking of the waxing and waning of each moon. '*I learned this rule from my father,*' said Agrasius, one of Varro's agri-symposium guests, '*and I keep it not only in shearing my sheep but in cutting my hair, for fear that if I have it done when the moon is waxing I may become bald.*' Written nearly two thousand years ago, the mentality has hardly changed in country areas.

Imposed on *Barba Nera*'s zodiacal calendar is the church calendar, the Feasts of the church and significant Saints Days. On the eve of St. John the Baptist, June 24, many of our neighbours still put out bowls of water in which petals of flowers are floated, for a refreshing and fragrant face wash in the morning. We too have some years filled our bowl with the petals of Mermaid, Albertine, the wild broom and acacia, in the spirit of the sceptical Varro who believed that nothing was lost by making offerings to the gods. In the same spirit we waited for the Count to plant with the approval of *Barba Nera* and the waxing moon.

The progress from planting, through three years of viticulture, to the actual business of vinification was a gradual initiation. In the first year the new vines were left to grow and sprawled or ascended temporary canes. But they had to be kept free of weeds.

We hoed and harrowed. In the autumn of year one came the first pruning, cutting the newly grown vines right down to the ground, leaving a couple of 'buds', as we had been assured those almost invisible swellings are.

In the second year the first signs of our deviation became visible to neighbours. As the vines shot up the sturdier supports which we had planted in the winter, and as they reached the metre-high first horizontal wire, the central growing trunk was severed at that height, two shoots were delicately attached to the wire, one heading left, one heading right, and all shoots below the bifurcation were rubbed or pulled off. No vines in this area are trained in this *bilateral cordon* style.

'Who did the pruning ?'

'I did.'

The Count's expression combined scorn and pity.

Hoeing and pruning, occasionally plugging into auto-prune from London or Melbourne and checking on serious advice from Sacramento still left time for contemplative pauses. Visible as I hoed, from the top of the vineyard, where the tooth-like Gran Sasso d'Italia pricks the Southern horizon, is the region of the Abruzzo, where Valentini, our inspiration, produces his red Montepulciano d'Abruzzo.

'I'm a compulsive reader,' Valentini explained to the writer Burton Anderson, 'and my favourite subject is oenology. I've read every work I know of on the subject, including the tracts on modern technology. And you know who my favourite is, the one I most often turn to? Columella. That's right, the Roman. Do you know that almost everything that's happening in oenology today was known to some extent by Columella? The secrets were there nearly two thousand years ago.'

So when winter snow blocked our road, it seemed a good idea to pursue Valentini's classical secrets, and, in front of a glowing fire, through the Loeb translations, I met the Roman agronomes. A bonus was in the introduction to Columella. Where else would our own John Milton's tart and puritanical advice to the young be found? '*After the scriptures, and after supper, schoolboys should devote their thoughts to the authors of agriculture, Cato, Varro and Columella. If the language is difficult, so much the better.*' Dozing with Loeb on winter evenings, we found ourselves in a world of *Barba Nera* without the saints' days. Beyond the practical were philosophical dimensions. Explicit was a general acceptance that there was an innate nobility and virtue in the ritual activities of tending the earth. Implicit was a religious awareness of the invisible world of the gods – the deities of nature, of the earth, of the sun, of the moon, of the grape, of the goatherds and the spirits of place.

Cato lived from 234 BC to 149 BC. Of country stock, he was a successful soldier, lawyer, administrator and writer on jurisprudence, military science, ancient and modern history, and agriculture. Shrewd, unvarnished, censorious, he was a voice of the old Republican virtues, taxing luxury, checking privilege and corruption, hating everything Carthaginian, despising the Greek sophistication which was creeping into Roman life.

'Our ancestors, when they would praise a worthy man, their praise took this form: Good Husbandman; Good Farmer,' from which point of departure he gave his agricultural precepts. *'What is good cultivation? Ploughing. What next? Ploughing. What third? Manuring; the master should have the selling habit, not the buying habit; when the weather is bad and no other work can be done, clear out the manure for the compost heap…'*

Cato preserves the ancient rituals in detail, like an agricultural Book of Common Prayer.

'In making the offering use this formula: Jupiter Dapalis, foreasmuch as it is fitting that a cup of wine be offered thee in my house for thy sacred feast, be honoured by the wine placed before thee.' He also hands on more down-to-earth advice. *'When a serpent has bitten an ox, macerate an acetabulum of fennel flower in a hemina of old wine. Administer through the nostrils and apply swine's dung to the wound itself. Treat a person the same way if occasion arise, or to prevent chafing, when you set out on a journey, keep a branch of Pontic wormwood under the anus.'*

Varro, 116–27 B.C. was an entirely different kind of man. Born of an equestrian family, he did his active service as a naval commander under Pompey, and had to tread delicately in the times before and after Julius Caesar's assassination and Antony's proscriptions. He studied in

Athens and was essentially a scholar. *Vir Romanorum eruditissimus* – the most learned of Romans – he was entrusted by Julius Caesar with the setting up of a Greek and Latin public library. He himself wrote on history, geography, philology, rhetoric, jurisprudence, music, medicine, architecture, literary history – and agriculture. His *Libri Rerum Rusticarum* of 37 B.C. is presented in a literary format, a series of discussions among friends on agricultural matters. It demonstrates the Roman love of logical, rational classification, the entire subject being put into categories, and sub-categories, and sub-sub-categories: choosing the land, erecting the buildings, cultivating fields, raising cattle, the husbandry of vines, olives, fruit trees, the game reserve, the aviaries, the fishponds, the apiaries, and even the management of snails and edible dormice. Not surprisingly for Varro, there are various references to the more bizarre experiments in country house living of the very rich. '*Under the same roof,*' he says of Lucullus, '*he had an aviary and a dining room, where he could dine luxuriantly and see birds lying cooked on the dish and others fluttering around the windows of their prison. But they found it unserviceable: for in it the birds fluttering around the windows do not give pleasure to the eyes to the same extent that the disagreeable odour gives offence to the nostrils.*'

Columella lived in the middle of the 1st century A.D., through the uneasy reigns of Tiberius, Caligula, Claudius and Nero. Originating from Spain, he owned and farmed estates in Central Italy and his *De Re Rustica*, written around 60–65 A.D. is by far the longest of the canon. It is the least idiosyncratic, the most informative – and in it are Valentini's secrets: which we failed to find.

Men experienced in war, politics, public service, the law, various branches of scholarship, these writers were equally familiar with agricultural matters. They give practical advice, some archaic and strange, some still valid. They record the immemorial practises of rural life, the sun, the moon, the calendar, appropriate sacrifices to the gods. Columella expresses the general admiration of a way of life epitomised by the heroic Cincinnatus, a farmer, called from his fields in 450 B.C. to solve a political and military emergency. Appointed Dictator, he solved the problem in sixteen days, resigned his position and went back to the plough. Horace had his Sabine farm, Cicero his country retreats for *otium cum dignitate* – worthwhile relaxation. It is a way of life which emerges lucidly from the letters of Pliny the Younger (A.D. 61–c112). He had several villas, famous for their architectural magnificence – but they were essentially country retreats from his work in the law courts, in political assemblies, in public administration.

The rich had several places in the country. '*Do you think I have not as much sense as the cranes and storks who change their habitation with the seasons*', said Lucullus, he of the dining room-aviary experiment. More in sympathy with today is the modest, cost-conscious advice of Pliny to one of his protégés, the historian Suetonius Tranquillus.

There is indeed much about this property to whet Tranquillus' appetite if only the price suits him: easy access to Rome, good communications, a modest house and sufficient land for him to enjoy without taking up too much of his time. Scholars turned landowners, like himself, need no more land than will suffice to clear their heads and refresh their eyes as they stroll around their grounds and tread their single path, getting to know each one of their precious vines.

February is the month of pruning. The pruning at the end of year two had publicly confirmed our deviant viticulture. However, the leafless vines looked fine, their young arms growing in strength along the wires. As the spring and summer of year three proceeded, with the promised first vintage in the autumn, the vines were tended with increasingly personal attention. The Montepulciano, slow and even sickly to start with, with an annoying tendency to droop, had picked itself up. Pruning it had shown the strong, firm-grained quality of its wood, hard like an oak. The Sangiovese was fast and forward, shooting up, full of show and *bravura* but a little soft in the centre. The Cabernet Sauvignon was treated with extra involvement and had begun to show its different quality – strong wood, a controlled growth, an elegance shared with its co-national, the at first more reticent Merlot.

In spring and early summer the vines grew almost visibly. Modern-style unecological systemic spraying was done regularly. Growing shoots were attached to the second and then the third wire, and then cut, on instructions from auto-prune. Miniscule grape buds in May turned into feathery flowers in June, converted into bunches of tiny but unmistakably real grapes in July, which swelled in August, turned from green to purply-black in September and continued to swell into October.

As the *vendemmia* – the vine harvest – approached, the weather was ominous: hot, close, storms building up. On a Wednesday, in the middle of the morning, all the church bells of San Ginesio rang out, just as they had done at each goal by Italy in the World Cup final years ago.

'To disperse the gathering storm. Hail would ruin the harvest,' the *Conte* explained.

'*The best protection is sending a plane to seed the potential storm-clouds with chemicals, so that rain falls rather than hail,*' says California.

No hail came. There was much talk of the moon. In the shops the Mostometer was everywhere on display, an instrument like a thermometer with, at one end, a glass bulb filled with granules of mercury. It measures the sugar content of grapes. We cut a bunch of each type of grape, crushed it in the kitchen blender, poured the liquid into a test tube and floated the Mostometer in it. Readings went up, day by day. On October 7 they reached the magic mean measure: 18, which means an alcoholic grade of 11.40, regarded as a minimum.

'*Go! Go! Go!*' whirred the fax from Melbourne.

We went out into the vineyard at ten in the morning, when the dew had dried off, my wife, Nello and I, armed with secateurs, a plastic bucket each and some bigger plastic boxes which were left at intervals down the row of vines. We filled the big boxes from our buckets and as each row was harvested, Nello and I carried the full boxes to the garage,

The Vendemmia

our vinification operations centre – or *cantina*. The boxes were weighed, type by type, for the record, the grapes tipped into the crusher-de-stalker machine, a metal bin with an electrically driven screw gyrating at the bottom, like a cement-mixer: it grabs, breaks and crushes the grapes. At one end, at the bottom, stalks shoot out. From the other end a plastic tube of wide diameter conveys the thick, turgid slurry into the fermenting vat. This fibre-glass 500-litre container, a rectangular cube, has a stainless steel bolt-on door pierced by a tap at the front, at the level of the bottom. At the top is a round hole into which the tube disgorges the liquid. This has a bolt-on lid, fitted with an air valve.

The harvest, the long-awaited *vendemmia*, was done by the three of us in two-and-a-half hours. The crushing machine was hosed down after its fifteen minutes of action and wheeled away to its corner in the garage 'til next year. Nello went home to lunch. 312 kili of grapes had been crushed, 250 kili of must was in the vat. No grape treading. No rustic banquet. No festivities but a slightly mystified, anti-climactic satisfaction.

Antero in the cantina

After dark, behind the shut garage doors, a dose of Metabisulphite of Potassium, was administered on fax orders and confirmed by a wine friend in the Veneto. *Everyone* does it, to control unfriendly yeasts causing unwanted biochemical molecular mutations, I think is what they said. Round here, *no one* does it: the wine must be *genuino* – untouched by chemicals.

Nothing happened. We weren't sure what was meant to happen. Day followed day. Neighbours asked: 'Is it boiling? Hasn't it started?' There was a nervous tone to fax messages and questions: '*Is the weather still warm? Are you keeping the garage closed?*' On the morning of the eighth day an unmistakably vinous smell permeated the garage, the house, the whole vicinity. A purring came from the vat and its sides were warm.

Three times a day the lid was opened and the thick cap of grape skins dunked with a wooden paddle, mixing it back into the *must.* The liquid tasted sweet, grapejuice. Then, after a day, it made the tongue tingle. It tasted sharp, and chalky. The mostometer came into use again, the readings dropping instead of rising, counting the sugar down to zero as the yeasts converted it to alcohol. After four days the bubbling stopped, the vat went cold and the reading was almost zero. We waited for it to reach zero. Then, a day-an-a-half later we ran the free-run wine out of the tap, through buckets and funnels into 55-litre demijohns. There was a nasty smell of sulphur. When no more liquid came, the low, oven-like front door was opened and the mass of gunge was shovelled into the press – the quintessential piece of winemaking equipment, unchanged in design since Roman times. We pressed down the soggy mass gently by hand and wine gushed out through the slats, into the holding rim and over the lip of the spout, into buckets and into the demijohns – the *fiore* as this second flush is called, the 'flower'. As the press is packed, the wooden top is fitted round the central screw, and then the wooden blocks, and the last of the grapey mass comes under pressure as we pushed, pulled and pushed on the ratcheted metal bar, as on a windlass. More tannin-full liquid came out. Then the press was dismantled, the damp cake of grape husks was chopped with a spade and thrown on the compost, the machine hosed clean and put away. The gas-escape valves were clamped onto the demijohns.

The news spread that our wine stank of sulphur. Though a deep red colour, it was disgusting, undrinkable. So much for new-fangled ways, was the local opinion. I had a guilty secret. In my furtiveness I had put in the wrong amount of *metabisolfito*. I had overdosed by a factor of ten, getting the decimal point in the wrong place.

The Count, satisfied with our failure, lent us a copper funnel. Run the wine over copper, he told us, and the smell will go. I did. It didn't go but it was slightly better.

To remove a bad odour: heat a thick clean piece of roofing tile thoroughly in the fire. When it is hot, coat it with pitch, attach a string, lower it gently to the bottom of the jar and leave the jar sealed for two days.

Fabrizio, the technician at the local wine co-operative didn't know Cato's recipe, but suggested amalgamating the wine with liquid Vaseline which would float to the top, bringing with it and away the smell. So the wine and Vaseline was duly whisked with a paint-mixing paddle attached to the Black and Decker. We skimmed off the surfaced Vaseline and tasted a slight but definite improvement.

In January we went, bearing samples, to our *enologo* friend in Conegliano near Venice. He gave hope. The overdose would have delayed the fermentation, improving the colour and flavour of the wine. The smell was because we had not moved the wine off the sediment quickly enough after the fermentation. Bad yeasts had been at work. But the wine was good in its heart. The smell would go. Patience and time. 'Re-ferment it' he said. We added yeast and sugar and it bubbled through a second fermentation, in April. The smell was *a lot* better. 'Now put it in the barrel and forget about it.' We put it in the barrel. Tactful neighbours didn't ask questions. Our reputation as failures was a fact of local life.

By the time of the next vintage, the '94, the oak barrel had done a wonderful job on the '93 wine, massaging away its rough edges, giving it a new suppleness. Some sulphur was still there, embedded in the wine, but the wine was just about drinkable, with apologies. The '94 vintage produced a heavier crop of grapes, more litres of wine, and this time it was removed smartly from the sediment just before the fermentation stopped. It did time in the demijohns and was duly put into the beautiful new barrels of French *Allier* oak. The Veneto *enologo* was enthusiastic after tasting the '93 and the '94. Then he surprised us.

'Cut the '93 fifty fifty with the '94. Barrel it. It will be good.' We did, giving us a barrel of '93\'94 and leaving a barrel of pure '94. Six months later, Therese, a fierce detector of imperfections, and I tried both. To our surprise, they were both drinkable, actually better than the wines we had been buying in the supermarket. An English wine importer \ exporter, at dinner in Rome, tasted, paused, named the varieties – Merlot, Cabernet Sauvignon, Sangiovese… pause…

Montepulciano. I was amazed at this expertise: and by his judgement. He said the wine was good.

We invented a label, from a miniature of the 15th century showing three people harvesting, one snipping bunches of grapes from the vine, a woman passing it to a man standing knee-deep in grapes in the fermentation vat – not orange fibre-glass like ours. We named the wine *Il Picchio* – the Woodpecker, this being the symbol of our region, the Marche, whose indigenous tribe was the *Piceni – the woodpecker people*. When they migrated from the Sabine lands, reported the Elder Pliny, *in vexilla eorum picus consederat* – on their standards was the wood-pecker. Our countryside is full of green woodpeckers.

A couple of cases went in the back of the car to England. '*But your wine is damned good,'* wrote a critical friend. '*It's not just that it's like real wine but it's far better than the plonk we drink here every day.'* Daryl the Fax, with professional tenacity, smelt an imperfection in the '93. '*The only negative with this wine is that I could detect a "chemical" trace in the flavour.'* However, his final judgment was friendly. '*I think both of these wines are well made and very pleasing to drink.'* Encouraged, we planted fifty Syrah vines to add quality and quantity in the future, and came to the '95 harvest flushed with confidence, with *hubris* – overweening pride, some would say.

Lino, the communist *contadino* turned goldsmith and watchmender, president of the local shooting association, had been haranguing me in his shop in the piazza about the unjust elitism of the English system of private shooting. The classic reply, about the slaughter of everything that flies was deflected by his argument that in Italy shooting goes with agriculture. The sparrows, the starlings – these are the birds that devour the fruits, the grapes. 'Talking of which,' he asked, 'have you done *questo lavoro* – this job', which he indicated by moving his hands like a desperately-digging dog, 'stripping the leaves to let the sun get at the grapes. Very important in these last days.'

Following Lino's advice, working through the vineyard in the last week before the harvest, pulling off leaves to expose to the sun (and hail…) bunches of grapes which were hidden like birds' nests, we found that the last row, the row nearest our bird-sanctuary cliff, the row of Merlot – had been stripped bare, giving new significance to fauna reports from English neighbours. They had been disturbed at night by wild boars rutting among their vines. Foxes had first pick of their grapes, then the birds. They recorded, in one morning, a buzzard, turtle dove, green and great spotted woodpecker, swallow, house martin, hoopoe, black cap, starling, nightingale, blackbird, long tailed tit, blue tit, nuthatch, tree creeper, yellowhammer, gold finch, green finch, serin, tree sparrow, house sparrow, golden oriole, magpie, hooded crow, not to mention a couple of amorous vipers.

So the '95 harvest was picked, with minimal Merlot. The weather being hot, the fermentation started quickly, in two days – the purring, the warm vat and the vinous fragrance. But the next morning it had stopped. The vat was cold, silent, still. Our previous fermentations had gone on for four days. A stopped fermentation is serious – some dire molecular-biochemical disorder, we were told. 'Bring a heating stove into the garage,' advised Fabrizio on the telephone. Daryl-the-Fax recommended patience. But after four days of inertia in the vat, he ordered emergency action. '*I think you need drastic action. Run off the liquid into large pots and gently raise the temperature to 25 degrees by cooking on the kitchen stove.*' Before cooking I took a sample of the wine to Fabrizio's laboratory at the *Cantina Sociale*.

'What's the problem? The fermentation is done, finished. Sugar is zero.'

'But it fermented just one day. Is it possible?'

'Rare. But possible. The weather has been hot.'

I telephoned the *enologo* in Conegliano. He was surprised but congratulated me on my oenological nerve. The concentration in the wine would benefit from having been left four days, after fermentation, on the sediment. He said I had done well. More colour. More flavour.

'But wasn't that, leaving it on its sediment, what caused the sulphur stink in '93?'

I couldn't understand his reply – talk of molecules, enzymes, yeasts. The new wine went into the well-washed and fumigated French barrels for its education. Two months later, when we came back from Venice – nemesis. Both barrels were vinegar though the thirty litres in excess, bottled for topping up the barrels, was in perfect order. Why? Why? Why? What had gone wrong? The puzzles of fermentation, pruning, grape-devouring birds and the sardonically critical face of the Count drifted in and out of the sleeping mind. When I woke in the morning, a possible explanation had come to mind. Perhaps, *perhaps* I had not cleaned and sterilised the wooden bungs with the same care and attention as the barrels. What's more, to make them fit more snugly, they had been wrapped in gauze, unchanged after various toppings-up: a warm, wet incubator of molecular-biological ferment if not of the dreaded vinegar fly itself. This was the only possible explanation – unhygienic, careless cellar work. I'm still not so sure.

The hundred-and-fifty litres of vinegar were duly pumped out of the barrels down the steeply sloping chicken run. A month later, a beautiful, ten-year-old walnut tree, in the path of the vinegar, wilted and died, to complete the fiasco of the 1995 vintage – *we thought*.

Wrongly: there was more to come. We were left in April with empty barrels, thoroughly washed but still with a taint of vinegar. Barrels once used should be kept full of wine, we were told. We had no spare wine, having just poured away the year's production. So? The barrel-makers in Piemonte said keep them dry. Burn a sulphur biscuit inside. Then keep the bung on. Once the sulphur smell had dispersed we detected a different but still nasty smell. 'Wash them with soda,' said another advisor. The smell stayed. 'You've got *puzzo di secco* – dry-stink. A problem.' A wine firm in the Veneto said try keeping them full of water. Emptying them after a month there was again a different and much nastier smell – of bilge water. The barrel stink problem did not go away.

The seasons in the vineyard proceeded. In deference to the fervidly green attitudes of Therese, we agreed that next year to compromise, to go on spraying with our modern, chemical, systemic mixture, but at half strength. By July I put on glasses to focus better on the downy grey bloom forming on bunches of small, green grapes.

'*Cenere*,' said Antero, who had become our regular helper in the vineyard. 'Ashes – the dialect word of *oidio*.' I knew the word *oidio*. It had a whole chapter to itself in the book on diseases. Antero wagged his head fatalistically at the question of a cure. 'It's everywhere'.

We drastically thinned-out the foliage to let air circulate better. We double-strength sprayed. We resorted to the traditional sulphur in powder form, and to copper sulphate crystals dissolved in water mixed with chalk to make it stick – the traditional Bordeaux mixture. The grape bunches grew greyer with mildew and started to shrivel. Then Antero pointed out yellow blotches on the vineleaves – everywhere. '*Peronospra* – it stops the grapes maturing.' More negative head-wagging. There was another chapter in the disease book entitled *Peronospra*.

So the 1996 vendemmia was a sad affair. As we snipped down the rows, we threw three-quarters of the blighted bunches on the ground, useless. In January we put the small quantity of characterless wine in an untainted barrel and consoled ourselves with the 1994 wine, steadily increasing in quality in the bottle. Occasional tastings of the '93-'94 mix gave hints of something even better to come. The sulphur was almost gone.

1997 was full of sun and movements of dry air, perfect conditions which finished in one of the best vintages ever in Italy. As we came to January and the moment to move the new wine from the demijohns into the barrels, the smell question was still unanswered. The problematic barrels didn't have an unquestionably healthy smell.

'Is it *puzzo di legno* or a *puzzo cattivo* – wood smell or bad smell?' asked the Conegliano oenologist on the telephone. How could we be sure? Fabrizio at our local Cantina Sociale couldn't help. They didn't use wooden barrels. 'Mere *chicquerie*' he said. We filled the least tainted barrels and left for Venice.

In our absence Antero had topped up the barrels weekly and reported no disasters. Back in April, we opened the bungs, extracted with pipette, looked, smelt, tasted. Clear. Good colour. Definite wood taste but not *cattivo*. With immense relief we emptied the wine into the large holding container, cleaned the sediment, washed the barrels and put the wine back. A week later, everything had gone berserk. The wine was alive and actively kicking – clouded, flocculent and reeking of wood as if the barrel itself had started to ferment.

'Don't worry,' said the *enologo*, 'it will calm down.' It calmed down, cleared but stayed far too oaky for drinking – virulently woody – another traumatic and mysterious experience. The newly-bottled, undrinkable wine packed our very small *cantina* from floor to ceiling. We remembered the legendary story of the experimental *Sassicaia*, pronounced undrinkable, bottled and forgotten for years to emerge in the end a princess of super-Tuscans but we didn't hope for such a far-fetched miracle. Occasional tasting showed some but little improvement. After another year I began surreptitiously sneaking the odd case into the back of the car and leaving it by the communal bin until caught red-handed by Therese.

'Don't throw it away. Taste it again.' As if by magic, the continual permutations, molecular rearrangements and growths of the living wine had indeed produced a miracle. It was drinkable: woody, but less so, and drinkable. Another year on and it had become our regular smooth, well-structured supper drink, even if occasionally referred to as *Old Smoky*.

The room where I write is above the *cantina*: bookshelves floor to ceiling over wine racks floor to ceiling, writing table over living barrels of living wine. Growing and tending the vines, making the wine and bringing it on are absorbing, irresistibly fascinating and humbling activities. '*The grape stock alone determines perhaps 90% of the flavour of the wine,*' wrote our original guide. We know what she meant. But that's by no means the whole story.

18

Floating

Selling our flat and cutting our costs in London put us out of debt. With the additional help of the American garden lovers the debt to Signora Laura was paid and in its lean-machine style of these later years the Pre-University Course continued. After the descent into the thirties, numbers moved about in the higher and lower forties and two years ago they went up to fifty-eight. Were we returning to the good old days, with sixty, seventy and even eighty students? Then, thirty-seven. Were we on the way out? On the wall was always the booking-chart – numbers at the end of each month over past years. It was often the ninth or tenth month before the numbers came up to the minimum needed and we knew that another course would happen. We were still afloat.

When we closed down the London office, our original part-time, long distance secretary in Oxford, Fleur Augarde wasn't able to take on the job again. But her sister Clare would. The Augarde name, familiar to so many students in our first phase, came back into our activity. Clare had spent time in Italy as a dancer so spoke Italian with a persuasive Neapolitan twang. As her children had finished school, she was, amazingly, willing to come out with the students to Venice and lodge in the notorious eye-of-the-storm, the second floor of the Hotel Atlantico. In recent years students have had the benefit of Clare's enthusiastic, worldly-wise, mildly chivvying presence to calm their late-night frenzies, take them to doctors' surgeries and, when necessary, to call a spade a bloody shovel.

Clare and Fleur Augarde with J.H.

In the interval between lectures, the bar opposite the little bridge, the Ponte del Purgatorio, the entrance into our part of the Arsenal, was crammed with our students. When the February sun shone, they sat or lay among the Peloponnesian or Delian marble lions which decorated the monumental entrance to the dockyard, the spoils of the last Venetian naval campaigns: *did* sit or lie. Now, the lions, including the one with the runes chiselled into its side by Viking mercenaries working for the Byzantine emperor, have become official art, protected by a chain fence. No more sandwiches between antique lions' paws.

Venetian painters, opera, iconography, restoration techniques, Michelangelo, Renaissance music, psychology, Machiavelli, 20th century art – each week two new lecturers, two new faces, two new voices, two new subjects. But what added the gold, what made the experience star-touched, for students, for lecturers, for me, was the city. Simply moving about, getting up, going to bed, browsing, shopping in Venice – *floating* – perhaps what Proust meant when he wrote: '*when I came to Venice my dream became my address.*'

The city's existence is a miracle of construction – palaces and churches rising out of water, built on tree-trunk-foundations sunk into mud, veined by tidal canals – an island. The fact of water everywhere produces particular light, movement and reflections. Instead of the noise, smell and clutter of the motor car, there is the essentially beautiful line and movement of an immense range of traditional boats designed for their various purposes: the tugs pulling large liners and freighters through the Basin of St. Mark's, the public transport *vaporetti* and *motoscafi* servicing their routes, the sturdy *caorline* carrying vegetables, cement, boxes, whatever had to be moved, and the narrow boats in the canals, the gondola, the *puparin*, the *sandolo*, easing round corners, gondoliers calling their warnings. Venetians commonly sing at work on their craft, out of pure *joie de vivre*. Who wouldn't, tiller fixed between knees, dog on the prow, the water of the Basin sparkling in the bright sun and a panorama of beautiful and familiar buildings streaming past to right and left– *La Ville Radieuse* as Le Corbusier called it, the Radiant City? Canaletto's – *The Basin of St. Mark's on Ascension Day*. Clear morning light, blue sky, a movement of air rippling the wide expanse of water. A crowd of craft, boatmen poised in a range of rowing movements and pauses, every detail pinpricked with light, bristling with movement, brilliant, bright.

At night, the *vaporetti* tied up together near the tugs on the Riva ride the movements of water, bang together and settle, bang and adjust, restlessly. The gondola, moored in its small canal, lifts and taps its fenders, responsive to every push of tide or wind. Visitors, in their first few days unaccustomed to the rise and fall of water transport, find the rise and fall accompanies their sleep. Canals were full to the brim or empty to their muddy bottoms, flowing in one direction, ebbing in the other, according to tide. Everyone knows the siren announcing an *acqua alta*, when the water fountains up with alarming force through the paving gratings in the Piazza and plank walkways are quickly put up throughout the centre by the municipal street-cleaners. Water, boats, tides and the salt smell of the sea give Venice its unique quality of fluid, perpetual motion.

Occasionally students were up in the early morning, goaded by our professional photographer to catch the sunrise and early morning light – the bright gleam of fish still moving on the slabs in Rialto market, the children thronging to school, the slamming-up of shop roller-blinds. More common enjoyments were the coffee and irresistible chocolate-filled pastries in mid morning, and maybe a gaze, in passing, at the San Zaccaria Bellini, its colours lit by the winter sun at midday, or a passing stroke of the booted foot of a 4th century porphyry Tetrarch, booty from Constantinople attached to a wall of St. Mark's.

In a conscientious mood, some may have browsed in the Accademia. Sitting comfortably on the well-upholstered sofa in the main room, they could absorb Titian, Veronese and Tintoretto. Free Art History lessons were provided by the steady flow of student groups. In an hour here they could know by heart the Art History A-level questions.

What was new about Titian's approach to painting? Was Giovanni Bellini in any sense an innovator? What were the advantages the Venetians saw in oil painting? Discuss.

In the course of half-an-hour, Veronese's wall-to-wall, floor-to-ceiling *Feast in the House of Levi* began to reveal its stature, like a mountain emerging from clouds – its breadth of organised composition, its binding swathes of colour and its brilliance in detail – virtuoso painting on a grand scale: a blank to the fast-art tourist.

There was also the alternative activity – looking at people looking at paintings, listening to teachers. The keenest, the early birds, passed through the gallery early. Bevy after flock after herd of English sixth formers, long of limb, short of skirt, flaxen-haired, came into the room and settled instantly on the sofa, like exhausted migrants, longing for Mars bars. A youthful teacher brought her wilting girls to their feet again in front of the Pieta, their last effort for the morning. She gave them Vasari's account, from Titian's own pupil, of how the master sketched in his picture with a great mass of colour. But the final stage involved his moderating here and there the brightest highlights by rubbing them with his fingers: in fact at this stage he painted more with his fingers than with his brushes.

'Personal expression – putting paint on rough canvas. Thick paint. Big, strong strokes. The beginning of everything you lot like – chunky, expressive painting, all right? Rembrandt, Rubens, Delacroix, Turner, the Impressionists… OK?'

Tired silence.

'OK? So that's it for this morning. First steps in Venetian painting in three hours. You've been very good. Thank you. I hope you've enjoyed it. Before we break up, are there any questions? Does anyone want to ask me anything? Amanda?'

'Please Miss Brotherton, these shoes?' Everyone looked at Amanda's kingfisher-blue patent-leather shoes. 'I paid sixty thousand lire. Do you think that's OK? I mean, was I ripped off?'

'I think that's quite reasonable Amanda.'

Chance bumpings into unexpected friends – 'My God, what are *you* doing in Venice?' – led to unplanned lunches which spilled on through afternoon lecture-time into early evening. 'Everyone comes to Venice sooner or later', an international art dealer who had chosen to live in Venice told me. 'And the scale is so small, it's a village: you can meet everyone. You always hear who is passing through.'

Reflections in the water and in the mind.

'One may doubtless be happy in Venice without reading at all, without criticising or analysing or thinking a single strenuous thought,' wrote Henry James.

Walking back late at night through the Piazza San Marco, empty except for one's own footsteps. Except one February midnight in 1976, when the solitary walker found the piazza a yard deep in newspaper, softly bunched, from the Ala Napoleonica to the columns of St. Mark's, undulating slightly in currents of air, like a ground fog. An unfamiliar figure had been seen for a few evenings, standing in Harry's Bar – big, bulky, with a black overcoat with fur collar. Ha Schult, the avant-garde German artist, it was rumoured. By eight the next morning every shred of paper had been collected and removed by barge, at his expense. A happening. Did it matter how few people had seen this extravagant gesture, spread just before midnight and gone by eight the next morning, signifying what?

All Venetian spaces, outside and inside, have the quality of *theatre*. The Piazza was charged with invisible energy, like the inside of an opera house or football stadium. The late night crowds milled while the midnight Easter mass was proceeding in the Basilica. As the sacristans moved slowly along the nave galleries, leaning over the parapets and lighting with long tapers the candles in sconces fixed to the marble walls below them, people flowed in and out, alternating liturgy with coffee and *grappa* in the bars open all round the Piazza and Piazzetta. But everyone was inside St. Mark's at midnight, when the liturgy reached its climax. All the candles were flickering. The gold and enamel splendour of the *Pala d'Oro*, the gold high altar cover, normally kept reversed and invisible except on payment, was revolved, at the magic moment, to show itself to the congregation, glittering with precious stones: at which moment the plain-chant changed to an explosion of choirs and organs from the galleries. And behind that, the pealing of all the bells in the Campanile outside. And beyond that, outside, the pealing of all the bells of the city.

Another Easter, after midnight, late revellers entering the Piazza were brought to silence by the expanding web of sound which the Clare College Choir was hanging on the surrounding buildings like invisible decorations: Tallis' forty-part motet, John Rutter conducting an impromptu after-concert, after-dinner performance for the satisfaction of his singers.

Carta alta a Venezia

Sarah Quill, Stella Rudolph and J.H. 1975

The age of burning the candle at both ends, a duty and obligation for modern Grand Tour eighteen-year-olds, was for me long past. After years of living in the pensione with the students, sleeping or not sleeping in the eye of the storm – that is, from midnight to 3 a.m. – a succession of responsible adults were enticed, lured, cajoled or bribed to occupy the hot spot or at least be first on telephone line for late night emergencies, whether a broken arm, a throat bleeding with excessive caustic *grappa* or complaints from the pensione's neighbours about too much noise. The first in this noble line was an old friend, Sarah Quill.

Sarah was working as a photographer before she became involved with the Course. Now that she is busy running her remarkable library of photographs, the *Archivio Veneziano* in its office in St. Marks' Square, she has less time for us though she still runs photography classes. But through the middle fifteen years of the

Course, she was a vigorous assistant, a dedicated instructress in photography and, above all, a loyal, humorous and wise colleague. Fragile-looking but with a spirit of steel, Sarah tacked through shine and storm with quiet style. Whenever the telephone rang at two in the morning, I knew it must be Sarah, and trouble. So on many occasions I joined her at the Atlantico, and got to know the *carabinieri*, the *Squadra Mobile* – the flying squad, the ambulance crews and the Civic Hospital.

Blue lights were still flashing and three *carabinieri* launches, as well as a fire-brigade boat were moored in the basin near the Ponte del Remedio, by the Hotel Atlantico watergate. The two boys, who were already in the office of the *Squadra Mobile*, had little to say, being stone-cold sober. The canal had been set alight by petrol thrown from an upstairs window in a bottle. It was the era of the Red Brigade bombings and kidnappings. The building across the canal from the Atlantico was a bank. The *maresciallo*, that is, the head of the *carabinieri* was not amused. It was the first time we had to use the morning BA flight back to London.

The *carabinieri* were less tense when interviewing the gondola-borrowers, and learnt the new word 'prank'.

'Don't put down *"ubriaco"* – drunk. Say *"brillo"* – merry, high-spirited,' one *carabiniere* insisted, helping the delinquent students with their declaration, cigarette in mouth, punching deliberately and slowly on a huge, antiquated Olivetti typewriter at two in the morning. In the fifteen yards of wall-bumping out of a side canal before reaching the Grand Canal and the *carabiniere* launch waiting to arrest them, £800 worth of damage had been done to the delicate gondola, which, as it happened, was the savings and pride and joy of a Venetian student.

Even in Padua the police were helpful and kind, though they didn't themselves come with us and knock on doors in the dangerous streets round the Santo, trying to trace our student who had gone, with his valuable French horn, to live with the *Children of God*, whose ritual murders round Europe were at this time being reported.

Over the years the Civic Hospital and many of its staff became familiar and reassuring. In spite of its antique location in the Dominican cloisters of the Basilica of S. Giovanni and Paolo, and in spite of occasional hiccups in the electricity supply – 'it all needs re-wiring', a doctor had told us – it was relatively efficient, had a friendly atmosphere and, in the middle of the night, service was quite prompt.

On one occasion when the telephone rang it was not for trouble at the Atlantico. Sarah had heard that an exceptionally high water – *acqua alta* – was building up. Why didn't we go out and take photographs? She would ring up Stella Rudolph too, who was here for her lectures, staying at the Dinesen just round the corner. It was one in the morning, not raining, but the soughing tepid *sirocco* wind, which pushes the tide up, was blowing in from the Adriatic. In these conditions, wellies are a nuisance. One has to sacrifice a pair of shoes, roll up trouser bottoms, immunise oneself with whisky and walk in the water. Outside the front door of my apartment, next to the old Barozzi gallery, it was three inches deep but by the *fondamenta* outside Cici's it was knee-deep, one of the lower parts of Venice. British consular parties have occasionally had to go on late into the night until the tide subsided enough to let guests pass out of the gate. Across the Canal, Stella reported, ladies in diamonds, evening dresses and furs, coming out of the opera house, had been carried away on the shoulders of men in black ties, with rolled-up trousers, caught by the rising waters during the first night of *Aida*. Only Stella could have done her double day's work, attended a performance of *Aida* and still be game to go out into the floods an hour or so later.

We all sloshed slowly, knee-deep past the door of the British Consulate and over the Accademia Bridge. Knowing the city well, we were not in danger of stepping from six inches of water into six feet, where paving ends and canal begins, with no visible difference under the rippling surface of water. Near St. Mark's, the smart shopping street, the Via XXII Marzo was illuminated and full of life. At two in the

morning, all the shops were open and lit up, the owners offering whisky among their antique statues, Persian rugs and model dresses – as many goods as possible lifted above water level. An unofficial street-shopkeepers'-association party was in full swing. In the fashionable clothes shop *La Coupole* whisky was pressed on us and dresses on Sarah and Stella.

The Luna Hotel entrance hall was ablaze with light and six inches deep in water, a translucent green over the marble floor. We sat, water above our ankles, in the bar and were brought more whisky by tail-coated waiters wearing green waders. The hotel was full with weekend bargain-price winter tourists, all sleeping upstairs, unaware of the waters below. A photo shows Sarah, thigh-deep in water, in the Piazza, leaning against a column of the Procuratie Vecchie which displayed a Fenice Opera House billboard advertising *Aida*.

Bookshops are a pleasure in any city. In the corner of the Piazza, the Libreria Sansovino: no bargains but a scholar-publisher in command. By San Moise, the Libreria San Giorgio, tiny, cramped, a range of tourist books and novels in English, French and German. Across the Accademia Bridge, the bookshop at the Toletta offered bargains. And down towards Rialto, by the Goldoni Theatre, the new Goldoni Bookshop: Art books.

It was difficult to believe. However could it be there, in Venice, a volume displayed in the window? Above the Van Dyck equestrian portrait of King Charles I, the title was in understated white lettering: *The Late King's Goods*. No publisher, no author, no hype. And on the back cover, in black on white, the royal monogram, the initials CR, Carolus Rex, below the crown. As I was buying this magnificent book, so indirectly relevant to Venice, the lady explained that they had this one copy only because the author had personally come in and left it with them. Not the author, I guessed, but the patron who had backed the Oxford University Press to produce this uncommercial collection of scholarly essays on various aspects of this greatest art sale of all time, of the collection of King Charles I. Which added probability to the village rumour that Lord McAlpine had bought a palace in Venice: his name was printed as co-publisher with Oxford University Press. All King Charles' Titians had started life in the studio in Cannaregio. Rolled up and sent down to Ferrara and Mantua, they had been the pride and glory of those courts 'til the sun set on the d'Estes and Gonzagas. The canvases came back with art dealers to Venice and were shipped to London.

Buying a good book before lunch sometimes led to the Ristorante Riviera, which was on the ground floor of the ex-*scuola* of the salami-makers. Its prettily-restored façade had a restrained elegance which suited the restaurant. In the warmer months there were a few tables with umbrellas outside on the Zattere, looking across the busy tideway to the Stucky Mill and the Giudecca.

'We have excellent crab. Try it?' No menu. A jug of wine arrived. The book took over.

Riviera was Franco's, with his mother in the kitchen. Franco had been a waiter at Harry's Bar, second reserve behind the bar itself, and he had the quiet class of that background, of the era when the team there worked with the flair, suppleness, intuition and morale of the Welsh rugby side in its then heyday. Connoisseurs knew where to find these stars in retirement, running their humbler bars and *trattorie* throughout the city, those who dispersed after the death of Giuseppe Cipriani, father and founder. At the Riviera, a hint of curry in a risotto, the crisp cream napery and the discreet attentiveness of Franco gave away the pedigree. No one stumbled on the Riviera by chance – it was so out-of-the-way and its opening hours were strange – in the evenings it was only open two days a week. Unlike most Venetian restaurants, Franco's had no bar at the front which was one reason to come here when in a reclusive mood. Or when one wanted to read a book, like then. It was quiet.

Wrapt in the symbolism of the coronation robes of Charles I, I had lost track of time. Had the crab come? Been eaten? Had I ordered, drunk coffee? Why was there an empty glass still scented with *grappa*, which I never drink after lunch? I never drink anything at lunch. It was two o'clock. Lectures started at two. I never missed lectures, was never late. From Franco's it was three minutes' walk along the Zattere to the stop. The vaporetto crossed the shipping channel and then looped along the Giudecca, stopping at all the Palladian churches – the Redentore, the Zitelle and San Giorgio. As the boat travelled, the Salute, the Customs Point and then, across the Basin of St. Mark's, the buildings of the Piazzetta and the Doge's Palace changed their relationships with each other, sliding into different combinations like dancers in a slow ballet. After coming face to face with the Doge's Palace, the boat moved east along the Riva and then turned left into the canal which led to the Arsenale. I got off at the last stop before it disappeared through the towered entrance into the deserted expanses of the naval dockyard, the Arsenale.

Across the Ponte del Purgatorio, a door in the high brick wall led into the naval library and, up spiral stairs, to the premises of the *Societa Dante Alighieri*. A large area with a coffered, painted ceiling was divided by curtains into unequal rooms. The furthest, darkest and largest was furnished with rows of chairs, two slide projectors and music-playing equipment, and was used for our lectures. Here sat my students, looking, listening, I hoped. The curtained-off space to the right had two windows which looked into the prohibited docks of the Arsenale, and it had a table surrounded by chairs including one armchair. In between was a smaller, 'dead' area where books and a blackboard were stored.

The right-hand room was perfect for a siesta after a post book-buying lunch. Settled in the canvas-backed chair, books spread on the table, it was possible to listen, invisible, to the lecture, and even, tiptoeing into the inner space, to peer through a crack in the curtains at lecturer and audience. Or one could doze at varying depths, regulating the intake from the lecture room. Depending on the themes of the afternoon, slumbers might have been enriched by the Tristan chord, by Callas's sleepwalking Lady Macbeth, by the iconography of the School of San Rocco or by Byron's accounts of the Carnival. That day it was a chronology of Titian's paintings in Venice which, like a sermon, set the dreaming mind in active pursuit along another trail. As the voice beyond the curtain proceeded through the solemn religious paintings on which Titian is judged here in Venice, from the Frari *Assumption* to the *Presentation* in the Carita, from the tumbling figures of violence in the Salute to *St. Lawrence* on his grid and to the *Pieta*, I put down my heavy book, open at *The Rape of Europa*. Thoughts drifted over Franca and Antonietta and the Cardinal Ippolito d'Este as he hangs in the Uffizi, painted during the two weeks he spent here with Aretino, Titian and the courtesan Angela Zaffetta. In Mantua Aretino had introduced Titian to the Emperor, with reverberating results: Titian as Knight of the Golden Spur, as portraitist of the jet set, of the d'Este of Ferrara, the Gonzaga of Mantua, the Farnese pope. He was their mail-order court painter, rolling up and sending off a succession of great paintings: the *Emperor on Horseback*, *The Emperor with a Hound*: and the steady supply to the emperor's son, Phillip II of Spain, of luxurious erotica –

of *Danae*, of *Diana*, of another *Diana*, of *Europa*, of *Lucrezia*, of *Venus* – the other Titian who is not to be seen in Venice.

'The statues and pictures of his majesty are daily visited here in Venice by all the great people of the city as well as by foreigners,' wrote the art dealer Daniel Nys. *'They all speak in admiration of their beauty and rarity, observing the King of England will possess the most beautiful works in the world.'*

In April 1628 the *Margaret* sailed out of Venice in a storm, with Titian's *Twelve Emperors* and other works. The *Unicorn*, the *Pearl*, the *Rebeck* and the *London* followed and what remained of the glories of the bankrupt Gonzaga's, bought by Nys for the King of England, were loaded in October 1630 onto the *Industry* and the *Peeter Bonaventura*. In the first room of the Privy Lodgings in the Palace of Whitehall, the royal inventory listed eleven Titians: in the second eight and in the third three. The *Emperors* were in St. James's Palace. Only Mantegna's *Triumphs of Caesar* were kept for the nation by the Lord Protector, after King Charles had stepped out of a banqueting hall window onto the scaffold on the snowy January 30 in 1649. The rest were auctioned. And the uninventoried Michelangelo Cupid, according to Nys: *'above price, the rarest thing which the Duke possessed.'* Did it go to Amsterdam? Was it the Michelangelo hinted at in the Rembrandt bankruptcy sale? Where is it now?

Silence.

Crescendo of *'Va Pensiero'* coming through the curtains penetrated my sleep and blew away any melancholy thoughts. Titian was over, Verdi beginning, and the light outside fading.

Emerging from behind the curtain at the end of the lecture, I found that James Martin, an English journalist living on and off in Venice, had sneaked in, to listen to Rodney Milnes and Verdi. Rodney, James and I left the Arsenale together and strolled in the brilliant light on the Riva. The sky and the water were amalgamated in a yellow sunset, flashing like a held mirror. Seen from the bridge of San Biagio on the Riva on this late March afternoon, the setting sun shone straight through the glass windows in the drum below the dome of the Salute. This was the moment of Turner, Turner of the 1840s – *Santa Maria della Salute: Sunset*: sky and water merge, forms recede into haze, light from the white wove paper shines through gold and blue water washes. In the real world, gold faded to green, to blue, to indigo, to violet. The lights came on, across the water, in the shop windows, in the bars, electrifying the magic hour of the *passegiata*. In Venice, *la bella gioventu* – the beautiful young people – were constricted by the city into the narrow shopping *calli* between the *campi*, into crowded *pasticcerie* to eat their chocolate *bignees*. Passing in opposite directions in the busy spaces, mingling like scintillating fireflies, female eyes greet male eyes, arms brush in passing. Brightness falls from the air and the adrenaline of the ritual chase, of flight, hesitation and pursuit rippled in the Venetian intonation of exchanged greetings: '*that soft bastard Latin, Which melts like kisses from a female mouth, And sounds as if it should be writ on satin*'.

Byron's gentle, gliding liquid Venetian language was exquisitely preserved, every Venetian cadence caught in Reynaldo Hahn' cycle of songs – *Venezia – Chansons en dialecte venetien*. Hahn, companion of Proust, was in the international musical line of Faure, Chabrier, Ravel, Stravinsky, Satie, de Falla, Kurt Weill, Milhaud, Poulenc – those who enjoyed the privileges offered by the Princesse de Polignac in her palace in *S.Vio*. His *Venezia* songs, put together in 1901, achingly conveyed the spirit of sensual pleasure which every young Venetian couple could, and still can enjoy on summer evenings on the lagoon – from the shop assistant in Standa to Angela Querini Contessa Benzon, the original *Biondina in Gondoleta*.

Madame de Bearn asked me to sing – just me and a piano – on the piccoli canali. Just a few gondolas – one or two friends hastily gathered together… *I was in one boat, lit up for the occasion, with my piano and a couple of oarsmen. The other gondolas were grouped round us. We found a place where three canals met beneath three charming bridges, and I sang all my Venetian songs. Gradually passers-by gathered on the bridges: an audience of ordinary people pressing forward to listen. The Venetian songs surprised and delighted this little crowd, which made me very happy. "Ancora! Ancora!" they called from above. These songs, both light and melancholy sounded well beneath the starry skies and I felt that emotion which reverberates in the composer's heart when it has truly been shared and understood by those around him.*

This was James' favourite moment of the day, he told us, recounting one of his Venetian anecdotes. In the Mascaron Bar, Philip, an English friend of his visiting Venice and he were sitting at a table with a jug of *prosecco* admiring Philip's newly published book. The blond lady, who walked a setter near the Accademia, came in with friends. She recognised James with a 'ciao' and a widening of her brown eyes as they settled at the next table. 'Why was she here, across the Canal, well out of her manor?' wondered James. A person obviously of a hyperactive and nervous temperament, a smile coming and going as she talked, her attention was straying in the direction of their table. She spotted the Holbein portrait of Henry VIII on the front of Philip's book. She lent back and over towards their table, to get a better look. 'May I? Who is he? The King of England?'

James too got a better look. Her mink coat was open. Her dress reserved nothing for the imagination. Her hair touched his cheek for an instant as she looked at the royal *homo erectus*. '*Che bello!*' The warmth of her breath moved James' mind away from Tudor politics. '*Mamma mia*. Six wives! *E vero?* Is it true? What a stallion!' With which explosion of mirth she leant back to her friends and repeated her remarks. Philip held up the picture of Henry VIII for their amusement.

'And who is *she*?'

She must live somewhere near the Accademia, James surmised. Two or three times he had observed her, always with the setter, and then she had walked into the *Bar Cucciolo* on the Zattere and ordered a cafe, standing next to him. They had got into conversation. Her eyes were fixed on James as they spoke. He complimented her on her fine dog.

'*Poverina. Ha bisogna di un amante.* Poor thing, she needs a lover,' she told James. Imagining often her slender form and attentive eyes, and taking some extra and futile strolls on the Zattere, only days later did he realise, as Geoffrey had immediately pointed out, that this dog-talk referred to herself. It must be an invitation. In Venice, in the village, sooner or later, in the violet hour...

James walked into the Pharmacy in Campo S.Stefano, on the other side of the Accademia Bridge, to get something for a lagoon sore throat. It was the violet hour. She was at the counter, demanding advice from the young male pharmacist.

'And these? *Sette Bello?* Or do you think *Contact* are better? What about these: *Amore Mio?* Extra Sensitive it says. Or these: *Do It* – King Size?'

She hadn't seen James. She was appraising the range of condoms so conspicuously displayed in modern Italy. He didn't wait to hear the pharmacist's advice. She would have to cross the bridge on her way home. Buoyant, he followed the click of heels up the steps of the bridge, walking in the slipstream of *Bal de Versailles*. As she turned left down the other side, into the intimate *calle* towards San Vio, he would spring his prepared proposal. 'If your dog *really* needs a lover, I know of one.'

She was now over the summit of the bridge and descending out of sight. As he came up to the top, he saw climbing up towards him the smiling face of the British Vice-Consul.

'Hello James! What a nice surprise. What are you doing in this part of town? We'll have a coffee in Paolin.'

The staff of Harry's Bar could be relied on to solve problems, from knowing where to hire a bicycle on the Lido to providing a pair of wellies if surprised by *acqua alta*, and specially for discreet biographies.

Ermanno lived not far from the Accademia. He would know.

James sat at the bar, absorbing a whisky sour. 'Ermanno. I've been meaning to ask you. You live somewhere near the Zattere don't you? I'm a great lover of dogs, did you know? There's a lady I keep seeing on the Zattere, with a beautiful setter. A lady with quite long blond hair. Who is she?'

'That's my wife. She told me you liked the dog. She's on heat. You don't, by any chance, know of a suitable male? She needs a lover.'

We had reached the end of the Riva. Rodney had to head for his type-writer. James was going to take afternoon tea in the *Danieli*, and write some notes. Like Lampedusa, he found bars conducive to composition and always carried paper and pen in his pocket. I would pick him up from there in an hour and we would have an *aperitivo* in Harry's Bar.

I went back in an hour. James was asleep in a capacious leather armchair, his literary notebook lying in his almost horizontally extended lap. We opened the swing doors of Harry's Bar and were greeted by Claudio from behind the bar. Ermanno attended our table.

'A *Whisky Sour* Mr. Martin?'

Dottor Arrigo Cipriani

19

Harry's Bar – A Digression

The corner table upstairs, the one looking onto the *Salute*, number twenty-nine, had been booked for lunch some six months in advance. When we arrived, we were greeted with discreet but special warmth. In the ladies' places was a small silk square, and in the men's a pocket handkerchief, dark blue with the *Harry's Bar* logo of hands shaking a cocktail in old gold, and underneath the dates 1931–1981. It was May 13, 1981, the fiftieth anniversary of the opening of the bar. Our favourite waiter Giuseppe – Merve the Swerve – placed a bottle of vintage Krug on our table, with the compliments of Dr. Cipriani. The style of the place was such that half the customers present would never have known that for the other half it was a special occasion.

Harry's Bars abound throughout the world but there is only one authentic *Harry's Bar, the Harry's Bar*, which opened its doors on May 13, 1931 and flourished under its originator, Giuseppe Cipriani. It continues under his son Arrigo. Two hotels in or near Venice keep the Cipriani name because of his original involvement with them, but none of the many *Harry's Bars* which benefit from the name has any connection with the original, which is unique, not the first of a franchise. *Was* unique. In the years after his father's death, Dr. Arrigo opened another bar, *Harry Cipriani's* on Fifth Avenue in New York, as well as a restaurant.

Here in Venice the swing doors open straight into the bar, all nine by five metres of it. The bar itself comes almost to the door and has room for only half a dozen stools. The rest of the narrow space is set with tables and comfortable wooden-armed chairs. At the end of the bar an opening leads between the cheerful kitchen and pantry, past where Maria hangs the coats to narrow stairs leading to the equally small dining room above. Up to the dado is brown, polished wood, then pale butter-yellow walls and white ceilings. When the fog bell on San Giorgio tolls across the water on blind February days, inside the bar there is a snug glow and warmth, like a well-settled wood fire. That is it – plain, simple, small – and disappointing to someone expecting the mirrored gilt of Florian or grand hotel grandeur. But not disappointing to someone like Truman Capote, who found that the most interesting part of his holiday in Yugoslavia was the return to *Harry's Bar* for the *gamberetti* sandwiches.

A stranger, hesitating at the door, is found a stool at the bar or a chair at a table by the barman Claudio, a double of Pisanello's Lionello d'Este. Whether he chooses the ice-cold brain-surgery of a dry martini, or a healthy mimosa of blood orange and sparkling *Pinot Grigio* – in summer a *Bellini* when the peaches are in season – he will feel instantly at ease and perfectly looked after. A plate of sandwiches, cut into manageable fingers, will materialise within easy reach: chicken, or egg and anchovy – fresh, light, full of flavour, to be taken or left. On Fridays a plate of *baccala mantecato* is offered: dried codfish beaten to a creamy paste, with a square of *polenta* to absorb the oil, a traditional Venetian plate which will be being eaten in gondoliers' bars through-out the city, washed with white wine, though at a different price.

Meals are served in the sociable bustle of the bar downstairs or, more privately, upstairs, looking across the water to *San Giorgio* and the *Salute*. The pale yellow table cloths and napkins, the gleaming glass, the minimal layout of cutlery, the simple menu – a short choice of Venetian and Italian food – is the same upstairs or down. The keynotes are friendliness, quality, simplicity, an absence of bowing and scraping and cooking on flames beside the table. The most austere dieter will find the home-made *dolci* or ices hard to resist, and, with coffee, it may be a surprise to discover how a Bassano distillery can refine the usually savage bite of a *grappa*.

Harry's Bar used to function, and, when the boss is present still does, like a machine invented and hand-built for human satisfaction. As in a Rolls-Royce, the engine purrs so smoothly that the ticking of the till, as it computes the steady consumption of cocktails, croquettes, dinners and digestifs is barely audible. It functions with such deceptive simplicity that the maestro's technique does not show. But what makes the place uniquely interesting is to discover that it is not a chance happening, but the conscious creation, from overall concept to minutest practical detail, of its founder, Giuseppe Cipriani. His autobiographical book *L'Angolo dell'Harry's Bar* reveals what went into the making of this expression of his ambition, ideals and imagination.

Circumstances prepared Cipriani for his future role. He went from Verona to Germany before the First World War with his parents, who hoped for better work there. After leaving school to earn, his job in a watch factory made him appreciate precision and order, and dislike 'pressapochismo' – his own word meaning 'more-or-lessness'. His mother took in lodgers, and he admired the way she had with them, being courteous and attentive but not servile. His vocation was conceived. Back in wartime Verona he found himself running a *pasticceria*: a pastry-shop, quickly mastered that art and began to realise the direction in which his future lay. So he travelled, working in smart hotels at Madonna di Campiglio, Merano, Palermo, Brussels and in France. He learned languages, observed critically and, being a true son of the Veneto, kept his feet on *terra firma*. In contrast to the grandiose traditions in which he was working, he believed that there should be a new style of service and cuisine, genuine, natural, without affectation and ornamentation.

Inevitably he came to Venice, fell in love with it and worked there. It was the era of grand hotels, the last years of Diaghilev and the twenties. The rich and aristocratic of Europe and the golden youth of Venice sipped cocktails among the cafes and bars of the hotels: the Grand, the Danieli, the Bauer, the Europa and others. Here he completed his training, perfecting the social art of barman in opulent surroundings, turning over in his mind the idea of opening his own style of bar, equal in quality to the hotel bars but without their pretentiousness. He wanted a small bar by a canal, the kind of bar which a client can enter without having to cross a foyer full of braided hall porters. At the period when wing collars and starched shirts were relaxing into a softer, casual informality, Cipriani was ready, in tune with the times. But he was married to Giulietta from Verona, she was pregnant and they had no money. He had lent his recent savings to a client in San Remo who had reneged on the debt.

At which moment, says Giuseppe Cipriani, the winter of 1930, Fate came to him in his bar at the Europa in the improbable person of Harry Pickering, a quiet, lonely young American sent to Europe to get over incipient alcoholism. Chaperoned by an elderly aunt, her gigolo and Pekinese, they passed two months in Venice, mainly in the bar of the Europa, occasionally taking a turn in the piazza, until the aunt and gigolo quarrelled with the young man and left with the dog. Pickering drank less and less as the money ran out and, before leaving, asked Cipriani to lend him ten thousand lire. The clinical eye made judgement and, with Giulietta's approval, the money was lent. Some months later Pickering came back, paid the debt and added forty-thousand lire, to open a bar. To be called *Harry's Bar*, decided Cipriani.

A few days later Giulietta tapped on the back window of the Europa bar. She had found premises – a rope warehouse nine metres by five with room for a kitchen and pantry at the back. It was exactly right and Cipriani knew how he wanted it to be. He asked the young Baron Gianni Ruban de Cervin, one of his Europa bar clientele, to help him with the design of furnishings. The result was simple, elegant, light.

It went well from the start. Cipriani paid attention to every detail, psychological as well as practical. The bar was near the door because he wanted the shy to feel at home straight away. He chose especially small knives and forks for the small tables and abandoned the elaborate cover normal in good restaurants. The democratic sound of activity in the kitchen – the cooks' voices, pans, plates – provided a lively background buzz. In fact, when the upstairs restaurant was opened in 1960, the kitchen was moved upstairs, but this produced such a polite silence downstairs in the bar that it was immediately moved back.

The sandwiches were soon famous, as they still are. The secret? Cipriani answers: bread kneaded and baked *con amore* – with love, cut *con amore*, mayonnaise made, chickens raised and cooked always with the same loving attention. If this warmth in the hard-headed, high-pricing, super-successful restaurateur comes as a surprise, in his own special field the King of the Cocktail waxes positively fantastical and almost untranslatable.

When a client enters, a glance is enough to know his tastes. The maker of a cocktail has his intuitions. There is the moment of magic, when the creative fire lights up in his mind and, through who knows what mystery in the cocktail, lights the same fire in the mind of the client. An exchange of looks, satisfaction on one part, gratitude on the other... ecco tutto – there you have it!

Legends of barmanship and cocktail connoisseurship accumulated. A particular aura surrounds the martini. Hemingway called his version a *Montgomery*. He wanted the same proportion of gin to vermouth as that Field Marshal expected between his soldiers and the enemy's – fifteen to one. Another client liked a little vermouth to be sprinkled over the ice in the shaker, then thrown away before the gin was put in. He called it the *In and Out*. For another it was enough that the bottle of vermouth should be shown to the gin.

Inevitably a bar of this character in cosmopolitan Venice attracted the famous which attracted the famous. 'Til the outbreak of war in 1939 it was a haunt of writers such as Maugham and Coward, Lifar from the former Diaghilev ballet, the tenor Schipa and Toscanini from the world of opera and music and assorted crowns, coronets, pens and brushes. In the post-war period it was the den of the North-American grizzly, Hemingway: '*Let's go to Harry's Bar and be famous people.*' Orson Welles, big as a wardrobe, habitually downed two plates of sandwiches and two bottles of chilled Dom Perignon before relaxing. The Aga Khan always had the same simple meal, caviar followed by tagliatelli. Lopez, a Chilean guano millionaire who had an entire floor of the Grand Hotel refurbished for his Venetian visits was a regular. His amusement was to circulate among the tables after dinner, dressed in his impeccable 'smoking', asking the clients if they had eaten well and were satisfied with everything. And there was the Milanese insomniac who would come in at the busy hour of seven on a summer evening, sit down with his *bitter campari* and sleep for twenty minutes – the only place where he could succeed in sleeping.

Venice in the tourist season can be a nightmare and *Harry's Bar*, bulging and blocked with summer people is unlike its winter self. In winter it has the personal atmosphere of a London club without the complacent exclusiveness. Hemingway describes it well.

There are hours when it fills with acquaintances with the insistent regularity of the tide at Mont-St.Michel, except that the hour of the tide changes while the hour at Harry's Bar is like the Greenwich meridian or the Paris metric standard or the high opinion French soldiers have of themselves.

'I am a simple man,' said Cipriani, 'and I believe that most people like simple things.'

'Simple sure enough,' commented an American journalist, 'nothing but the best.'

In *Harry's Bar* Cipriani put into practice his ideals and at the *Locanda Cipriani* on Torcello he created an equivalent idyllic retreat in the lagoon. His remaining dream, unrealised, was to open a genuine *osteria*, large, dignified, full of the sound of voices, festive, where tumblers of local wines – *Merlot, Tocai, Cabernet, Prosecco, Verduzzo* – are slid across the wooden bar, clean but not too done up, easy-going but civilised, a real Venetian tavern.

In May 1980 Giuseppe Cipriani died – King of Hoteliers according to the press, humble barman according to himself. His son Arrigo carries on the family business. Being born into *Harry's Bar*, his upbringing was entirely different, as is his personality. Giuseppe had a natural, understated conviviality. His genius was to create atmosphere and cocktails. Arrigo is by nature less genial, less relaxed, more private and more speculative – in philosophical observation and in business enterprise.

It's said that Arrigo wanted to be a racing driver and the story went of his driving from Venice the seven-hundred-and-fifty kilometres to Bari, where he interviewed a cook, and back, between closing time and opening time. That was in an Alfa Romeo. But his present car is the best ever, he told me, when we met by chance waiting for a *vaporetto* at the *Piazzale Roma*, the Venice car park. A Mercedes, normal body but special engine.

'An hour-and-a-half from the centre of Milan to Venice.'

An average of 184 kilometres an hour puzzled me, knowing that there are now camera speed controls and the fine, or disqualification, arrives by post.

'Too fast for the camera system,' he thought.

In the 1980s Arrigo opened in New York, a bar and then a restaurant, and he continues there, as well as in Venice, not without visible stress. At this time the prices printed in the bar in Venice went up to equal those in New York. For American summer visitors the prices seemed normal, but for others, English visitors for example, they were outrageous. For regulars it made no difference, the monthly, annual or casually irregular bills being at the discretion of Arrigo. Adjustments, crossings-out, revised additions and subtractions are approved with ambiguous phrases – *totale parziale*, meaning biased or incomplete total, *voce amica* – a friendly voice in the ear.

Poised like a discreet falcon by the far angle of the bar, he chats for a moment with a client, the while observing the bar, the kitchen, the waiters and other clients. His presence guarantees the established standards. But not even Arrigo can be in New York and Venice at the same time, to the loss of both places. Sometimes, arriving and with overcoat removed hovering while two newer waiters chat among themselves, one ends up taking it oneself to Maria in the cloakroom – not a great fatigue but a hint that things are slipping. Copious helpings of food are not always prepared or presented with the *amore* prescribed by father Cipriani. Often the place is so jam-packed with tourists audibly puzzled by the fame of the place that it's enough to open the swing doors and exit on their rebound. These minus points are not missed by some of the food-guide writers. Nevertheless, certain individuals, like club members, are always there at their regular times. There are occasions, some Sunday evenings when the tourist tide is low, when by chance there are several tables of different friends and acquaintances – Venetians, foreign residents, regular visitors – all familiar to each other in the village that Venice is. Barmen and waiters know and are known to everyone and the evening has a mellow sparkle, the atmosphere of a festive family rather than an exclusive club.

Even when he is in Venice, apparently surveying the action in the bar, he may be somewhere else in his creative imagination: in Beirut for example. *Harry's Bar* in Beirut in the year 2000 is the setting of his novel *Heloise and Bellinis*, about the passionate romance of an American army private and a stunning Czechoslovakian widow, 'a woman always aquiver.' The story chapters are interleaved with letters – *intermezzi* – from the author to a confessor-friend Abelard, giving the author freedom to range with ironic, sometimes smouldering humour over an assortment of topics: meanness, the beneficial charms of the long-closed brothels, harmonious atmospheres in bars, hangovers, clients' unpaid bills, the sex-appeal of his sister-in-law, the sense of smell, Primordial Woman and, recurrently, his father, which adds a mellow dimension to the reticent figure in the grey suit.

The father's book is the book of a barman. If the son's bar is the bar of an ironic writer, the machinery still purrs, sometimes on auto-pilot, with the traditional quality and smoothness. For some years in advance, table twenty-nine had been reserved for the evening of December 31, 1999. '*Unfortunately I am not able to tell you the exact price per cover,*' faxed Arrigo Cipriani, in characteristically enigmatic vein '*but the amount will be very near to the cost of 99 kili of fresh butter, per person.*' When the Millennium came, considering that half our large party were children, with considerable regret we decided not to pay the 99 kili of butter for buckets of Beluga caviar and Dom Perignon '92, with no *voce amica*.

You missed something. The best night we have ever had. Dancing 'til 5 a.m. But of course the real Millennium is December 31, 2000. You've got another chance!

20

Expatriates

It is a fact that almost everyone interesting, appealing, melancholy, memorable, odd, seems at one time or another, after many days and much life, to gravitate to Venice.

Henry James could not have said this of the Marches, even if he had heard of the region. Before I arrived for the first time to look at the house, rumour had reached Peter, the Yorkshire solicitor that another Englishman was coming to San Ginesio. And as Giorgio Lauro and I arrived at the hotel late that bright, freezing night, the only words from the landlady were: 'there's another Englishman here.' I had imagined English teeth grinding behind a firmly-bolted door at my intrusion into his territory, but not that we would be searching for those same teeth among soiled bedding and broken glass on the floor in a room in our own house fifteen years later. The eccentric, combative character of Peter at his zenith came across strong and clear when we first met in the piazza. In his decline, accompanied, even caused partly by his animals, he lost little vehemence.

Peter had the animal-loving quality of St. Francis. His five dogs were all strays, rescued from the communal pound's death row. Luca, meaning no ill but possessed of a scientist's urge to know what is inside everything, has for the second time destroyed the covering of all six chairs in my *soggiorno*, he had written to me. The interest of his dogs in the rats nesting in his oven presented a dilemma of considerable moral and practical complication. As for flies – how can you swat them with those eyes looking at you... A pity about the field mice. They are such delightful little loveable creatures that it pains me to hear of their being disturbed. After being banished from San Ginesio on account of his uncontrolled dogs, he returned to Pellestrina, where he found more animal-haters. He was left with one dog.

'I'd love to visit you in San Ginesio but alas I'm tied here by my beloved dog. The Pellestrinotti would rather drink a tumbler of Prussic acid than look after a dog for a day.' The dog was killed by a youth on a motor scooter on the tarmac road. Peter took in stray cats, which perched all over him like the pigeons on corn-offering tourists in St. Mark's Square. His letters were fewer and his condition bad. He walked with difficulty. Volunteers from the Comune brought him meals, which he fed to the cats. They didn't like going into the house because of the atrocious smell. When they forced a public health visit, they discovered that a dead cat had been on his bed for a week.

Back in San Ginesio, in our *stalla* now converted to a temporary refuge, the doctor was horrified to discover a deep and septic wound in Peter's shin, a cat scratch. We came to know better the world of hospitals – a world which expatriates regard with apprehension. With drips his fever went and strength returned but he stayed in Tolentino hospital for five weeks, on antibiotics to combat the threat of gangrene in his leg. Tolentino hospital is a modern concrete block in the new concrete suburb of this ancient city, treeless, airless, a furnace in summer. A background smell of urine and excrement pervaded the air inside. Male nurses in off-white coats and slippers wheeled trays of syringes and pills along corridors. It was here that Therese had come when her first pregnancy ended. On that occasion, through the unclosed door of the treatment room I had watched the nurse smoking. The doctor had come out in a stained white coat, cigarette in mouth, bringing to show me the lost foetus in a kidney dish. It was here too that we had visited Osvaldo, finally pinned down by cancer, before he was taken home to die. '*Cosa voi fare?* – what can you do?' he had whispered.

Peter Young

When it wasn't Tolentino it was the cottage hospital at Sarnano, a little ski resort town at the foot of the Sibilline mountains. The *primario*, the elderly doctor in charge, a thin, Germanic disciplinarian, was not pleased to receive yet another elderly patient.

'I don't like the English,' was his opening remark to Peter.

'I love Italians,' was Peter's effortless leg-glide, reminding me of a youthful cricket team photograph of him, padded up and smiling in the front row, ready to open the innings for the Gentlemen of Yorkshire. It was in this hospital that we got to know the company of ladies who appear from the shadows when needed: an unofficial but essential part of the system. They are available to look after patients who have no family. Washing, changing bedding, helping feeding, are functions done by family, or paid helpers, not by the nursing staff. When a patient's night alarm bell rang and rang and rang unanswered, we found three nurses playing cards in the duty room where the bell was ringing.

When finally the ambulance from Rome arrived with a Yorkshire male flying nurse, Peter shook hands from his stretcher under the fig tree outside his room, more a curse than a farewell salutation, as he most reluctantly had accepted an old friend's proposition that he should return to a nursing home in the bleak East Riding. The distancing of time puts these last months, of Peter's rage at the incapacitating pain in his bones, into the context of a long friendship. His memory cruises, like a brisk frigate, guns run out, in his favourite waters – among our books, in the garden, in the sun outside the bars in the piazza. Recently he fired a long shot from the grave, spinning with his particular style of humour. One of his old letters which I was re-reading spoke with unbridled enthusiasm of the Victorian writer Augustus Hare's *The Story of My Life*, some of which was in Italy. '*You must,*' underlined three times, '*read it. It's excellent*', underlined twice. Heywood Hill was faxed and two weeks later three heavy parcels arrived, each containing two 500-page volumes of *My Life*. The bill for £125 was annotated: 'association with Tom Driberg', as the book was inscribed by him to a friend, with the words: 'a further overload for the top shelf.'

After Peter had gone, his title of *l'Inglese* – the Englishman – was vacant. When we moved to San Ginesio permanently, our lower ranking, *l'altro inglese* – the other Englishman – dropped out and the senior use settled on us. When ordering quintals of grain for the hens, or answering misdialled telephone calls, it was much easier to say *l' inglese* than the name Hall which is unpronounceable to Italians.

At an early stage in the manual demolition of an outer stone wall, the *contadino* who was helping me, Ugo, from Cerreto across the valley asked if I had a friend wanting to buy a house. But not like ours. Much better – a *good* house, big and in good repair. He admitted reluctantly that it was old, relatively old, and quite isolated. And it had a view of the mountains, which he had learnt that the English like. Our good friend Nicholas True was due for a visit that week. After grilled fish and white wine at Pippo's, a meal which began in heavy rain and ended in bright sunshine, Nicholas viewed the house and fell in love with it. They bought the house and ever since he and his family have come in school holidays.

We enjoyed the fact that, wherever we went in the area, life was old-fashioned, unsophisticated by the presence of foreigners and extremely cheap. The word foreigner was used for those locals who had gone to work in Rome or Milan and came back to their relatives in the summer. Few other outsiders ever came. Publicity came to the area with the disappearance of Mrs. May-Rothschild, last seen in a gathering snowstorm on her way to an appointment in Sassotetto, the little ski resort in the Sibillini above Sarnano. She had bought and was restoring a farmhouse. Her bones were found in the mountains eighteen months later – a mystery still unsolved and almost forgotten. We had read Raymond Flower's description of the colonisation of Chianti and were pleased not to be in that kind of Italy: an attitude which is incomprehensible to Italians, for whom a deserted beach is hell. Like eels collecting in pipes, they like to rub shoulders – as do some English.

Then came the first light smack of new reality. A lorry horn brought me to the door. It was Renato from the builders' merchants.

'Where do you want it?'

It was a *pozzo nero*, a concrete septic tank. It was twenty years since my septic tank had been delivered and dug in, I reminded Renato. And then he realised.

'My father said it's for *l' Inglese*. He must have meant the *other* Inglese. Didn't you know? There's another Englishman, restoring a derelict house across the valley.'

The other Englishman turned out to be a barn-conversion builder from Worcestershire who had arrived more or less by mistake. A deal on a house in Umbria, seen in *Exchange and Mart*, had fallen through so he'd taken the alternative offer of something across the Apennines. He'd never heard of the *Marche* before arriving here. He has stayed, succeeding in getting work as a builder, though he spoke no Italian. He lived through the summers and survived freezing, long winters. A good stonemason, he now is always in work, on houses for the steadily arriving English.

We enjoyed being almost the only English in the area 'til one day neighbours told us with enthusiasm that another Englishman had bought a house near Gualdo, not far away – a fortified Medieval mill at the bottom of a dank, dark dell on the little Tennacolo stream.

'He was here. Yesterday. At that table. *Molto simpatico*' Pippo told us. 'A Siena number plate.'

Back in 1976, our hearts sank. We were sure it was Flower's first move into Marchigian property. A year or two later a long-abandoned house with a fallen-in roof down in the valley below the Trues' was said to have been bought: it was rumoured by an Englishman from Tuscany. The mud road from it came up to join the Trues' narrow track. On one occasion a large car came up from below, at the very moment Nicholas was passing. Both braked, stopped and politely waved the other on. A fair-haired, very English-looking man sat in the Mercedes which had a Siena numberplate. Siena is the capital of Chiantishire. Our conviction grew that Chiantification of the *Marche* was imminent, though for years we saw no palefaces. Advertisements appeared in the *Spectator* for houses in *Le Marche*, giving an English name and a Macerata number.

Not many years later, American friends from Venice, who had moved to London, telephoned. We *must* meet friends of theirs who had bought a house in our area. They were coming out next week. We were given a local telephone number where messages could be left. The telephone number, we discovered, was Monica's, a neighbour of Raymond Flower in Tuscany, she told us: she had moved here three years ago. We had never met her. She lived in the *comune* of Gualdo, whose towers we look out at on a skyline, seemingly close but two valleys away. The Londoners came over with Monica for a drink. All was revealed. They had bought from Raymond the *Frantoio*, the olive press house next to Raymond's mill. We were invited to drinks at the *Frantoio* – a full-scale English drinks party with about thirty English and no Italians, a network who had bought holiday houses in the Gualdo area: bankers, Oxford dons, diplomats, children at public schools and English universities. Some had bought through Raymond, some through an enterprising surveyor of Gualdo who had a flair for imaginative and stylish conversions and had latched onto how to advertise in England. This summer population in the Tennacolo valley, a veritable *Happy Valley* of holiday homes was completely concealed from us by the two steep-sided valleys which directed them towards Sarnano or Amandola for their shopping. There was nothing to draw them to the froward town of San Ginesio.

Summer migrants can't wait to party with birds of a feather as soon as the Volvo engine is switched off. Permanent expatriates tend to be less frenetic in their socialising and more conscious of social space. After all, if we don't see each other this week then next month would be nice or, better still, wait 'til October 'til things are back to normal.

In the winter, at the builders' merchants, we came across an English couple. They had bought from Raymond Flower the house with the fallen-in roof below the Trues'. With the help of the Worcestershire builder at first, and then on their own, they laboured for two years, husband and wife, teaching themselves bricklaying, stonemasonry, carpentry, plastering, plumbing and electric installation. They ended with a beautifully-restored house which they sold instantly to the first viewers, a German couple. They immediately bought another shell and started on its conversion. Having come from Sussex via Thailand, they had been shocked by the Marchigian winter and now, thanks to the Germans, may be able to avoid the snowy months here. But their roots are strengthening, friends and family have bought nearby and Roger, builder's bad back and knees permitting, paints mountain views and portraits.

Through Venetian friends we met a couple who had bought an 18th century farmhouse on a hill-top outside Sarnano, cheek by jowl with the Sibilline summits, it felt. Crispin rebelling from an English public school, went to manage herds of cattle in the Australian outback. He is a hard man of many parts, himself single-handedly clearing and bringing under cultivation the scrubby acres of his hill. He plants English varieties of apple and pear with a missionary zeal. In winters he has made the windows, doors, staircases and wooden floors of the house, a self-taught carpenter and a connoisseur of timber.

'Pear wood. Nothing like it. It's the most beautiful wood. Plant it.'

Married to an Italian lady, the couple previously had bought and themselves restored a 16th century palace in Venice, where his skills are admired to this day by the critical builders and carpenters of Cannaregio. The fact that he could be seen rowing his timber down the Rio della Sensa from the yard to palace in his own Buranello *sandalo* added to their approval. After Australia, he had taken a degree at St. Andrew's in Classics and Modern Languages, and had done time teaching English at a university in Milan, interspersed with working as an Alpine mountain guide. His two-volume textbook of English literature is used in the *Scuole Superiori* throughout Italy.

Also at the builders' merchants we met the retired Brigadier Robert Ockenden and his wife Pat. Like ourselves, they were private people, more than content to work in the garden which they had created, to tend their grafted English apples, experiment with grapes, and study the stars. Although they had already lived nearby for several years, it was by chance that we met. The acquaintance developed at first slowly, with reluctance to intrude on privacy and it was a great pleasure gradually to find many mutual interests. These included gastronomy and wine and an old-fashioned enjoyment of dining with a hint of formality: so at what became our regular dinners, more or less at monthly intervals, home and away, there would be candles and, occasionally, a tie might be worn as a surprise. They recently went back to England for reasons of health, and it is a sad gap, particularly in our winter season.

In due course Monica introduced Raymond Flower, whose loyalty to Tuscany has waned – too many people, far too expensive and you have to book in advance at even the simplest country *trattorie*. More and more he likes the *Marche*. A tall, often straw-hatted Englishman with a colonial flavour – he had spent much of his youth in Egypt – he has sold his tower in Chianti and lives in one of the several houses he has recently bought near Monica's. With Raymond, finding and buying houses is an absorbing passion and selling them on is an irresistible and profitable consequence. To follow his idiosyncratic and enjoyable book on Chianti he is working on a *Marche* book. In the winter he goes South, to Singapore, to Penang, to Australia, to more benevolent climates.

His fortified mill was bought unseen by David Laws, the London-based international interior designer who has already revamped the inside into a well-heated and comfortable habitation – and he has made a pleasing meadow-copse garden among the trees by the stream in the dell. David is a positive addition to our country-mouse existence, coming for a week every six weeks or so, often with friends from the *metier*, bringing an exotic whiff of Mayfair to the backwoods.

The presence of resident English in small numbers has made a difference. The tribal settlements are two valleys away. As those few we know are dispersed in dingles or on hill-tops over a wide countryside, bumping into each other by chance hardly ever happens. However, it is sometimes a pleasure to chat in English about how the world goes on – our local world and the big wide world.

We were visited by a team of lecturers – geographers and gerontologists – from Sussex University who were doing a research project on retired expatriates in Spain, Portugal, Malta and Italy. They were amazed to find that round here almost none of us was retired or thinking of retiring, whatever our age might be. All of us are busy building our own or other people's houses, cabinet making, writing, painting, planting and growing things, making wine, breeding pheasants or other absorbing activities. We all have plenty to do. In the other countries, the gerontologists told us, golf, the English Club, the English local newspaper, the Bridge Club were the rule, the antidotes to boredom.

The question 'but what do you actually *do* all the time?' comes up regularly and in the early expatriate days could still produce a flutter of guilt.

Up at sunrise. Shutters closed. Dictated 'til 11. Continued on terrace. Ride in chariot in countryside. Light lunch. Siesta. Walk in garden, reading aloud. Another walk. Oiled, exercise. Bath. Dinner at sunset. Read to. After dinner, music and entertainment. Bed.

We are aware of the horrendous example set by ancient Romans, those who were active in politics and government at the highest level, commanded armies and fleets, and in their spare time, the virtuous *otium cum dignitate*, wrote authoritative books on a wide range of subjects. The industrious younger Pliny, whose country routine is listed above, had obviously paid attention to his uncle who had told him off for walking to work in Rome. How could he afford to lose the reading he could have got done if he had been carried in a chair? But what do *we* do all the time, in the middle of nowhere? ask our friends in England. The more years go by the busier we seem to be and the more difficult it becomes to think of what we have actually done on any particular day.

A more fascinating role-model might be Vicino Orsino, of Bomarzo, neighbour and friend of the 16th century villa-building cardinals Alessandro Farnese at Caprarola and Gambara at Bagnaia, who retreated into the creation of his mysterious and disturbing Sacred Grove, having witnessed massacres and horrors including the burning alive of a church-full of women and girls in sanctuary during his military service for the Spanish-Neapolitan Carafa Pope Paul IV. In a letter to Cardinal Alessandro, he gave his reply to the same question.

Item: looking after my offspring, both he and she, both great and small. Item: the harvest, which, since I have no hope of selling the grain, is unpleasant. Item: I look after my whores of whom, being thank God now over forty, I keep more than one for my own use. Item: granting a delay to my debtors until they come again which seems to me no small thing. Item: putting the fountains in my grove in order; it is a burden to be about this every day. Item: apologising somewhat to the Cardinal of Trent who I am sure will complain of me.

In contrast to the half-provocative, self-questioning, ironic listing of a castle-and-land-owning, privileged but cauterised military aristocrat of the noblest Roman lineage, our own activities, the trivia of ordinary life, are like a million other middle-class families' and most of them don't depend on being in Italy. We could follow the duke's style of answering the question.

Item: taking offspring to school, both she and he; taking them to airports. Item: cultivating the vineyard. Item: making wine, bringing it on and looking after it. Item: maintaining cypresses, roses, yews, bays, fruit trees, olives – hundreds of shrubs and trees. Item: cutting three fields including awkward and precipitous edges with dangerous, whirling instruments, collecting and getting rid of the cut grass. Item: keeping the fountains in order. Item: looking after an assortment of dogs, cats and fowl. Item: teaching English at the local school...

and so on, all of which tends to evaporate into a hazy blank when someone asks the question. Even with the help of a diary, it's difficult to find a typical day.

Young Kate, and later Sam, went to the local nursery school and elementary school up to a certain age, and Kate added a year at the *scuola media* and *liceo linguistico*. Taking the children the four-minutes' drive up to school and collecting them was a satisfactory routine, rarely recorded. The memory of high-spirited children running into school and out, greeting and embracing their teachers, is like a perpetual spring field of wild daffodils. Parents' meetings, particularly those which go on into the night discussing with cook and headmistress, after parental complaints, every detail of the menu of what we thought were excellent school lunches, queuing to talk to each teacher about the child's progress, hours of waiting, talking with other parents was a routine which we remember with nostalgia. Later, driving or going by train to Bologna and putting them on a flight back to school in England, and meeting them coming back, were recorded though even these highlights have become routine. Both children, without the slightest conscious effort, are bilingual: more if you add our local Marchigian dialect, and the Venetian they used in the terms they spent in Venetian schools during the Venice courses.

From the moment long ago when Therese came back from market holding two white hens and two red hens, live ones, we have had a fluctuating population of fowl, and a rousing salutation each day before dawn. Therese can recognise each cockerel by its crow. '*Three goslings, four bantam hens, two ducks, two mute ducks, eight chicks – from Signora Faraona, Sarnano market,*' is the kind of entry which featured frequently. Therese knew all about such matters and we became used to drenched chicks drying on towels under the hairdryer on our bed, cardboard boxes of peeping, newly hatched birds in various rooms and the frequent depredations of the fox. '*June 4 – Fox took eight fat marram hens.*' We accumulated a fine colony of hens, fiery cockerels, wild bantams, secret guinea fowl, deliberate snake-killing turkeys – favourite of foxes, delicately-nasal mallards and noble geese. After a successful year with ordinary pheasants we brought in the back of the car from England three Silver pheasants and four Reeve's pheasants, which reproduced well and were a constant interest and pleasure in all the stages of their growth – and excellent at winter dinners.

With curiosity aroused by reading *Alice in Wonderland* to Sam and by seeing the bright red example in the Lauritzen's palace, I brought home as a surprise present from Venice a pair of blue-cheeked loreys which lived in a cage in the Sibilline room. On one occasion, at feeding time, one flew out and up into a plane tree. We put the cage outside

Therese and Sam

with the other lorey still inside and, after an exchange of calls with the lorey inside, the escaped bird flew down and stepped into the cage. More remarkable was the experience of Fefe Sensacqua, the retired stonemason, who fed our stock one year while we were in Venice. Again, a lorey escaped and Fefe couldn't find it. When he arrived back at his house in San Ginesio he was called by a peeping sound on his roof. The lorey had followed his van. So he drove back down to our house and indeed the bird again followed him. Again, after exchanging calls with its mate, it flew down and stepped into the cage.

We have four Springer Spaniels, an Alsation and a Dalmation, plus a Yorkshire terrier. The dogs range freely. When the fowl are grazing the dogs are put on chains at the bottom of the field by the wood, on fox watch. Romeo barks all day, Sybil digs, Zoë lies down but her ears are constantly on the twitch, listening, Stella and Ben sleep. At night they sleep in the kennel when the cold winds blow and in their individual cool corners on summer nights. On winter evenings they often come in, in front of the fire until we go to bed. Zoë did not have the springers' fatal weakness for bantams but on a rare occasion seized a peacock.

She is shut up when the replacement peacock takes a walk.

Our uncounted cats have all lived outside, their function being to control mice. Having coexisted from kittenhood with the dogs, they feed with the dogs, follow us for walks with the dogs, come to the whistle and sleep in heaps on top of dogs on cold nights. Their names, often repeated, turn up irregularly in the diary: Tom, Inky, Streaky, Snowy, Moppet, Blue, Lavender, Mittens, Silly Billy. Births are natural, in log piles often, and kittens have to be hidden away from the attention of dogs, so we see mothers carrying kittens, one by one, in their mouths, to improbable safe places like the dovecote, in the heart of an impenetrable bonfire-in-preparation, in the compost heap and even in the top of a chimney. Therese detects the tiniest kitten miaow with the perception that spotted the minuscule gold heart on our wedding day. Occasionally a litter goes in the bucket and an occasional kitten is found a home: most follow the chances of natural law in the country-side. Because of the cats, dogs and fowl, we rarely now see a snake near the house. Sadly, lizards are rare too.

May 16. Another day of torrential rain and wind. Last night, in the raging storm, there were horrific screams and prolonged cries and today we found two pigeon squabs bloodless in the dovecote, two pigeons missing and the rest terrified. A polecat?

Noises in the night are part of life here. On still nights there is a range of rustlings, creaks, secretive footsteps, tappings from the roof above our heads, from a variety of birds and cats which nest, roost or hunt there. Often we hear the harsh barking of the fox, marking its travel from over the ridge, across the fields, down into our wood, then blood-curdlingly close as it skirts our chicken enclosure and fading as it heads off towards the abandoned church and the free-range chicken establishment in the adjoining house. So awesome is the sound that neither Kate nor Sam would permit the concept of Fox to enter their minds after dark: the word, and any reference to it was banned, though

J.H.

in recent years Sam has taken to sleeping outside on the terrace on his own in the summer. Round the camp bed sleep five dogs.

Inspired by the beautiful movement of trout in a local mountain trout farm, we decided to see if we could keep them in the round fountain.

May 18 1984. Yesterday Kate and I brought home four beautiful mountain brown trout from the mill at Sarnano. It was a race against death by lack of oxygen, one rolling onto its back in the bucket on the fifteen-minute dash home. It revived in the fountain. They are a truly wonderful sight – symmetry, poise, speed, economy, colour.

June 1. Had fixed two air pumps to oxygenate the fountain for the trout and a magnificent sight they were, cruising and flashing at accelerating turns. But while I was in Florence a hurricane scorched the garden plants and left so much debris in the fountain that the pump was choked and the water so turgid that the fish were invisible. Three died. Yesterday Kate and I emptied the pool, moved the three survivors which were living a lethargic, scum-covered, un-troutlike existence into a large plastic bath while we cleaned the pool: they visibly revived their mettle. But this morning all three are stretched out on the grass, having jumped out of the bath which had been filled to the brim by torrential rain in the night.

'Are you accepted by the locals?' is another and slightly strange question, frequently asked by friends in England. Unless you keep unruly dogs in the centre of town, the answer is 'yes.' Like everyone anywhere, we have our continual contact with shopkeepers, builders' merchants and, more closely, with our neighbour *contadini* who often do work for us: harrowing the vineyard, carting firewood, mending the road and ditches. We are often asked to lend a broody bantam. At certain periods, when Kate and Sam were at school here, we knew all the teachers and the children in their classes and their parents. In the years when I taught English at our *Liceo Linguistico* I was part of a functioning institution and knew all my colleagues and the young from the area, aged from thirteen to nineteen. And perforce we all have contact with *statali* – those who work in the state bureaucracy, in the *comune* – for certificates of residence and paying the refuse-collecting bill, in the post office tracing registered letters gone astray, at the local health service centre for inoculations. We are treated like anyone else. In an English context, the question means dinner parties – 'are we asked?' We aren't: they don't have them round here.

In another sense one is very much an outsider. The foundation of Italian society and survival, the defence against corrupt administration, unemployment, financial disaster, illness, old age is the family which is a very safe stronghold. Although one is sometimes asked into houses, and the tradition of hospitality to strangers is alive, social moral obligations are limited to the family. None of Peter's friends would have thought of caring for him in hospital. When the young marry in our area, many of them live in the same house as their parents. And there will be grandparents and sometimes great-grandparents. There is automatic baby-sitting, washing and ironing in the household. And the bleakness of old age is softened – a benefit not extended to outsiders.

Most of us are not estranged from England. We ourselves spend a working month each year in England, and are in almost daily touch by fax and telephone. The BBC World Service crackles through a more pleasingly sieved version of life than the raw actuality we can now watch via the satellite on television, which tends to remind us of why we aren't by choice in Britain. *The Field*, the *New York Review of Books* and *The Art Newspaper* arrive monthly, *The Spectator* weekly and fascinating bulletins from the World Pheasant Association irregularly, plus *Hortus, The Journal of Garden History* and the magazine of the Garden History Society. London bookshops have faxes and parcels wrapped in brown paper arrive from Heywood Hill and John Sandoe and the London Library provides a superb service by post. What with bookshelves of the English classics, some still waiting to be read, and the regularly updated list of set books of contemporary writing prescribed by our children for the re-education of the *terza eta* – the old – we are not out of touch with our own civilisation. A shelf includes at least a yard of books, increasing a few inches each year, by the English about the English in Italy, not all recommended reading, but curiosity has to be satisfied. It is true that absence makes the heart grow fonder, and there are moments of nostalgia. Having not been involved with cricket for many years before we left England, I now ask for the Band of Brothers cricket fixture list to be sent and, as I cut the field into long swathes and smell new-mown grass in May, am aware that I Zingari are at Torry Hill or the Yellowhammers at Tonbridge.

'*However long you live here, you will always be playing a role, and while you can learn to think in Italian, you will never feel in Italian,*' wrote one introspective expat to another. Would an Italian in England expect or need or want to feel like an Englishman? We breathe the freshest air. At night, mountain mist permitting, we look at bright stars. There is absolute silence. We are content in Italy. As the patient said to the psychiatrist at the end of treatment: 'My life is still confused, but on a higher level.' We came back to San Ginesio after a couple of months in England to find that we had left the large and conspicuous key in the front door while we were away. As we believed would be the case, the house was un-entered. After this, recorded in the diary, is the sentence: '*We are glad to be back to our own version of normality.*'

Statue of Alberico Gentili in the piazza of S. Ginesio

21

San Ginesio

The steep walk up from the house is through the cultivated vines and olives of the contrada all the way to the Porta Ascarana. Through the walls, under the gate-tower into town, up to the left is a large garden of grass parterres, gravel paths, lime alleys and a fountain, the Colle San Giovanni, an extensive platform set inside the lip of the town walls. From this *Balcony of the Marches*, as the guidebooks call it, there are magnificent views southwards down the chain of the Sibilline Apennines, west to the hills round Camerino and north over the fertile March of Ancona with the sea a pale strip to the north-east. The cobbled street dips down from the town summit, Capocastello, down-hill to the piazza, framing the tall facade of the Collegiata, the principal of the parish churches. References in the parish archive of 1054 and in a Vatican archive of 1171 record its early foundation on the site of a country chapel in which was an image of the Roman martyr, Saint Ginesius. Around this time, hereditary remnants of long-ago imperial invasions – Langobard, Carolingian, Ottonian and Byzantine nobility, scattered in the countryside in fortified villages and towers, were moving towards safer strongholds and alliances in the towns growing up on defensible hill-tops. For the next three centuries a main theme in the town archives is the buying up of surviving fortified towers in the contrada, the offering of citizenship and alternative buildings inside the walls to these old feudal clans followed by the immediate pulling-down of the potentially threatening towers in the country – a strand in the story of the growth of the Italian city states.

Sitting at a table outside the Bar Centrale, it was easy to see why Peter Young, having scootered round most of Italy, had settled for San Ginesio – the most beautiful place in Italy, he judged it. Over *cappuccini* our guests admired the intimate grandeur of the piazza, the Romanesque and Gothic front of the Collegiata attached to the ensemble of surrounding buildings from different centuries unified by harmonious materials and colours: sandstone, pink brick, washes of various shades of ochre and by the overlay of light and shade, brilliant sunshine and black shadow. *'Here all the cities are capitals and have not that provincial tone of secondary cities of other kingdoms.'* We could see what Byron meant. But who, they wanted to know, is this Alberico Gentili, whose bronze statue complete in Oxford hood and gown, stands in the centre of the piazza, erected, it is written, on the 300th anniversary of his death? When I took them through the little archway into a small back piazza their curiosity was positively excited by the plaque they saw on the wall.

Piazza Sir Thomas Erskine Holland
17.7.1835 – 25.5.1926
K.C., D.C.L
English Jurist
Professor of International Law in the University of Oxford
1874 – 1910
Who honoured and made known the Virtue and Greatness
Of Alberico Gentili.
Honorary Citizen of San Ginesio

Alberico Gentili is now generally regarded as the 'founder' of International Law. Born in San Ginesio in 1552, he graduated in law at Perugia University in 1572. In those perilous times of the Counter-Reformation and the Inquisition, his family was suspected of protestant activities and in 1580 Gentili escaped from Italy to England. In the London of Elizabeth I and Shakespeare, Italian civilisation was high fashion at court and jurists rigorously trained in Roman Law were in demand. Gentili was introduced to Secretary of State Walsingham, to Sir Phillip Sidney and to the Earl of Leicester, then Chancellor of Oxford University. He was installed as Regius Professor of Civil Law in 1587, though not without opposition, which persisted throughout his tenure. The other side of the Italian coin was the anti-Rome Puritan persuasion, articulated by schoolmaster Roger Ascham as *An Englishman Italianate is the Devil Incarnate.* A virtuoso dispute, initiating out of the performance of undergraduate plays, was joined by Gentili and the Puritan theologian John Rainolds, arguing on the principle of who decides what is acceptable – a theologian or a lawyer – with obvious extensions upwards from student theatricals to affairs of state.

In those days intellectual battles did not exclude crude insults. As well as being labelled *Italicus, Machiavellicus, atheus,* Gentili was accused of the stock Italian vices (from the Puritan point of view): breaking one's word, sodomy and lechery. Rainolds was no mean opponent: he later became President of Corpus Christi College and a prime mover in the Authorised Version of the Bible. Gentili's lasting reputation in the field of International Law was founded on his *De Jure Belli* published in 1598. He died in London in 1608. '*Alberico Gentili, doctor of Roman Law, was buried in the cemetery in the corner under the window by the gooseberry bush less than two feet from the railings, June 21, 1608'* runs the parish register of St. Helen's, Bishopsgate. He sank into oblivion. Until November 7, 1874 when Thomas Henry Erskine Holland, Fellow of All Souls and Professor of International Law and Diplomacy started his series of inaugural lectures. Speaking on the Life and Works of Alberico, he showed how much the well-known international lawyer Grotius owed to Gentili. Echoes of Holland's major re-assessment reached the University of Macerata and a committee was formed to erect a national monument to Gentili. On September 26, 1908, three hundred years after his death, his statue was finally displayed in San Ginesio. VIPs flocked to the celebrations. Among them was Professor Holland on his fourth visit to the town, who was applauded by the population with shouts of '*Viva il rivendicatore della memoria di Alberico Gentili! Viva il nostro concittadino onorario!*'

A *Centro Internazionale di Studi Gentiliani* still flourishes in San Ginesio and regularly invites eminent jurists to give papers. One such visitor was a recent Fellow of All Souls and Regius professor of Civil Law. On the occasion of his paper in September 1988 the little piazza by Nicola's bar was renamed after Professor Holland.

Ruminating over this improbable information, our guests went to cash travellers' cheques in the bank, I went to have a document photocopied. Baldoni's shop was inexplicably closed. In the *Cartoleria* Adele's machine was again out of order. On the door of Luciano's *Agenzia Ginesina* was pinned a note 'Back soon', which meant in three hours, his neighbour told me: he had gone to Macerata and would be back on the midday bus. So no photocopying. And no money in the bank today. Our friends had been told to try again tomorrow. Somewhere nearer Rome than Florence an invisible frontier divides Italy separating North from South. In its dilapidated inefficiency, San Ginesio is well inside the psychological territory of the south, the *mezzogiorno*. There are some compensating charms. In high summer, when industrious Lombard Leaguers are in bed by midnight, here the entire population is socialising in the piazza 'til 3 a.m., eating ice-creams and sorbets, sipping *amaro* digestives, playing cards in the Circolo Cittadino or ambling, arms linked, round the established route of the *passeggiata*. Round the piazza, up to Capocastello, round the Colle San Giovanni lime alleys, back down to the piazza, up to Capocastello… against a background of revving *motorini* and scooters ridden by the *bella gioventu*, the girls side-saddle on the back, detonating up and down the narrow streets.

Over the first *cappuccino* the piazza and the town itself seem to have a stylistic unity, giving the feeling that you have gone back in time and are in a medieval town. Gradually, common sense and closer looking make us realise that we are in a *modern* medieval town, the present moment in a chain of development and change stretching over centuries. If many of the stone walls look remarkably well-preserved it is because our builders today are all practised stonemasons. They can break and chip and square blocks of stone exactly as their forbears did, in a tradition which has never stopped. Most building work here is and has always been making-good and updating existing structures. Occasionally there are surprises, major changes. At the bottom end of the piazza, an inconspicuous and narrow arch leads towards Nicola's bar. On the wall of the arch is a plaque, which reads: '*Paid to the family of the Prior a pound of candles for the lighting of the palazzo and locking up the gates of the piazza. Public Annals 1390.*'

And below this on the plaque, a Latin inscription by the 16th century historian of San Ginesio – Severini: '*Then our piazza was closed by twelve gates, all of which existed in my time though now only one remains. The keys were given to the deputy at sunset and the place was protected by Andrea de Pitino and a troop of soldiers.*'

Now, the little arch to Nicola's bar is the only trace of the gates and of the fortified centre of the original town. The gracious and spacious piazza where we sit, presumably was opened up in the time of Severini, leaving the newer curtain walls to protect the town, then at its most prosperous and populous. Wandering round the narrow streets which make up the town, following the circling contours of the hill, our friends began to sense how this small town of 4,000 inhabitants might once have had 28,000, as is claimed. We looked at its three other parish churches, at the Franciscan cloister now the Municipio, at the still-just-functioning convent of the Poor Clares and the Benedictines, at the fine cloister of the Augustinians now the *Liceo Linguistico*, at the Great Bell hung in the bell-tower of the Collegiata. '*The history of civilisation leaves in architecture its truest because its most unconscious record,*' wrote the architect Geoffrey Scott. At the bottom of the town, set in the walls just inside the Porta Picena is another plaque recording a visit to San Ginesio of the 19th century historian Theodor Mommsen.

'In these walls can be read the history of San Ginesio. They tell its history better than any document.' The walls, the churches, the squares and streets of the town are indeed witnesses of times past – inscrutable witnesses.

Walls may have ears but they don't talk. Thanks to Professoressa Anna Maria Corbo there are other witnesses – documents on parchment and paper which she recently rescued from oblivion in the town archives. The archives, a collection of 2,600 documents dating back to the 1190s, had been neglected by successive administrations, moved from building to building, dumped in piles on floors of store-rooms and in cupboards and had suffered from damp, mould, insects and mice. Then and now photographs in her modest publication of 1993 *The Rescue of the Historic Archives of San Ginesio* show piles of bent and twisted manuscripts now classified and arranged in orderly shelves. Early documents record town statutes, concessions of privileges by imperial, papal and feudal authorities, many contracts to do with the acquisition of castles and towers in the contrada as well as innumerable registrations of legal acts between citizens.

May 10 1194 Copies of process of Curia General of the March against the Comune of San Ginesio for the construction of a fortress without the required licence; June 1250 Concession of Cardinal Pietro to the Comune of San Ginesio to build new walls, moats and gates; February 15 1228 Obligation on Gualtiero Abbraciamonte to reside in San Ginesio and to sell his castle of Brugiano; May 13 1250 Innocent IV confirms San Ginesio's buying of the castles of Ripe and Giuffone; June 3 1377 Act of peace exchanged between Giacomo Masino and Angeluccio Massoni for injurious words exchanged ; May 4 1282 Condemnation by the judge of the General Curia against the Comune of San Ginesio on the non - payment of 10 libri ravennate as salary to Sig.Berardo of Tolentino, master of grammar in the Comune of San Ginesio.

The archive documents breathe the reality of the moment, visible and touchable presences. Their rare, direct references to the big issues of the times put a brake on those historians who select and simplify for the sake of the comprehensible pattern of history, the aerial view.

Capocastello was destroyed by Percival Doria, Vicar of King Manfred of Sicily, in 1258. The San Ginesini rebuilt it and on the orders of Pope Benedict IX put it under the command of Giovanni Spoletano, Rector of the March. In 1436 it was conquered by Francesco Sforza, rebel against the Holy See, and was then destroyed by Niccolo Piccinini, condottiere of the Pontifical Army, and it was never rebuilt.

This is a guide-book potted history, of unannotated significance, of the castle of San Ginesio. The true flavour of those harsh centuries, whose tides flowed and ebbed round the walls of the Marchigian towns, can be savoured in the many bitter contemporary accounts of and comments on events and people.

The Italian context was the growth of the cities through various forms of government, from transient republicanism usually ending in the rule of a powerful lord. The larger context was the fluctuating presence in Italy of Germanic emperors, with claims on Italy dating back to a remote memory of Charlemagne's alliance with the Papacy and coronation in Rome.

It is our duty, with the aid of divine religion, to protect with our arms the holy Church of Christ from the incursions of pagans and the devastations of the infidel without and within to support the catholic faith. It is your duty, most Holy Father, to raise your hands to God with Moses and to help on our campaign.

Charlemagne's letter to Pope Leo III in 796 left plenty of room for dispute between Imperial and Papal claims and the question of who appointed bishops and abbots, possessors of large territories, incomes and political, military and financial powers reverberated down the 11th, 12th and 13th centuries. Added to which was the ancient contention that the Frankish King Pepin had donated to the Papacy extensive territories, particularly in the region of the Marches and Umbria, confirming the even more ancient Donation of Constantine. The Roman emperor, apart from endowing the church with wealth and lands, raised the Roman clergy to senatorial rank, gave them the privilege of riding on white horses and of wearing the insignia of patrician rank, giving rise to Dante's comment: '*what ills Constantine fathered when he made the first rich clerk.*'

After the protagonists – popes, emperors, princes and despots – another class left an indelible mark on the records of the late Middle Ages in Italy, the mercenary soldiers, the *condottieri*, who pursued war with a most savage dedication and enthusiasm. Rulers – papal, imperial and city-state, increasingly used mercenary captains to conduct wars. Some came from country nobility unassimilated into the towns, based in castles with cavalry retainers, who offered their services. Others, like Sir John Hawkwood brought his private host, the White Company into Italy after campaigning in France in the Hundred Years War, in the expectation of employment. Other wandering companies of professional soldiers moved in Italy, battening on the countryside, an uncertain threat to rulers but also available as an ally, on payment. The profession of *condottieri* was potentially profitable and, in their own eyes, honourable. The attitude of the *condottiere* could hardly be more clearly put than by Jacopo Piccinino, surrounded by other *condottieri* in the employ of the opposing side and asked to surrender.

Unless Italy is ablaze with war we can scrape together nothing from her. In peace we are looked down on and forced to the plough. In war we are famous. Our trade is to bear arms. Do not let them rust in idleness. Consult for the common good. Vote for war and arms. Why should priests have such wealth and power? Who can endure that the pride of Venetians should lord it over land and sea? What more shameful than that the Florentines should rule over Tuscany? Is it not fair that those who wield arms should be the ones to rule kingdoms? I applaud the power of Francesco Sforza which was won by military prowess. It is base and disgraceful that loafers should be kings. Let merchants sweat at buying and selling wares. Let priests administer the sacraments. Lordship belongs to us.

In a region and time when the law of the land was in a state of flux – was it the law of the Holy See, was it imperial law, was it the law of individual towns? – force ruled and allegiances were continually changing. The Cantinelli Chronicon records events in 1281 when the *condottieri* Guido da Montefeltro led the army of Forlì against Ravenna: '*They destroyed all the corn and trees, vines and plants and carried out the maximum devastation right up to the walls of the town itself both on that day and during the night. On the following Sunday they returned honourably to Forlì during the evening, burning all the houses that they passed on the roads by which they came back.*'

The 11th century Pope Gregory VII's exhortations, in the words of Jeremiah – '*Cursed be he that keepeth back the sword from blood*' – fitted well with the methods and policies of the Spanish Cardinal Albornoz, sent by the Popes in their Avignon residence to bring back under control the papal territories in Italy. He ruled with mercenaries. In 1354 he was employing thirty banners with 600 horsemen, in 1355 fifty banners with 1,000 horsemen and in 1356-7 a hundred banners with 2,000 German horsemen.

Nor were princes averse to violence. Of the Renaissance Lord of Rimini, Sigismondo Malatesta, Aeneas Piccolomini, the future Humanist Pope Pius ll wrote: '*He hated priests and despised religion. He had no belief in another world and thought the soul died with the body. Nevertheless he built at Rimini a splendid church dedicated to St.Francis, though he filled it so full of pagan works of art that it seemed less a Christian sanctuary than a temple of heathen devil-worshippers. In it he erected for his mistress a tomb of magnificent marble and exquisite workmanship with an* inscription in the pagan style as follows: 'Sacred to the deified Isotta.' The two wives he had married before he took Isotta for his mistress he killed one after the other with the sword or poison. When his subjects begged him at last to retire to a peaceful life and spare his country, he replied 'Go and be of good courage; never while I live shall you have peace.' Of all men who have ever lived or ever will live he was the worst scoundrel, the disgrace of Italy and the infamy of our times.'

'Peace is the one thing I have not found,' wrote Petrarch in 1336. 'The shepherd goes armed to the woods, the armed labourer uses a lance instead of a goad ... at night time there are dreadful cries without the walls; in the day, cries of "to arms, to arms".'

A hundred years earlier, the chronicler Salimbeni, describing conditions in the region to the north of the Marches, wrote: 'And all day, armed soldiers guarded those who worked in the fields. And it was necessary to do this because of the murderers, thieves and robbers who had multiplied out of all measure. And they took men prisoner to gain their ransoms and they stole and ate their cattle. And if the prisoners would not pay, they hung them up by the feet or hands and pulled out their teeth, and, to force them to pay, put toads in their mouths, and this of all forms was most cruel and detested. And in those days seeing a stranger on the road was like seeing the devil, for each thought the other would capture and imprison him.'

All of which gives a more sombre significance to the walls of San Ginesio: and to works of art, which leave less to the imagination. Inside the Pinacoteca is a 15th century panel painting. In front of the Porta Picena, knights and foot-soldiers fight with swords and lances, those from the nearby enemy town of Fermo against the San Ginesini. In the foreground lie dead and wounded. Over the slaughter, behind the tower, stands a giant Saint Andrew, protector of the gate, presiding over the just cause of violence. In the Collegiata itself, the theme of religion and violence is again evident. On the north wall, a recently restored panel painting shone in the sunlight. Saint Ginesius to the left and a Dominican saint to the right hold back the gold-embroidered

*The 15th century panel painting by an
Anonymous Master (1400-1450) inside
the Pinacoteca*

blue cloak of the Madonna of Mercy. Sheltering under the cloak is a crowd of citizens and patrons and above them scrolls of Christian scripts: *'Come unto me all who seek God; Mary – unto your care we fly; O Mary, intercede for your devotees.'* Beyond the pale, outside the holy cloak, are other scripts: *'We suffer because we do not love; we are here because we did not believe.'* Barely visible on the edge of the panel are depicted fortified town walls. Barbed arrows fly downwards. Some, having entered the aura of divine power, are snapped or bent. On the ground outside the cloak are many people, dead or wounded, lying in contorted positions, each and every one with an arrow sticking into a cheek, a mouth, an ear, an eye, with atrocious precision and detail. Iconographically unusual, we are told, to have all the dead and wounded. No record of the commissioning has yet been unearthed in the archives but it clearly related to dire events.

Many Italophiles love the extraordinary beauty of Italy, of its cities and towns, its countryside and its people. And we have a tendency to love ancient things, to explore in the direction of that foreign country which is the Past, towards a classical, possibly illusory Golden Age. Even in the bleaker centuries, there were lights. In the war-ravaged Italy described above, people in towns and countryside may have taken heart from the spiritual inspiration of St. Francis and his followers. Ugolino, a Franciscan monk who lived in Montegiorgio, one of the little towns whose distant lights we see at night, wrote of the many Franciscans who had settled in the 14th century in the Marches: '*The Marches were in olden times adorned, even as the sky with stars, with brothers that were patterns of holy life: the which, like shining lights of heaven, have illumined and adorned the order of St. Francis and the world with ensamples and with doctrine.*'

Coming back to the sunny present I was able to point out the ten Olympic-standard all-weather tennis courts under the Medieval walls by the Porta Picena. The Italian National Tennis Federation had invested in San Ginesio for one of its youth training centres, for reasons written in its brochure: '*All our centres are in healthy, unpolluted environments but this is our only one in a truly historic architectural setting.*'

To say that life in San Ginesio today is relaxed, unfraught – at least for outsiders – would be an understatement: park where you like, leave the keys in the open car, there is no stress. From the barber's shop on the sunny side of the piazza Valerio waved a greeting, obviously curious at the sight of foreigners. Like most barbers' shops, Valerio's is a centre of information and misinformation. Here I am given the latest gossip about town politics, about the gambling and womanising of the GP, the latest stage in the feud between the President of the Liceo Linguistico and the Civic Architect: '*he's worse than a serpent – he's a worm.*' Valerio claims to take no sides in the always bitter divisions of the community though it is clearly a pleasure for him to have a naïve foreigner eager to understand these violent and invisible currents. There are still arrows stuck in eyes, ears and cheeks but metaphorical ones or at worst injuriously verbal.

On my last visit he had told me he had again that night dreamt of his first love, now married in Torino, daughter of the then gaoler of San Ginesio. The gaoler had been given an ultimatum by the marshal of the *carabinieri* when yet again the overnight prisoners, probably the gaoler's drinking companions, had walked out of the unlocked gaol. *'Either be the barber or be the gaoler. You obviously can't do both jobs properly.'*

He chose the state pension and young Valerio was brought in from nearby Urbisaglia to be the new barber. He lodged in the gaoler's house, fell in love with his daughter but was not approved of by her parents. Valerio still dreamed of those days. *'I should have persisted'*, he sighed, *'she loved me'*.

In a flank of the local count's palace which dominates a corner of the piazza, in deep shadow, is the jewellery and watch shop of Lino, who would certainly have been watching us as we sat having our coffees. More or less here the Count of Cerreto had been stabbed to death, pursued by his enemies, the majority of the moment, at the words *Et est incarnatus* in the Easter mass in the Collegiata in the 15th century. Lino, a tall, strong, grey-haired man in his sixties had started life as a *contadino*. He knew all about growing potatoes, about the vineyard and about shooting – he had been president of the local Shooting Association and a partisan. He had been and still was a staunch communist. Like the barber's, his shop is a place where many people pass time, another centre of information and misinformation. He had made me aware of another dimension in community life, invisible to an outsider. 'No – I *never* go to the mass. Never. And do you want to know why?'

His father had been a Baptist, an almost unheard-of sect in Italy. When Mussolini had signed the Concordat with the Vatican, enthusiastic and loyal catholic fascists in San Ginesio had taken it as an order for a second Counter-Reformation, a second Inquisition against heretics and non-conformists. Lino could remember his father being brought by the town police into the *Collegiata* one Sunday and execrated publicly, from the pulpit, by the parish priest. He was then led, in the following week, to the various schools in San Ginesio and again publicly humiliated before the assembled pupils and teachers. The mayor of the time was the present mayor's grandfather. The President of the Liceo Linguistico's grandfather was an active fascist. The intensity of hatred, and of active or furtive involvement for or against the regime was extreme. It continued into the relatively recent period of German occupation. Those memorial plaques to martyrs fallen *'under Fascist lead'*, partisans executed: behind each one was an informer, a betrayer. This is recent history. The families are alive. In a community as small as this, *'everyone knows who did it but no one talks.'* Telling me about this one day, he had to stop talking as a lady came into the shop to look at watches.

The parish churches are full every Sunday and religious institutions continue to exist, even if on the wane. The Poor Clares' convent at the end of the road, by the Porta Ascarana is an active and admirable community, working in the world. Our daughter Kate spent several months there when she was at the Elementary School and we had to go to England. We got to know them all – the elderly Suor Germania in her wheelchair; Suor Pacifica who looked after the chickens and always had eggs in her pocket; the cook Suor Agnese; the young Colombian Suor Stefania who took Kate to school each day before going on to the *Scuola Superiore* herself; Suor Teresa the nurse, whose brother is a *contadino* near us; Suor Valeria who cultivated the kitchen garden; Suor Angela who took Catechism classes and chased the young to take part in the processions, dressing the Princes, the Papal Guards, the Madonninas.

Like most Italian towns, San Ginesio has its round of festivals and its wardrobe, traditionally supervised by the wife of the marshal of the *carabinieri*, of splendid silks, satins and velvets for Madonnas, angels, virgins, dames, princes, Swiss Guards, archers and crossbowmen, cavaliers and standard-bearers that make regular appearances. The first

San Ginesio piazza

procession is on Good Friday, a lugubrious spectacle led by the *sacchoni* – the confraternity that wears sacking hoods – carrying their heavy, rough-hewn cross, usually in drizzle. *Corpus Domini* in late May is often bright and cheerful, flocks of children press-ganged by Suor Angela leading and strewing the route with flowers from the country-side. Later in June there are the processions of the *Madonna of Mercy*. Each evening for a week, a large, photographic reproduction of the *Madonna* is taken from the *Collegiata*, mounted in a car with an accompanying priest praying through a distorting amplifier and driven through the countryside. The motorcade winds through roads illuminated by flaming torches, stopping overnight after a mass in the church of the *contrada* whose turn it is. At this season, every third year, the 'return of the Exiles' is re-enacted – thirty citizens banished for factious behaviour who had been allowed to return through the mediation of the Siennese: a rare reconciliation in the annals of San Ginesio. They returned in 1451 with a beautiful wooden carved crucifix, a gift from Sienna, now in the Collegiata. Being before the holiday season, these are local spectacles, most of the population attending and participating: this is living tradition as still found in the former Papal States.

In August, with the population quadrupled by Milanese and Romans and with holidaymakers from around coming into town, events have a more touristic and less religious quality. The town is decked with heraldic banners, the colours of the four *rioni* – areas of the town – named after four gates. Each *rione* has two consecutive evenings of *festa:* dinners served at long, trestle-tables, games and *ballo liscio* – ballroom dancing in the old-fashioned way: the waltz, the tango and the wild traditional Marchigian *sardarellu*, a peasant dance with a strong beat to the skirling music of accordions. After sunset the town is magically transformed by the flickering lights, the flags of the *rioni*, the aroma of grilling meats and the music. Milling people, some tourists and many mainly *contadino* families in from the *contrade* perambulate, eat, dance and catch up with each other's news in the balmy summer night. The dance floor, elevated and illuminated like a boxing-ring, is packed, with children, youths, the middle-aged and the old, all going flat out. On *Ferragosto* – August 15 – is the *Palio*, a tournament where

The relics of the arms of S. Ginesio in procession

Suor Angela

riders compete to pierce a suspended ring with a lance. The first records of the *palio* preceded the famous Siena *Palio*. San Ginesio claimed that it was their exiles who introduced it to Sienna. Finally, on August 25 there were celebrations for the Patron Saint, San Ginesio – high masses, processions, outdoor banquets, dancing, banner-throwing and the tolling of the *campanone* – the great bell. After midnight a firework display of magnificent extravagance is set off at the top of the town, visible and audible for miles around.

'So it's not all gloom and doom, vendettas and blackguarding, Montagues and Capulets?' asked our friends.

That evening, a *cinquecento* arrived at our house just before dinner-time. It was the bank manager. 'If your friends want to change their travellers' cheques, I've got some money now. I'll open the bank for them.'

22

Coda

Beginnings and endings and the pattern of the seasons stand out.

Another Venetian year. By nine o'clock I was, as usual, in the Piazza waiting for the new students, to lead them on their first day into the labyrinth of Venice – their orientation walk-about. It was Monday, always the last in January or the first in February. A freezing *Bora* blowing off the Adriatic cleaned the atmosphere to extra-terrestrial brightness. Diagonally across the Piazza paving and up the Procuratorie Vecchie like a dark finger lay the shadow of the *campanile*, the sundial of the city, moving, shortening and lengthening as the sun arched the sky, from rise to set. The bells tolled, buildings and ground vibrated and another year was beginning.

What would the students be like? We had been through the liberated and creative late sixties and early seventies, through the cool *Monty Python* years, into the big-time era of the *Sloane Rangers' Handbook* top rating and then the brash Thatcher years. Over many years the students had been active, enthusiastic and a pleasure to be with. It has to be admitted that communication is less total now that the age difference has moved from twelve years to forty-eight, though having a sixteen-year-old son helps the language problem. If one remembers a fluctuating minority, and more clearly those from earlier years, it's more to do with an ageing brain than less memorable students.

My role had become like a resident architect's, seeing if the structure works, checking the foundations, opening up a new window occasionally. To the students, in recent years, I seemed a remote figure, though I knew far more about each of them than they ever would have imagined. Clare was the administrative and pastoral miracle, reassuring parents over the long booking period, collecting the fees, noting every student's allergies and special diet, diplomatically keeping hotel staff and students in friendly equilibrium, offering tea, sympathy and, in the early hours of the morning, an occasional verbal cuff.

The first tourist group was there in front of the basilica. A new-style guide addressed his throng of Japanese, amplifying microphone attached to his jaw like a bird's beak. His metallic voice grated, in the level tones of a robot. At five-past-nine the *carabinieri* launch tied up at the Molo. A line of three unshaven prisoners, chained together, was escorted up the Piazzetta and across the Piazza to the temporary law courts under the Procuratorie Vecchie. Lumps of vaulted ceiling had started to fall in the old Rialto courts, where Shylock might have pleaded. If the inert plastic sheen on the replica horses of St. Mark's brought a sinking feeling to the pit of the stomach, an inhalation of *Bora* carrying the tang of seaweed off the ebb tide restored a sense of proportion. The Palladian churches – San Giorgio Maggiore the Zitelle and the distant Redentore – looked across the water, changeless. The noble pile of the Salute presented its angled facades at the mouth of the Grand Canal. The Doge's Palace held the waterfront and the Piazzetta and the ring of Palladian buildings across the Basin of St. Mark's together, like a commanding magnet. Which familiar sight proved that the heart could still leap, the adrenaline produce that intensification of life, that wrapt enchantment which Bernard Berenson, the American art connoisseur, recorded as the driving force in his long career.

From this year's rented apartment we watched the weeks pass, looking out over the Giudecca Canal at the Redentore and beyond into the southern lagoon. The established pattern of our lectures unfolded, the eyes, ears and minds of our students were opened as the city unwrapped itself from winter and moved towards spring in its own predictable sequence.

First, the clear season of the *Bora*. From the back windows, we could see the snowy Dolomites at Cortina d'Ampezzo to the north; westwards from the terrace, the breast-like Euganean Hills south of Padua and at night the line of lights on the Lido horizon right down to Pellestrina, fifteen miles away to the south. This was the season of Peter Lauritzen's lectures on the History of Venice and of Nicholas True's Byzantinism and visits to the draughty spaces of Ravenna, its brilliantly-coloured mosaics sparkling like frost.

When the *Bora* had blown itself out, then followed the February mists. When the mist was at its most fluid and Turner-esque, thickening and thinning minute-by-minute in the changing evening temperatures, the domes of the Redentore, the Zitelle and San Giorgio floated like detached segments of moon in the reduced illumination from the pavement lamplight. The Greek cruise ships of the Minoan Line were at their most romantic, throbbing down the tideway with windows and portholes glowing yellow – *Daedalus*, *Phaedra*, *El Greco*. Photographers Malcolm Crowthers and Sarah Quill taught the students to manipulate their apertures and exposures to catch the changing light. At the Arsenale, Peter Phillips brought them from plainsong to the grandest Mahlerian orchestrations in parallel with Charles Hope's instruction on iconography and the Venetian painters.

Then the seasonal high-pressure clamped on Northern Italy: brilliant skiing weather in the Alps, fog in the plains, its densest concentration on the lagoon. The same liners slid past, entirely invisible though within a stone's-throw, their engines shaking the buildings and their radar signals twittering, like tangible bats' wings, brushing the outside walls by our terrace as they felt their way blind towards the sea. The Giudecca Canal was filled with hooting traffic, the inshore *vaporetti* flashed their searchlights in warning and the fog bell on San Giorgio rang steadily. With the airport closed, our lecturers came and went via Treviso or the dreaded Trieste. The students were lead by Rodney Milnes or John Allison, escaping from the *Opera Magazine* editor's chair, from Rossini via Bellini, Donizetti and Puccini to Weill, from Verdi and Wagner to Gershwin and Britten. Caroline Villers from the Courtauld Institute explained the techniques of paint pigments and mediums and led them through oil glazes to impasto, *pentimenti*, X-rays and infra-red explorations and all the mysteries of restoration and conservation.

Throughout this period, from February to mid-March, a little group of us, local Venetians and myself, waited down the Zattere near the Gesuati at nine each morning for the doors to open into the Palestra Delfino, the gymnasium recently opened by Giuseppe, the now twenty-five-year-old miracle son of Gino and Rosanna. We each had our printed-out regime, moving at prescribed intervals among the latest electronic health machinery: bicycles, rowing machines, apparatus for toning up the lower back, the upper back, the rowing torso, the thighs, calves, arms and heart. Saddle adjusted for height, weight, level of difficulty and time tapped in and entered, away we went on the bicycles, the favoured warming up machine, building our revs to what the red dials told us to maintain.

On my right a man in skin-tight silks and gloves pedalled fast and broke sweat quickly, obviously on a high level of difficulty. 'I've got to. I'm a spare-time racing cyclist.' He watched himself steadily in the mirror. The whole room was mirrored from floor to ceiling. The music kept us happy – the *Macarena*, salsa, *Evita*, swing, *Fats Waller*, *Volare*.

Usually to my left was Luisa, the blonde wife of Adriano from the Accademia Bar. '*Odio la bicicletta* – I hate the bike,' she would say every morning. The dark-haired girl from the *pasticceria* at the Toletta on the bicycle beyond said that her aunt expected her to come down from skiing in Cortina to make her mid-Lent confession. She must be joking. I asked Luisa if she had been given flowers. She had forgotten it was St. Valentine's Day. So had Adriano. 'My boyfriend was singing outside my window at seven o'clock,' said the dark girl. '*Basta*.

J.H.

Ho capito. Via – Enough. I get the message. Go away'.

To the right the athletic lady from the *Sacca Fisola* was pounding at speed on the *run-race*, after taking her children to school and crossing on the boat from the Giudecca. In the mirror I could see the overweight taxi-boat driver making faces at himself in the mirror, puffing and grunting as he wrestled the wheeling hand-pedals of the upper-back machine. '*La vecchiaia,*' he often repeated – old age.

The Contessa, in white tracksuit, earrings and long bead necklace, perspired gently on a second-row bicycle, sitting back in the saddle reading the *Gazzettino*, the Venice daily paper.

'Look at this. Have you seen this?' she was asking the taxi driver, reading from the *Calli e Campi* column of daily Venetian anecdote. 'The parish priest of *Santa Lucia* wants to regain possession of the crypt which contained the remains of the saint but which has been used since 1960 by a nearby pizzeria as a deposit for hams. The pizzeria refused the priest's written request to keep the *salumi* in a more suitable place. The priest padlocked the crypt. The pizzeria owner broke the lock and denounced the priest to the *Pretura*. We wait the reply from the *Pretura*.'

The village atmosphere and attitude – someone had said that it came from the tradition of all so often being literally in the same boat together, reminded me of long-ago dinners in Count Cini's palace, where everyone spoke in the Venetian dialect and the white-gloved-and-stockinged footmen behind each guest's chair often joined in the conversation as they refilled the gold-engraved glasses.

Selected reading from the newspapers by the ever-bicycling Contessa, or the sight of the doe-eyed architecture student Manola who takes the coats in the evenings at the Ristorante ai Gondolieri lying on her back in a minimal leotard and slowly flexing her legs 'til they touch the wall behind her head, or Luisa two yards away, opening and closing her strong legs on the thigh-exerciser, smiling at me to Harry Bellafonte's *Banana Boat Song* could be distracting. But printing into the computer ten minutes on the *run-race*, ten on the bike, five on the upper-back developer, five on the lower-back did provide periods of isolation in committed, uninterruptable time and the bicycle was not a bad context for hearing the delicate thunder of local and foreign attitudes to Venice and its problems, its past and its future.

'*Do we want or not want the Carnival, Mayor Cacciari asks the citizens. Did you see that yesterday in the* Gazzettino? *Don't go on moaning. We can have it – or we can stop it. The city must decide.*'

No one bothered to answer the taxi-driver's declamation. Another Carnival had just passed, an abysmal lack of organisation and flair, 'But it's appalling. What a missed opportunity! Think of what the city has to offer. The setting. A tradition of processions – look at the Gentile Bellini procession-painting in the Accademia. A tradition of music, of ceremony, of theatre. Why don't they find a Diaghilev, pay an impressario, a Carnival manager?' had asked a visiting English architect.

Treading the *run-race* among chatting Venetians induced a relaxed, or resigned attitude to the righteous indignation of the Englishman. Many Carnivals had intervened since my naively optimistic letter printed in *The Times* in 1974, enthusing over the plans of the new enterprise: *Venice – Island of Studies*. The population had diminished in that time from 108,000 in the historic centre to 73,000. 'Even the *lucciole* have left Venice,' said Luisa, noting the disappearance of prostitutes – *fireflies*.

If Giorgio Lauro's brief promotional tour had resulted immediately in twenty-seven foreign universities setting up programmes in Venice, surely a deputation from Cacciari, the mayor, could lure one Japanese electronic industrialist to set up business in the vacant spaces of the Arsenale or on one of the inner islands? What is needed is work, employment, prosperity – the rest follows. 'Cacciari is *bravo. Bravissimo*, 'said the taxi-driver. 'His father was a wonderful paediatrician. All the children in Venice loved him. *Veri Veneziani* – real Venetians. They lived near the *Frari*.' 'From Brescia, by origin, his family,' added the Contessa. 'Anyway, why Japanese? The *Veneto* is one of the richest regions in Europe. Why not one of our own, local geniuses – Benetton, dalla Vecchia, Gaggia, Marzotto? After all, when it was most needed the Venetians were able to produce the body of an evangelist.'

The Chamber of Commerce hired an outside team of urban consultants to study the economic and social problems. When the consultants submitted their final report, they appended a note saying that in the course of their research they had asked twenty prominent citizens where they thought the city would be in five, ten, fifteen years. None of them had ever given the matter any thought.

Venice? In fact, Savannah. In his book *Midnight in the Garden of Good and Evil*, the American author John Berendt concluded: '*The city looked inward, sealed off from the noises and distractions of the world at large.*

It grew inward, too, and in such a way its people flourished like hothouse plants tended by an indulgent gardener. The ordinary became extraordinary. Eccentrics thrived. Every nuance and quirk of personality achieved greater brilliance in that lush enclosure than would have been possible anywhere else in the world.'

While living in the body of Venice, like a child in the womb, one heard muted sounds from the remote outside world. Hardly audible were the strident voices raised in New York or London prescribing ways of saving this city which, outsiders insisted, belongs to the world. However, on the level of dogs, cats and pets in general the city worked extremely well.

Not liking being without dog-company when we had to leave our family in San Ginesio, Therese had bought a Yorkshire terrier, Poppy, a portable dog. We had both become very fond of this courageous and spirited small animal. Returning from shopping, Therese had released him from his lead outside our front door in Campo Santa Margherita. In a flash he had dashed off, following other dogs, and disappeared. I found there were no fewer than twenty-nine calli – exits from the campo. Therese was tearful and in a fury with herself, stamping her foot, surrounded by sympathising neighbours. Of course, we hadn't got round to putting his telephone number on the collar.

Announcing the disaster in the gym, I was calmed and soothed by everyone. 'Don't worry. He'll be found. No one steals dogs in Venice. What you do is… ' So I had enlarged a snap of Poppy, typed out in large letters a description of the Lost Dog with our address and telephone number, and sellotaped it up in the vaporetto stops of our quarter – the Zattere, San Basilio, Santa Marta, Piazzale Rome, San Toma, Accademia – and in many bars and shops: all were more than willing to have the notice put up. I did about fifty. Therese and I separately combed the labyrinth.

In the afternoon I visited the car park and bus stop area, the Piazzale Roma, a centre of population movement and information. In a canal corner is the Cooperative of Luggage Transporters, a group of boat-porters who move in the bloodstream of the city: most of them were acquaintances, having carried our cases up to inaccessible attic flats in various quarters of the city over many years, when we arrived in January and left in March. Yes – they had seen a woman in a fur coat with a lost dog. Just a few moments ago. She had been putting up notices of a Dog Found. In fact there she was, they showed me, just getting into her parked car. Amazingly she had Poppy! She had found the obviously lost dog near her sister's flat in Santa Marta, had taken Poppy in to be shampooed, had had him photographed and had put up announcements in bars and vaporetto stops. She refused any reward and was in tears of joy. I went round collecting the notices I had put up, and in many places found the Dog Found notices too. For several days we received telephone calls from strangers, of enquiry, commiseration and joy.

One morning we would notice a more insistent chorus of birdsong at five in the morning. The mists were gone. The rising sun was back, pouring into the flat but with a different intensity. The sky was a darker blue and by nine in the morning it was warm. We had gone into March. Late at night, lone fishermen stood under the lamplights where I had perambulated on those first freezing nights thirty six years ago, by the Customs Point, holding a rod and line to 'swim' an attached female seppie-squid, and a long-handled net to catch the attracted male. 'It's the *stagione d'amore* – the season of love.' The last lecturers from England were in action. In a single memorable day Jane Glover presented Mozart, from infant prodigy to the final curtain. Edward Lucie Smith, or sometimes Louisa Buck, led them to the wilder shores of contemporary art, stabilised by Nicholas Penny's lectures running in parallel, confirming the classic measures of excellence established by the *greats* – Raphael, Michelangelo, Leonardo, Titian and Correggio. The course was nearly finished in Venice. With the arrival of spring Peter Lauritzen took them into the countryside for their introduction to the Palladian villas – the *Cornaro* at Piombino Dese, the *Emo* at Fanzolo

J.H. with Jane Glover

and, after lunch in Asolo, to the *Barbaro* at Maser. Daffodils and narcissi in the Veneto turned our minds to San Ginesio. Suitcases in store since mid-January were brought out for the return.

Before leaving Venice we visited the Island of *San Michele* and in the Evangelical Cemetery left flowers on Christina's grave and pruned the English rose *Shakespeare* which we had planted there. We noticed that this year Olga Rudge had joined Ezra Pound.

After the week in the schoolroom atmosphere of Florence, crowding in with the teachers and taught of all nations, the students were amazed by the gold, marble and *lapis lazuli* caverns of Roman Baroque churches. At the end of their private visit they lay on the floor of the Sistine Chapel, gazing up at gaunt Sybils and contorted *Ignudi*. A walk among the fountains of the Villa d'Este, a vinous final lunch under the wisteria by the Roman Temple of the Tiburtine Sybil in Tivoli and it was time to say goodbye. As they piled into the coach to take them to the airport and back to England, many watery eyes showed that another year's students had the virus in their blood. The strange ache in the heart, they began to realise, was Venice.

Moving from gondolas to grapes, from sea level to two-thousand feet, with plenty of snow still lying low on the *Sibillini* was, often literally, a cold shower after city life. The vineyard, pruned and harrowed in our absence, was immaculate. Daffodils and narcissi were finishing. Cherry blossom was out and wisteria showing blue. The late mountain spring softened into summer and led into the growing seasons – the cutting of the grass, the tying up of the vines and the lazy-looking slow evening sprayings. Summer holidays brought *il gran caldo* – the great heat, with Sam, tall and sunburnt, on the mountain bike, playing tennis, running with the dogs. Occupying alone, with the many creatures of his imagination, the spaces where other children had been in years gone by. Over the years, diary entries follow a similar pattern.

April 2. A fine day. In the morning we moved wine from the barrels to the container, cleaned the barrels and put the wine back. Everything in good health thank goodness. We lay naked on the terrace in the sun for an hour after lunch. At night there was a low, golden full moon. Thunder and rain in the night.

April 5. We walked to the old church and picked deep-blue irises. Beyond, the fields are full of jonquil-like wild daffodils with the delicate scent of spring. In the evening the old Franciscan priest arrived in his cinquecento to give his Easter-season blessing. He stood outside the house facing east and blessed la famiglia inferiore – the livestock – with a prayer and a sprinkling of holy water. Then he faced west and did the same for the attrezzatura – the farm equipment. Then he came into the house and with longer prayers and more sprinklings we and the house were blessed.

May 10. Busy with spring. Emptied the round fountain and cleaned out last year's plane tree leaves. Sam caught four frogs in his fingers. Cut the grass for the second time, a most enjoyable task walking up and down behind the motor cutter. The smell of cut grass and the striped look of the cut fields took

Ready to plant the rose Shakespeare *by
the grave of Christina Thoresby*

me straight back to Canterbury, Colin Cowdrey batting for Kent on a fresh
morning against the Australians, on the occasion when he scored a century
in each innings, the second in ninety-three minutes.

May 31. We have moved into glorious weather. The countryside is
awash with the colour and smell of acacia and broom, the air
snowing with poplar cotton – all bad for Therese's allergies but
spectacular. The honeysuckle is nearly blocking the study door from
opening onto the terrace, the yellow water irises are standing tall in the
fountains and most of our roses are in the best flowering we have ever
seen – after so much rain I suppose. To make up for last year's time in
hospital in London, Therese has planted no less than fifty-five vases
with geraniums, surfinias, petuneas, lobelias… for instant colour. Our fields
are cut and raked clean. The vines are growing well and the new young
Syrah are shooting up their poles. I gave the first spraying today. It is the
season for the hatching of fowl from eggs so we have cardboard boxes in
many rooms full of peeping Reeve's and Silver pheasant chicks plus some

Mikados, Mandarin ducks and an assortment of jungle fowl and bantams.

June 5. All four springers were clipped, changing them from furry, Highland cattle to thin, quivering, suede-coated whippets. They were almost unrecognisable in their summer coats.

July 2. Tractors working by headlights all night, harvesting the grain. The almost continual bleeping is their electronic warning that they are working at a dangerously steep angle. Warning obviously ignored.

August 22. Blazing heat continues- cloudless, hazy skies.

August 29. A cataclysmic storm. Thunder, lightning, torrential rain. Having learnt hard lessons in the past, this time our deep and well-maintained ditches, wide iron grilles across the road, our cement tombini which swallow spate water and convey it under the road to other,

The old Franciscan Priest

bigger ditches are working well. The countryside is roaring with water. A drainage system working in full flood is one of the most pleasing satisfactions in our steep terrain, equalled only by a well-stacked supply of dry logs in winter.

September 5. The dogs barked a lot in the night. A flock of sheep has been brought down from the mountains and is pasturing by the old church, on their way to lower ground. We hear the clonk of the bell wether and the angelic higher tinkle of other sheep bells. The Sardinian shepherd sleeps at night in his rug under an oak and his white Maremma dogs keep watch.

About this time, when the sheep are coming lower and nothing more can be done in the vineyard except hoping for no hail, we drive to England for the season of promotional visits to schools. Two nights in country inns in France, then the Tunnel and the astringent realities of London and England. We see family and we see friends. I give talks on Venice and the Course, a school a day, from Somerset to Kent, from Yorkshire to Shropshire, in Manchester, Birmingham, Edinburgh, Oxford, Cambridge, London and it's a pleasure to see again so many congenial and dedicated people in the teaching profession, most of whom have recommended children to Venice. After being in a country where historic city centres mostly missed the industrial revolution, where one can still enjoy walking and sitting among the palaces and piazzas of the Medici, the Gonzagas, the d'Estes, the Visconti and the popes, and where industrial estates are efficiently planned round the peripheries, one regrets more keenly the bleak aspect of our English cities, golden names from Shakespeare's history plays overspread with ugly growth and choked with indigestible traffic. Oxford High Street has more charm in the Ackerman print on my wall at home than in its raucous actuality. In spite of which England has its quality and charms which one savours all the more for enjoying them rarely. It is a strange fact that, in the old days when we were still based in London, at the end of our period in Italy we returned to England with a sinking feeling in the heart. Now, when we go to England for a month, we go in high spirits and at the end head back for Italy with elation: and a little apprehension for our rendezvous with the grapes – it's time for the *vendemmia*.

October 14. These are golden, precious days – peace, tranquility, benign air, no pressure. The grapes are in and the vinous smell of the fermentation oozes out of the garage and from the many cantini in town permeates all the narrow streets, emanating from cellars. Therese has been organising her plants and vegetables for winter, her bulbs for the spring.

October 25. Went to Beppe and Anna, the nursery gardens, and were shown the demolished gate column on the main road where Gabriele, our second builder, finished his life two weeks ago. We hadn't heard the news.

November 8. Everywhere ancient women are stooping under oaks, collecting acorns for the pigs. The first snow has arrived on the mountains.

November 28. Yesterday we brought in the lemons and geraniums. Today, heavy white frost. All the fountains are frozen, In the middle of the day the icy mountain ridges and surfaces shine silver in shadow, gold in the sun, appearing to float in the palest blue sky as if hanging in space.

December 6. Porridge. A cold wind blowing snow on the mountains, a big log fire. Last night we had our first winter Saturday dinner - home-reared pheasant, candles, a bottle of claret and the dogs stretched in the warmth.

December 15. Dario, a shepherd across the valley from whom we had bought peacocks, appeared with a lamb, skinned but still warm, in payment for a few hours tuition I had given his son. When we checked the weight and cost of the lamb it was precisely the cost of my lessons. We hung it on the terrace beam.

Christmas is pleasingly unstressful and there is very little commercial madness. We follow English customs many of which overlap with Italian, some of which don't. Italians prefer stewed eel on Christmas Day. Kate sings, or used to sing in the choir and we went to midnight mass. Although there are no English carols, *Silent Night* is international. There is an unfamiliar familiarity in the service. *'And there were shepherds in the fields abiding, keeping watch over their flock by night,'* suddenly has a real meaning, as does *'and they laid him in a manger'* – the *mangiatoio* being part of every local countryman's daily furniture. We have our Christmas dinner in the late afternoon as the light is fading, Christmas lights outside on the fig tree at the front and plane trees by the fountain at the back. A log fire glows, candelabra blaze with candles, surfaces are stacked with Christmas cards, the table laid with English crackers – all the reds and greens of a traditional English Christmas complete with home-reared turkey, Christmas pudding and mince pies. Sometimes more, sometimes less family are present, and sometimes occasional friends. There are telephone calls from and to those absent.

At the New Year, we see and hear fireworks sprouting and detonating from all the ten or so near or distant hilltop towns which we look out at from our terrace. Up in the piazza, pastas, pigs' trotters with lentils, *dolci* with *spumante* are consumed in large quantities in Terzo's pizzeria and in the Albergo Centrale.

Then cases are brought out in readiness for going to Venice. Antero and Palmina are briefed in their dog, poultry and house-minding duties in our absence. With the help of Antero the new wine, sitting calmly in glass demijohns, is moved into the French oak barrels to begin its mysterious elevage. Finally, in the cantina under the house, carefully sterilised bungs are tapped with the wooden mallet into the full barrels, a final ceremony of shared memories and annual hopes before leaving for the new season in Venice.

It is a long way from a peak in the French Alps to here, from the first *fragoline* in Frascati to the mountains of the *Marche*. The plane saplings

Family Christmas 2000

by the round fountain are now trees. The little cypresses are a thick hedge. In relation to the slow yew hedge, which has moved from ankle to shoulder height, Therese and I grow smaller. As one has been recording the passing of time, things don't stand still. In Venice the Atlantico's lease came to an end and we had to find another hotel: we are now back where we started, near the Salute in the hotel next to Cici's. The Dante Alighieri were moved out of the Arsenale to make room for a school of naval warfare. We have found an excellent lecture hall in the cloister of the Gesuati on the Zattere. The born-free Geoffrey has become domesticated and lives with Holly, a bright Seattle lady who teaches in Venice University, their child Lucy Mae and dog Perdita. The sanguine and energetic Gino, husband of Rosanna, Gino of the bar and the football matches, died suddenly in his son's gym after his daily spell on the bicycle machine, at the age of fifty-nine. In San Ginesio, our past and present have taken on a future tense and new dimension: continuity. The long-abandoned farmhouse below us, where the road ends, where Rita and Osvaldo used to live, was bought three years ago by my oldest son Nicholas: he, wife and children come each summer. And now, as these last chapters have been written, Nicholas' brother Charlie, on the brink of marriage, has bought the house and outhouses across the field and below the abandoned church where Antero and his ninety-three-year-old mother lived 'til three years ago. So now we are once again in the grip of dealings with builders, on Charlie's behalf, against the deadline of their arrival after the June wedding. Next week, they promised, weather permitting, the bulldozer and excavator man will start.

Geoffrey, Holly and J.H.

The Family – Summer 1999

Acknowledgments

I thank my daughter Katharine for her drive and enthusiasm which have brought about this actual physical book. It has been a great pleasure to work with her team: Karen Homer as editor and Elizabeth Wickham as designer.

In the many years of revisions, momentum was helped by the critical encouragement of friends who read various drafts – particularly Caroline Harris, Crispin Mason and, most of all, Hugh and Georgina Seymour-Davies. I thank Crispin also for his dust-cover pen and ink drawing.

Although dining by candlelight on the Orient Express (Chapter 1) remains a clear memory, as does the conversation with the horse-buyer from Treviso, the other passengers have faded from memory. To enliven the occasion, I have taken the liberty of borrowing some of my favourite characters from other people's writings. Some details come from Agatha Christie's *Murder on the Orient Express* (Harper Collins 1994, originally published 1934). The American mother and daughter are from Osbert Sitwell's *Winters of Content* (Duckworth 1932). Celestine and her aunt and the Bellaires' conversation are for ever in perfect focus in Ezra Pound's *Lustra* (from Collected Shorter Poems, Faber and Faber 1952).

A paragraph from William Rivière's *A Venetian Theory of Heaven* (Hodder and Stoughton 1992) is quoted on page 62, Chapter 5 to add a fictional impression of Venetian life.

Parts of Chapters 14, 16 and 17 have appeared in the magazine HORTUS and are reprinted with kind permission of the editor, Simon Dorrell as is his pen and ink drawing on page 8. HORTUS website: www.hortus.co.uk

As a general guide to tone, tact and selectivity I acknowledge a humble admiration for the writing of Iris Origo, particularly in her two books *A Need to Testify* (John Murray 1984) and *Images and Shadows* (John Murray 1970).

Picture Credits

Malcolm Crowthers *p.60, p.277, p.280*; Simon Dorrell *p.8*; Kate Hall *p.277*; Katharine Hall *p.135*; Sam Hall *p.262 (top right)*; Il Gazzettino *p.239*; Crispin Mason *pp.1 and 92;* Museo del Settòcento, Venice *p.130*; Hugh Palmer *p.298*; Sarah Quill *pp.30, 42, 47, 61, 120, 129, 152, 240, 243 and 252*; Daryl Weate *p.181.*

Pre-University Course

— entirely different from any other cultural programmes in Italy

John Hall Pre-University Courses
London VENICE Florence Rome
for Gap Year Students of the Arts and Sciences

John Hall's *Italian Journeys*
organised for Venice parents, past students and friends

Administration: The Secretary, 12 Gainsborough Road, Ipswich IP4 2UR
Tel: 01473 251223 Fax: 01473 288009 www.johnhallpre-university.com

Bibliography

So many bits and pieces from yards of bookshelves are embedded in my mind and book that it would be impossible to remember and acknowledge all sources. Books which have been particularly relevant to *Gondolas and Grapes* and which others might enjoy reading are:

History – Mediaeval and Renaissance
The Lands of St. Peter Peter Partner (Eyre Methuen 1972)
·*The Lords of Romagna* John Larner (Macmillan 1965)
The Italian City Republics Daniel Waley (Weidenfeld and Nicolson 1969)
Memoirs of a Renaissance Pope The commentaries of Pius II (George Allen and Unwin 1960)
The Archives of the Comune of San Ginesio

Art History
Titian Charles Hope (Jupiter Books 1980)

Italian Gardens
Italian Gardens Georgina Masson (Thames and Hudson 1961)
Hortus Sitwellianus Sacheverall, Osbert, Sir George and Reresby Sitwell (Michael Russell 1984)
The Villa in the Life of Renaissance Rome David R Coffin (Princeton Univ. 1988)
Gardeners and Gardening in Papal Rome David R Coffin (Princeton Univ. Press 1991)
The Letters of Pliny the Younger.
On the Art of Building Alberti (MIT Press, Cambridge, Mass. 1988)

Viticulture and Oenology
Vines, Grapes and Wine Jancis Robinson (Mitchell Beazley 1986)
Vino Burton Anderson (Papermac 1982)
Life Beyond Lambrusco Nicolas Belfrage (Sidgwick and Jackson 1992)
The Great Domaines of Burgundy Remington Norman (Kyle Cathie 1992)
Exploring Wines and Spirits Christopher Fielden (The Wine and Spirit Education Trust 1994)
General Viticulture Winkler, Cook Kleiwer, Lider (University of California Press, Berkeley, Los Angeles 1962)
On Agriculture Marcus Porcius Cato (Loeb Classical Library, Harvard University Press)
On Agriculture Lucius Junius Moderatus Columella (publishers as above)
On Agriculture Marcus Terentius Varro (publishers as above)